GLOBAL CITIZENSHIP EDUCATION

Global Citizenship Education addresses the intersection of globalization, education, and programmatic efforts to prepare young people to live in a more interdependent, complex, and fragile world. The book explores topics such as sustainability education, cultural diversity, and human rights education, offering critical insights into how these facets of GCE are interpreted around the world. The book also strives to give voice to student populations within historically marginalized communities, rather than focusing solely on the role of GCE in elite schools. Gaudelli blends theory and practice both to provide an overview of GCE and to examine current efforts to develop more globally conscious classrooms. Blending empirical research and practical illustrations, this important volume encourages educators to take seriously their own call to prepare young people to engage global challenges with a sense of urgency and helps chart a new direction for global learning that is increasingly expansive, dialogic, and inclusive.

William Gaudelli is Chair of the Department of Arts and Humanities and Associate Professor of Social Studies and Education at Teachers College, Columbia University, USA.

GLOBAL CITIZENSHIP EDUCATION

Everyday Transcendence

William Gaudelli

Routledge
Taylor & Francis Group

NEW YORK AND LONDON

First published 2016
by Routledge
711 Third Avenue, New York, NY 10017

and by Routledge
2 Park Square, Milton Park, Abingdon, Oxon, OX14 4RN

Routledge is an imprint of the Taylor & Francis Group, an informa business

Library of Congress Cataloging in Publication Data
Names: Gaudelli, William, author.
Title: Global citizenship education : everyday transcendence / William Gaudelli.
Description: New York : Routledge, 2016. |
Includes bibliographical references.
Identifiers: LCCN 2015040970 (print) | LCCN 2016000199 (ebook) |
ISBN 9781138925939 (hardback) | ISBN 9781138925946 (pbk.) |
ISBN 9781315683492 (ebk) | ISBN 9781315683492 (e-book)
Subjects: LCSH: World citizenship–Study and teaching. |
International education. Classification: LCC JZ1320.4.G38 2016 (print) |
LCC JZ1320.4 (ebook) | DDC 323.6–dc23
LC record available at http://lccn.loc.gov/2015040970

ISBN: 978-1-138-92593-9 (hbk)
ISBN: 978-1-138-92594-6 (pbk)
ISBN: 978-1-315-68349-2 (ebk)

Typeset in Bembo
by Out of House Publishing

To Liz and Alex…no place I'd rather be.

CONTENTS

FIGURES

ACKNOWLEDGMENTS

The work of writing a book only appears to be a singular act; it is in fact a social effort through and through. Teachers College, Columbia University provided me with a sabbatical and funding for data collection for which I am thankful. The participants in this study whom I refer to by pseudonyms have given so much time and energy—I am deeply grateful to all of them. I am also indebted to many individuals who supported this effort in various ways over the four years of its development, including:

Catherine Bernard, Margaret Crocco, Daniel Friedrich, David Hansen, Olga Hubard, Gowri Ishwaran, Patrick Keegan, Ching-Fu Lan, Megan Laverty, Grzegorz Mazurkiewicz, Merry Merryfield, Dana Mortenson, Janet Miller, Melissa Mitchem, John Myers, Ari Paloniemi, Walter Parker, Sandra Schmidt, Avner Segall, Brett Shanley, Els van Wezel and Scott Wylie.

While all of those named and others contributed generously, the limitations of the book are solely mine.

INTRODUCTION

A poor, dirty and unkempt man is aimlessly wandering a town square. He enjoys the company of dogs, marveling at how genuine they are, the way they seem to experience the world immediately in the present. Dogs are not much for pretense as they satisfy bodily needs when the urge strikes without regard for the situation, regardless of who else happens to be present. The man thinks, "how contrived people are, always presenting and pretending so as to shape the impressions of others about them." The man wishes to shake off this way of being as he has purposely removed the trappings of normal life to actively question those conventions, to speak truth to others as a symbol of an alternative way of living.

People about town seem to know this man's story. He was from another town, one quite far away, but was banished for destroying currency, an act that violates the law of the state as well as the conventions of reason. Why would someone destroy money? He claimed that he was told to do so by a voice he heard, which raised questions about his mental stability. Some might say that it was an adolescent rejection of his father, who was a money trader, while others might suggest it was only the beginning of a lifetime of calling into question all that society determined necessary and right.

The man could be seen walking through town in the bright midday sun carrying a lamp. When asked what he was looking for he would reply simply, "I am looking for a man" (Laertius, 1925: 6.43). His ironic disdain for people was storied far and wide and he had little regard for people's social position. When a famous leader once visited him on the street, having heard of his earthy charm, the leader asked if there was anything that he could do for the street-wandering man. He replied, "Stand out of my light" (Laertius, 1925: 6.41).

The man believed people adulterated the simplicity of what the gods provided. Arrogance was a source of these changes and a cause of much human suffering.

The desire to constantly tinker and make supposed "improvements" only made life less livable. These improvements invariably became distractions such that people were moved away from the immediate experience of living, separated from the bounties of nature while focusing too intently and starry-eyed on the artifice people had built. The rules of social life often stood in the way of living freely and consciously. The man would mock such contrivances by going to the marketplace to purchase food and flout the rule not to eat in the marketplace. When confronted by the shopkeepers about his indulging in the food in the marketplace, he replied, "Well, it was in the market-place that I felt hungry" (Laertius, 1925: 6.59).

Before the man died people in the town asked him what should be done with his body for a proper funeral. The man asked that his body be thrown over the wall of the town and left there to be eaten by the animals that would gather. People were aghast at the suggestion, asking why he did not care about the prospect of being eaten by wild animals, to which he replied "as long as you provide me with a stick to beat them off." This seemed odd since after death one could not use a stick, to which he said, "If I lack awareness then why should I care what happens when I am dead?" (Cicero, 1574: 1.43). And so it was that the old man died though the stories told about him have lasted for ages. They even built a statue for the old man in the town where he lived: a resting dog at the top of a pillar.

The soul-searching wanderer is Diogenes of Sinope, the ancient Greek cynic who once declared "I am a citizen of the world" (Laertius, 1925: p. 6.65). One might say that global citizenship, despite the popularity of its utterance today, springs from humble, ironic and perhaps even absurdist origins. What could it possibly mean to be a *world citizen* when the one who made the declaration had scarcely seen a fraction of the planet and knew only a relatively small amount of what existed beyond the city-state of Athens? Diogenes may seem an odd progenitor for global citizenship but the more that I wrestle with understanding how this idea came to be, the more I come to understand the appropriateness of these peculiar origins.

We can only speculate about what Diogenes might have meant by his proclamation of world citizenship. Was it a statement of true affiliation with all people of the world? The world, for Diogenes, was likely a small subset of people actually inhabiting the planet at the time, namely those of the Mediterranean basin and central Asia, people he may have encountered in the crossroads that was 350 BCE Athens. While we may read his claim as celebrating all of humankind, why would one with such a dark view of people that he preferred the company of dogs make such proclamations? Was Diogenes' invocation of world citizenship intended as a slight, a reminder, particularly to the learned and aspirational Athenian intellectuals, about how fundamentally parochial their outlook was, how narrow and selfish their view despite their big thoughts?

There is something naive in talking about global citizenship even in today's integrated planet. Most people do not make declarations about being world citizens, including someone like me who chooses to write a book about it, as it seems too grandiose to get one's head around. We are much more likely to describe our civic identity in national or even local/regional terms than in such all-encompassing ways that *global* connotes. So can it be of any more use than to say we are *global citizens*? Is it a discourse on the fringes of society, only to give us pause and wonder about our assumptions related to nations and other territorial units, testing the limits of our sense of belonging, affinity and responsibility?

Global Citizenship Today

Global citizenship resonates today in part due to the attention global issues receive in the media along with how ubiquitous that media has become. Reports about global happenings, such as earthquakes, severe weather, contagious disease out-breaks, internet security breaches, terrorism, acts of civil unrest and ongoing wars, are all broadcast through various and multiple outlets in a 24/7 media churn. The intensity and repetition of the flow of information coupled with the enormity of circumstances can quickly leave one feeling overwhelmed both by the range and complexity of events.

Thinking about global citizenship conceptually is a starting point for this book, though at core I am most interested in education, or how one prepares the next generation and those beyond it for inhabiting this complicated and troubled world. The central argument of the book is that what is needed in education for global citizenship is a coupling of the everyday and transformative, the mundane and transcendent. What does that mean? How does one ponder the meaning of the universe and one's minuscule place within it while eating a sandwich? I want to suggest that both activities—pondering and eating—are fundamentally wound within what it means to be a global citizen. Thinking big or transcendently about our lives is perhaps the same insight that inspired Diogenes to utter his famous claim to world citizenship over two millennia ago. And our daily eating habits are so intimately woven into the fabric of a networked planet within a beleaguered biosphere that one is *literally* eating from around the world at every meal. As Martin Luther King reminds us,

> All life is interrelated. We are all caught in an inescapable network of mutu-ality, tied into a single garment of destiny. Whatever affects one directly, affects all indirectly…before you finish eating breakfast in the morning, you've depended on more than half of the world.
>
> (King, 1967)

So, the question I address is how to make that possible, that sense of being rooted in a particular place while connected to the broad issues that shape what it means to be human.

A necessary piece of this *everyday transcendence* is the material conditions of life for people around the planet. The ability to gauge and track economic development has been of particular interest in the present era, as a means of demonstrating the ranges of wealth and poverty and the challenges of economic stratification exacerbated by globalization. The World Bank uses four quartiles of income to illustrate relative wealth by country, for example. The lowest category is less than US $1,000 annually and includes countries such as Cambodia, Bangladesh, Mali and Tanzania. The next quartile includes incomes from $1,000 to $4,000 and includes the likes of Guatemala, India, Mongolia and Ukraine. The third quartile represents average annual incomes from $4,000 to $12,000 and includes Brazil, Russia, China and Mexico, and the last quartile includes those over $12,000 and comprises most of Europe, Australia, the US, Canada and Japan. This is a useful heuristic since approximately 1 billion people, or 15 percent of the world's population, live in the highest quartile, 5 billion exist in the middle quartiles which is equivalent to 60 percent of the world's population and about 1 billion, again 15 percent of global population, occupy the lowest income group (New Country Classifications, 2013). Globalization has exacerbated the challenge of having an adequate living standard for billions of people on the planet, particularly those in the lower two quartiles, as many are increasingly beholden to the flow of capital that is virtually boundless within a global economic network. The fact that over 2.2 billion people lack basic sanitation and 780 million do not have access to clean drinking water suggests the extent of deprivation that exists in the lower ranges of the classification (UNICEF, 2012).

There is a sense that the world has become integrated too rapidly, particularly since the late 1990s, a period characterized by hyper-globalization, specifically economic integration (Tabb, 2012). In the past 15 years, for example, three-quarters of economically developing countries have experienced growth rates over 3.3 percent of gross domestic product, with much of this economic boom growth occurring through increases in world trade (Subramanian & Kessler, 2013). There are now deep grooves—or some might say scars—of interactions largely cut by post-national dimensions of capital, as investments and profits are shifted and hidden with relative ease such that the global tax base of national governments is eroding (Subramanian & Kessler, 2013, pp. 31–2). Revenue shortfalls reduce a government's ability to address social problems, which has broadly created a fiscally strapped public sector in the North and an inability to meet the rising needs for infrastructure development and human services in the South.

Another point of friction around rapid planetary integration has been significant environmental challenges. We inhabit a biosphere of limited resources that cannot foreseeably sustain the economic and environmental consequences brought about by the transition to an Anthropocene, or an age of human planetary control lacking a plan (Crutzen & Stoermer, 2000). The gravity of the situation is difficult to ignore and potentially overwhelming in its proportion. Humankind has since World War II the ability to alter life on the planet in fundamental and permanent ways, unlike ever before and distinct from the capacity of any other species. Governments remain unable to achieve an agreement that will make a relatively small sacrifice of economic growth, perhaps a year's worth of economic growth distributed over four decades, to stave off the most extreme repercussions of a warmed atmosphere (Singer, 2002). The Kyoto Protocol, ratified in 1997 by most nations who symbolically agreed to proportionally reduce carbon emissions into the future, has taken a serious hit as of late, as Canada joined Russia, Japan and New Zealand among highly developed economies to pull out of the climate agreement (Pearce, 2013). The recent Lima Agreement of 2014 overwhelmingly assented to in Paris, 2015 holds out some hope given that 200 nations participated, including carbon giants such as the US, China and India. The planned reductions, however, are aimed at cutting carbon production half as much as needed to stave off a 3.6 degree Fahrenheit temperature increase by 2050 (Davenport, 2014).

Educators like me believe that teaching the next generation to think of the world less as a repository of resources and a dump but more as an inviolable entity is a vital dimension of what it means to be educated in the 21st century. Also, we believe that humanity can live justly without gross maldistribution of wealth to avoid the grave suffering of so many. We have responded to globalization with increasing attention to the complexity and interdependence of life and it has renewed a sense of urgency about re-examining how, what, where and whom we teach (Andreotti, 2010; Kissock & Richardson, 2010; Merryfield, 2000; Myers, 2008). In high immigrant regions that have experienced changing demographics, for example, students are often the bellwether through which globalization's changes are most apparent. The New York City Department of Education educates approximately 1.1 million students of which roughly 20 percent are themselves immigrants, 41 percent are living in homes that speak a language other than English, with those students representing over 160 languages (Demographic Report, 2013). These figures do not come close to capturing the ethnic and linguistic diversity of the school system as a whole, as those whose parents are immigrants are not included nor are students who hold dual citizenship. These data illustrate the substantial demographic changes that are the new norms of this century in metropolitan centers the world over.

Governments, corporations, non-governmental organizations (NGOs), educational institutions and international organizations all deploy global citizenship education (GCE) in numerous ways. Given the array of participants shaping the discourse, it is of little surprise that "there can be no one dominant notion of global citizenship education; 'global', 'citizenship' and 'education' all are contested and open to further argument and revision" (Peters et al., 2008, p. 11). Those engaged in GCE at various levels struggle with how to conceptualize and implement such programs in a manner that respects the local contexts from which they grow while pointing to other places and towards an uncertain future. These educators seek learning that honors the challenges and possibilities of the global situation today while orienting young people to act in local communities beyond their immediate surroundings and in an indeterminate future.

What does it mean to educate for global citizenship? The broadest invocation suggests an aspirational sense of being human as a universal condition coupled with openness to the plurality of people and their environs. Also, it suggests that all people have the capacity and access to participate in multiple communities, often simultaneously, at a wide range of scales from local to global. Last, GCE points to students learning about the world they inhabit and gaining experience and reflective insight to act. The breadth and expanse of the phrase thus calls into view a multitude of conceptions that can at times be read as contradictory. A CEO of an international corporation might create a new division for global citizenship that mirrors the efforts of an NGO to promote a technology transfer program. In addition, the technology transfer might be viewed by an anti-globalization political advocacy group as action that imposes Western values of consumption while exacerbating a North–South economic gap. Many presume that *education* within the phrase can be left unexamined, as inordinate attention is paid to what *global* and *citizenship* mean while assuming that *education* speaks for itself, as if to say that content/information matters, while the processes or pedagogy for engaging content is simply given.

I join others who identify significant tensions in GCE, specifically how it normatively presumes that all people have equal access to social engagement and political participation (Myers & Zaman, 2009). The aspiration to open communities, local to global, to wider participation is critical; yet, scholars engaged in this area of research have acknowledged and must continue to acknowledge the built-in inequality that prevails in the world. These conditions are part of our global inheritance from legacies of oppression and exploitation that shape interactions, including the trafficking of women and slavery to colonialism and subsequent misdistribution of resources to mass violence and genocide. Some champion a global society that has been flattened by equal access to technology and commerce, asserting that the contemporary era lifts all boats (Friedman, 2005). Though there is some evidence to support this worldview, in the main it is little more than wishful thinking coupled with historical forgetting. Rather, the GCE that I wish to examine is one that robustly engages the inheritance of a global legacy and how we can educate to address past harms towards contemporary and future redress.

The educational programs profiled in this book are purposefully diverse. The range of practices oriented by *global citizenship* aim to avoid a tight focus on one type of practice while foreclosing a consideration of how diversity nourishes the concept and its significance in all educational practice. At some level of analysis, there is no education undertaken today anywhere that is not global, since all learning occurs within the confines of the planet and in some way aims to orient students towards this awareness. Also, the presence of the world in our minds, or that each of us has some full conception, however fragmented and limited, of the wider world in which we are situated, suggests that all learning could conceivably be dubbed global learning. I tighten my conception considerably when looking at practices that constitute GCE, however, examining those that specifically focus on civics/human rights education, sustainability, and intracultural/intercultural learning. My intention is not to solidify a singular way of conceptualizing GCE and identify exemplars to be replicated, but rather to explore diverse possibilities that strive towards a common understanding of shared humanity on a fragile planet coupled with a commitment to addressing social problems through engaged public participation. The cases reflect this diversity, with illustrations from the global North, in the US, Canada and Poland, as well as the global South, in Thailand and India. And while the number of cases examined herein is more numerous than one might anticipate in this genre of research, the breadth of GCE as a topic begs a wider set of illustrations.

I realize that I write from a particular situation and time; notably the US in the second decade of the 21st century. This location orients my thinking about GCE in a particular way, most often as a response to a more popular version of what it means to engage in global learning. This book is in part a response by counter-illustration to the dominant narrative of *learn-to-earn* tropes that are typically invoked when referring to *global*, *international* and *education* now in the US and increasingly beyond (Parker, 2011). My sense is that GCE must speak to and beyond a singular rationale of preparing young people for global economic conditions. Education for economic development alone is insufficient given the significant challenges we face on the near horizon as a planet. This book shines a spotlight on efforts to educate otherwise that do not preclude economic development but those that also choose not to fetish it as well.

What follows is my story about the efforts being made by educators to engage GCE. We are inheritors of a somewhat strange legacy of some 2,400 years ago, that of Diogenes the wandering stoic paradoxically seeking transcendence and rootedness, immediacy and distance. What are we to make of the fact that he destroyed money, sought otherworldliness and lived a relatively local existence, all while declaring himself a world citizen? I suspect that as we progress through the illustrations that follow you will find traces of these moorings, expressed as desires to live peaceably, justly, sustainably and in robust, engaged communities such that the past will not seem so distant. My hope is that you will gain sharp insights about the rich diversity of ideas relevant to practices of GCE, insights that can inform your work as a scholar, educator, student and perhaps even as a global citizen.

1

GLOBAL CITIZENSHIP

> We must foster global citizenship. Education is about more than literacy and numeracy. It is also about citizenry. Education must fully assume its essential role in helping people to forge more just, peaceful and tolerant societies.
>
> (UN Secretary-General Ban Ki-moon, September 26, 2012)

Global citizenship presents a certain amount of ambiguity given its aspirational qualities. No one is a global citizen in a legal sense and so the phrase can invoke uncertainty, disbelief and even disorientation. What is a global citizen, or global citizenship, exactly? Some consider the term offensive, as it suggests arrogance about the privilege that is often connoted by one who declares such membership. Others believe that it is urgent to act on this aspiration in developing educational programs and civil society to promote world-mindedness. Still others contend that global citizenship is indeed urgent, which requires a more measured response and greater patience. In the words of Bayo Akomolafe in his recent keynote to the DEEEP (Developing Europe's Engagement with the Eradication of Global Poverty) world citizenship conference, referencing the words of his West African elders, "The time is urgent. Let us slow down" (November 19, 2014).

I want to briefly sketch some ideas about global citizenship, addressing some of the larger issues in the discourse taking shape today. I explore a variety of points that have been raised about global citizenship, from advocates and critics alike, as a way of setting the broad context for understanding what it means to educate for global citizenship. I surely will not address every issue, but I hope to give the reader a working understanding of the discursive terrain. The backgrounder offers a broad context for interpreting and understanding the local acts of education related to global citizenship that follow.

Ambiguity, or What is Global Citizenship After All?

I was engaged in guest teaching with colleagues in Nijmegen, Netherlands in 2004. After a 10-day stay in a small village near the campus with my family, we decided to rent a car and drive to Germany for the weekend. We had recently visited the overwhelming serenity of acre upon acre of soldiers' graves, killed in the liberation of this region in 1944. As we left for Germany, I recall driving across the international border, which still had an immigration house, though completely vacant, left over from an earlier time. We talked about how incredible it was that this border, a center point of world conflict just 60 years prior, was hardly noticeable now. Did this brief moment point towards a larger trend, a citizenship or belonging beyond a strictly national one that was once so foundational to the 20th century and now rapidly disintegrating?

People have wrestled with what global citizenship means for quite some time, increasingly in the past two decades. These debates, though, have largely centered on the *global* aspects of the phrase and less on *citizenship*. I want to begin, however, with citizenship since this term is at least as problematic as the term global. Leaping ahead from the time of Diogenes, what it means to be a citizen in early modern Europe raises doubts about the solidity of citizenship as a concept. Europe's transition from the feudal era prior to 1500 to the revolutionary period of 1770–1810 had much to do with reconfigurations of what it meant to belong somewhere and therefore to have rights and responsibilities in and to a particular place. In the old regime of Europe, one's standing in a community was related to one's descent or identifiable lineage such that the "law came with the person" (Fahrmeier, 2007, pp. 10–11). This principle helped preserve rank and social hierarchy thus maintaining an aristocracy throughout much of Europe during this period. Early modern states, such as France and Sweden, were relatively weak as compared to estates and provinces that collected taxes and provided some social services, not the least of which was protection. And, the primary purpose of revenue generation was not social services but rather to wage warfare. This was among the most violent three-century era in the history of Europe, from 1500 to 1800, due in part to the consolidation of power by sovereigns and the raising of armies to build, maintain and extend spheres of economic and political control.

The revolutionary period in France and the then-fledgling US generated a deeper sense of citizenship vis-à-vis the state while ironically excluding large segments of society from the category of citizen. In the former, a citizen was one who was a political actor, a conscripted soldier, or a passport holder, but in relation to the latter, these privileges were not available to women, ethnic minorities and the poor (Fahrmeier, 2007, p. 29). The divisions within citizenship became more pronounced throughout the 19th century for a number of reasons. The shift from agricultural to industrial economies in the West slowed demand for farm labor—comprising enslaved persons or indentured servants in North America, South America and the Caribbean—and generated demand for factory labor, especially in industrial centers. These changes caused the migration of previously conscripted labor to the industrial North in the latter half of the 19th century along with increased flows of immigrants leaving Ireland, Poland and Italy for industrial, urban centers elsewhere in pursuit of economic opportunity. National debates about immigration and citizenship were troubled by a rising discourse of scientific racism, a movement fueled in part by the publication of Charles Darwin's (1909/1859) *The Origin of Species*. This era contributed to a widely held belief that genetic stock of "preferred races" contributed to national prowess. Though race-ability discourse ebbed considerably following the atrocities of World War II and the Holocaust, eugenics remains a residue of significance in the West, particularly as espoused by right-wing identity groups angered by and anxious about demographic changes.

Citizenship in the post-World War II era thus shifted increasingly away from ethnic/racial identity and gravitated towards nation-states and the making of new, aggregate identities. The period 1950–2000 was perhaps the zenith of national power as previously colonized countries were granted independence, the Cold War created a dualistic environment (e.g. US or Soviet) for national alignment and nations increasingly and generally diminished legal constraints on granting citizenship. And with the expansion of national power, and subsequent growth of international relations, there was an expansion of projects aimed at protecting the social welfare of an increased number of citizens while expanding the duties and entitlements of citizenship to a widening circle of people. Problems of disenfranchisement persisted, however, throughout this era as they continue into the present. In the US, for example, 12 states may deny convicted felons the right to vote in elections, even after their prison sentences have been completed (Pro-Con.org, 2013). Or, the presence of undocumented residents in the US, now estimated above 11 million, continues to challenge what it means to be a citizen (Undocumented Immigrants in the US, 2013).

Turning to consider global in this compound phrase, it too inheres some of the uncertainty of citizenship. Global can be found periodically in the latter half of the 19th century, as a way of naming the growth of industrial capital and the expansion of international trade. It was and still is often used as a synonym of universal or worldwide conditions. An element of conjecture accompanies global as a way of articulating a representation of the world, a way of asserting that a condition exists similarly in multiple locales, rather than a unique circumstance all its own. Marshall McLuhan popularized the phrase global village in the 1960s as a way of expressing the relatively small size of the planet, the interconnectedness among people, while ironically connoting a degree of intimacy by invoking a tight-knit community (McLuhan, 1964, p. 34).

Global characterizes a diversity of phenomenon, from trade and commerce to environment and sustainability, from peace and human rights to cultural diversity and religious affiliations. Global could be used to describe any range of phenomena, including a marketing campaign, outbreak of a contagious disease, crop failure, financial portfolio, aesthetic sensitivity and architectural style. In all of these illustrations the common element is the conception of scale, that global has application elsewhere and around the world. But must it be applicable everywhere to be global or only somewhere else? Say, for example, there is a loss of habitat that is happening in a limited number of places around the world. Does that somewhat particularistic version of global connote the same as the always/everywhere term before? I would like to think that even the "few-case" scenario does since the value of global, in part, is the ability to understand through comparison to similar circumstances, which does not require that one look at many or every situation.

Taken together, *global* and *citizenship*, what can be made of this conglomerate phrase? Might it be that global citizenship is part of the logical progression for humanity, from living in small bands in our origins to living in increasingly larger and intersecting groups over time? If we consider the short trajectory of citizenship highlighted here, a few patterns emerge. Citizenship is a term, though Western in origin and arguably exclusive in application, increasingly used throughout the world to describe the relation of self-to-sovereign as well as the relationship one has to other citizens. Citizenship's history illustrates a broad arc of moving from exclusion to expansion as its circle has tended to grow wider over time, though with significant challenges of exclusion remaining. Last, as suggested by the Netherlands–German border crossing, a tendency towards larger and larger political units is both characteristic of globalization and epitomized by the European Union's push towards economic, political, legal and to some degree, social integration; but it is challenged as well, for example, by flows of migration from war-ravaged areas of North Africa and Central Asia.

The *global citizenship as logical progression* thesis may seem to make some sense but there are counterpoints that also need to be considered. As citizenship in nations has increased, there has been a weakening of people's sense of affiliation to nations along a similar trajectory. Consider the rise of pan-Islamic identity demonstrated in the Arab Spring of 2011 or the subsequent rise of ISIS in 2015. One way to read these events is to argue that certain Muslims feel more affinity with fellow Muslims beyond their national boundaries than with those non-Muslims with whom they happen to share a national citizenship, say in Egypt or Syria. Centrifugal forces related to multiculturalism of the past three decades in the West, for example, take shape diversely and yet share a similar antagonism towards hegemonic national containers. Furthermore, global citizenship may be viewed as a way of ironically reinscribing the privilege of earlier applications of citizenship. As Fahrmeier (2007) offers,

> An extreme projection of some present-day trends suggests a return to some pre-citizenship practices. At the very least, there are indications of the emergence of an international class (or estate?) of "high potentials" distinguished by wealth, common educational experiences, cultural codes and employment practices, who communicate in an international language

(English) and who may have more in common with each other than with their fellow citizens.

(Fahrmeier, 2007, p. 232)

The increase of gated communities, quasi-public/private housing arrangements, may foreshadow a new mode of social organization that oddly resembles older versions.

Global citizenship might be read in a totalizing manner, meaning a person with rights and privileges as a citizen everywhere, or might be read as a person developing their identity as rooted in a particular community but with a sense of connection, responsibility and concern for people elsewhere. Again, it may not be global in the comprehensive sense of everywhere and anytime but rather in the particular situation that one is found. Hurricane Sandy's aftermath in the northeastern US, for example, has drawn a closer link to engineers in the Netherlands who have tried to hold back the sea for nearly a century and are increasingly learning to mitigate rather than prevent inevitable flooding in such lowland areas of Earth (Kimmelman, 2013). The exchange of expertise and insights generated from such living conditions being shared between at least two locales around a public problem suggests a practice of collaboration, and perhaps an act of global citizenship.

Scale, or How Big Can a Civic Be?

The Greek city-state serves as a historical and etymological grounding point for citizenship, through the combination of *polis* and *civitas* (Dagger, 1997, p. 155). Aristotle and Plato both speculated about the issue of scale. Plato offered an exact figure, some 5,040 families, that would constitute a healthy polis; Aristotle, on the other hand, offered criteria of (1) self-sufficiency, and (2) knowledge of each other's characters (Dagger, 1997, p. 156). The ancients could not envision communication technologies such as Twitter, YouTube and Facebook that allow people to reach out to wider circles of others to share ideas and insights and, in so doing, permit knowledge of themselves to be known. Do these technologies make the scale of a civic unit limitless? It depends. We know that communication technologies do not necessarily lead to engaged public discourse; indeed, it may create the opposite as incidents of flaming, or public insults, are much more likely to happen in a-synchronous conversations than in face-to-face ones. While technologies offer platforms for dialog about substantive issues, it is difficult at this stage to imagine them having the replacement value of live, embodied speech. And yet without that, it is difficult to imagine a civic on such a scale as the planet—or even for that matter on the scale of a large urban center.

Distance itself does not seem to be the trouble, as citizens living in the US, for example, have a relatively strong sense of shared political identity despite the size of their civic. Approximately 6,000 miles, a quarter of the circumference of the

Earth, separates the westernmost island of Hawaii from the easternmost coast of Maine, and yet it is politically singular. As Peter Singer (2002) notes, "geographical proximity is not in itself of any moral significance, but it may give us more opportunities to enter into relationships of friendship and mutually beneficial reciprocity" (p. 166). Or, to invert his argument, distance allows us to avoid witnessing the situations of others. Wing-Wah Law suggests that it is the lack of territorial symbolism, or that, "There are no commonly shared symbols to arouse people's sense of belonging to the global society that are comparable to those associated with national identity, such as a flag, anthem, or emblem" (Law, 2004, p. 273), that creates a stance of disinterested bystander among those seemingly unaffected by a problem far away. While the lack of emotive symbols complicates the emergence of global citizenship, the trouble lies beneath these construed objects, pointing to the narratives they convey. Flags, anthems and emblems signify shared sacrifice and values. The lack of a mythos, or a story of shared origin and common experience however fictionalized such a story may be, undergirds these symbols. The "abstract universalism" of global citizenship has created a yawning gap of meaning, an insufficiency of connection such that most people prefer the tangible stories of ethnicity, religion or region to the somewhat utopic and futuristic pull of global citizenship (Castles & Davidson, 2000, p. 6).

Mobility bears on this conversation as well. Part of what has sparked discourse about global citizenship has been the increasing number of people who travel and work beyond national borders. The ease of intercontinental travel has increased dramatically since 1950 along with the proportionally decreasing costs of these excursions, making them available to those other than elites. Yet as people are more mobile, and often do not live for extended periods of time in the same community, they may be disinclined to feel a part of that community. The tension exists between a conception of civics that is rooted in embodiment, inhabiting particular places and feeling a sense of attachment to those places, and their development in tension with a disembodied, technologically connected and seemingly placeless type of global belonging. When combined in this manner it is difficult to imagine how something can be both *global* and *civic* since they have highly different meanings.

Facebook has become a sort of virtual community of enormous scale with nearly 1 billion users globally and 3.7 billion dollars in revenue, arguably a global civic space. People are able to communicate with a diverse community of associates, or friends, in ways that are simple, direct and easily accessible across the planet. And yet the sense of connection that people share when they like a photograph, watch a video or read a posted link is less intimate than talking over coffee, attending a public meeting or participating in a demonstration. As Stephen Marche (2012) cryptically offers, "We were promised a global village; instead we inhabit the drab cul-de-sacs and endless freeways of a vast suburb of information." Advocates of global citizenship therefore have to confront how scale may contravene efforts to build a community of the world, one that still breathes with life and fullness. Spaces such as Facebook, which are designed to keep people in touch but literally at a distance, are not sufficiently robust for what global citizenship might become. Rather, such media may also suggest its opposite, a dystopic digital wasteland filled with ephemeral images that are no more about connection than about simple appearances. The question of scale is not simply about "how big is too big" but more about what types of connectivity, listening and sharing do we imagine constitute a meaningful civic engagement?

Politics, or What are the Power Structures of Global Citizenship?

Globalization is typically understood as a powerful economic force, one brought on by the liberalization of financial markets in the latter half of the 20th century. In what William Tabb (2012) has called the *era of global neoliberalism*, major economic shifts identifiable in the past three decades include rapid increases in foreign direct investment, speculative transactions in international markets by a growing investment class, currency fluidity and the sale of derivatives, or a financial instrument based on the exchange of an asset (Tabb, 2012). The recent wave of debt crises in southern Europe and how each day's news roiled and soothed financial markets around the world demonstrates how deeply interwoven the world economy has become. The economic dimensions of globalization represent an important piece of infrastructure as to how the world is connected, though they alone do not capture the breadth of what is taking place. Globalization is rightly associated with economics, specifically international finance, capital shifts and technology flows. But this "electronic herd," or the rapid and intense flow of capital into and out of particular countries due to political circumstances there, moves quickly and voraciously around the planet with relatively little regard for what is left in its wake (Friedman, 2000).

While the economic aspects of globalization are largely the drivers of the changes we have witnessed and will continue to witness, the political dimensions are more prominent in public consciousness and are therefore more likely to be part of how global citizenship is talked about. Human rights, for example, are in a way the public face of global citizenship, perhaps due to the transcendent quality of both discourses, imagining a civic location that is not state-bound but created simply by being human. The codification of global human rights laws is among the most significant results of the post–World War II era. Drawing from the broad decree that is the Universal Declaration of Human Rights (1948), a variety of internationally binding agreements have been established: the UN Convention on the Prevention and Punishment of the Crime of Genocide (1951), the International Covenant on Civil and Political Rights (1966), the International Covenant on Economic, Social, and Cultural Rights (1966) and the Convention on the Rights of the Child (1989). These conventions among others represent efforts to codify international law with respect to the treatment of people, one that respects the rights of sovereigns and yet grants protections for individuals and collectivities vis-à-vis states.

A recent complication in the reconfiguration of power between states and citizens is that of universal jurisdiction. Universal jurisdiction is

> the right of any country to try a person who has committed crimes against humanity, irrespective of whether the country in which the crime was committed is a signatory to a convention that provides for international criminal responsibility in respect of that crime.
>
> (Singer, 2002)

The notion here is that anyone who commits a crime against humanity, such as murder, genocide, enslavement, deportation, torture, rape, disappearance or apartheid, can be held to account for this crime anywhere in the world, without safe harbor or refuge and regardless of national borders. This is a fairly controversial legal principle since it may undermine the sovereignty of states, calling into question a long-standing principle of diplomatic immunity while opening wide the possibility that unscrupulous individuals may exploit this standard for political gain (Singer, 2002, p. 116). Yet, that universal jurisdiction is an open question suggests the extent to which individuals are recognized as having standing and are sovereign in relation to states. This change represents a dramatic shift in civic and legal identity of people around the world.

The establishment of the International Criminal Court (ICC) under the Rome Statute (1998) identifies four domains of international crimes (genocide, crimes against humanity, war crimes and crimes of aggression) that can lead to adjudication by a tribunal in The Hague. Currently, there are 121 parties to the Statute, which operates on state consent. In effect, countries must assent to be governed by the ICC and can make exclusions/exceptions even when they choose to participate. Enforcement of the Rome Statute, however, will be an uphill struggle as the recent presidential elections in Kenya illustrate. Uhuru Kenyatta, son of Jomo Kenyatta, Kenya's first president after independence, was elected president in March, 2013. Kenyatta is charged by the ICC for bankrolling death squads during the bloody 2007 elections in Kenya, charges that he denies. The North–South, colonizer–colonized tensions are reanimated by this case, as Ugandan President Museveni declared at Kenyatta's inauguration in April, 2013 that the vote indicates "the rejection of the blackmail of the International Criminal Court (steered by) arrogant actors to install leaders of their choice in Africa and eliminate those they don't like" (Gettleman, 2013). Perhaps most ironic is that countries who refuse to participate in the ICC, such as the US, have until very recently kept Kenyatta at a distance for his refusal to be held accountable before the court. This political episode represents tension between a state-based politics of sovereignty emblematic of the 20th century and the emergence of an individual/group-based sovereignty more in keeping with the current time.

The rise of a global conception of jurisprudence is a distinct pattern among constitutional courts globally. This cross-fertilization of legal reasoning, which has been called variously legal comparativism and transjudicialism, demonstrates the leading edge of how states are increasingly cooperating on matters of constitutional law (Gaudelli, 2007; Slaughter, 2004). As Slaughter suggests, "the emergence of a global jurisprudence refers more to the existence of active dialogue among the worlds' judges based on a limited number of precedents...no one answer is the right one; the principles of pluralism and legitimate difference again prevail" (p. 78). As institutions like the European Court of Human Rights, the European Court of Justice and the various supreme courts of European states demonstrate, there is greater collaboration among judges across borders and along with an emerging sense of order even in cases where no supranational institution or laws exist. Comity, or the respect of courts as legitimate arbiters of conflicts regardless of where they may happen to be located, is an important principle that increasingly comes into play with transnational litigation related to business law, for example. The overlay between commerce, which increasingly does not recognize international boundaries, and courts, that are still somewhat tethered to national laws, can create sharp disputes. In *Kaepa, Inc* v. *Achilles Corp.* (1996), Kaepa was the plaintiff in a federal court case filed in Texas against Achilles Corporation, a Japanese company (United States Court of Appeals, 1996). The case involved a breach of contract dispute, one that Achilles agreed to have heard in a US court. Achilles then filed a mirror case of breach of contract against Kaepa in a Japanese court. The US District Court in Texas granted an injunction against the same case in the Japanese court, an edict they could not enforce but one that the Japanese court abided by based on the principle of international comity.

Slaughter's conclusions about an emergent global legal order suggest that sovereignty is redefined as a disaggregated phenomenon engaged by a variety of actors—legislators, government administrators, judges, NGOs and government ministers. Rather than thinking about power in the hands of the state as solitary and singular, or a 20th-century conception of states, she contends that sovereignty is "relational rather than insular." Slaughter (2004) writes,

> In a world in which sovereignty means the capacity to participate in cooperative regimes in the collective interest of all states, expanding the formal capacity of different state institutions to interact with their counterparts around the world means expanding state power.
>
> (Slaughter, 2004, p. 268)

Perhaps this is the state of the world, legally, in the early 21st century, though my hesitation is to suggest there is much more to any civic arrangement than a body of laws, courts, legislators and enforcement agencies. This worldview is demonstrably Western and one would have difficulty mapping a disaggregated view of sovereignty onto a deeply divided world. I recall giving a talk at a conference in India about international law and human rights, engaging a discussion about this contentious global/legal framework. A former member of the Indian military approached me afterwards and said that while he appreciated my thoughts about global citizenship, he was convinced that it was a discourse most appropriate for the West, where national sovereignty and identity are more concretized than in India where a sense of nationhood is still developing. I found his remark compelling as it reminded me of the significant limits of GCE as a global framework.

Subjectivity, or Who Do We Think of Ourselves in the World?

The sense of who we think, feel and believe ourselves to be generates both from within and without, through an individualized sense of ourselves coupled with a relational sense of how we understand the world, other people, and various groups. It is a vital dimension of global citizenship. Subjectivity is constantly on the move, of course, as people learn, develop and change over the course of their lives and in relation to the changes that are occurring in the people and social environments that surround them. As we move on our personal horizons of development, and so too does the world around us, we find points of awareness where we can identify a significant shift in our thinking, feeling and believing from a previous self.

A recent study confirms how people change over time along with the limits in being cognizant of those changes in the future. Some 19,000 people were surveyed and the study found that most believed they had changed a great deal in the decade up to the present but did not imagine themselves changing much in the decade to come, what the researchers dubbed the "end of history illusion" (Quoidbach et al., 2013). I most often witness this blind spot with graduate students, who will often report how much they have changed as a result of their studies to date, but rarely believe that these changes will continue, indeed with increased velocity, over time. There is something about society that implicitly teaches us that it is best to be completed, to have reached closure, rather than embracing the fact that we are incomplete, in process and as yet, not fully known even to ourselves.

I once led a group of US high school students for a month of home-stays in St. Petersburg in 1992, not long after the city was renamed from the Soviet era, Leningrad. We did an initial side-excursion to Moscow to visit museums, palaces and the ballet, but my students were abuzz with the idea of going to the newly opened McDonald's there. I recall thinking how odd it was that they were intrigued by this particular hybrid. The narrative that they were abiding, though I think unaware of it, was that the change sweeping Russia was a result of economic liberalization coupled with democratic participation, symbolized for these students in the free choice to go to McDonald's. If they knew then what is happening now in Russia, with its oligarchic and autocratic governance, I doubt they would be as sanguine about the changes. The response of this student group captured the irony of globalization at that moment: that the world was being remade in the image of the West and how enamored the West was with its export. These students were in some measure trying to find their American selves in Moscow.

The flow of people and media around the world is nothing new, but the rate of flow is remarkably fast and some would argue fundamentally reconstituting subjectivity. Arjun Appadurai suggests that electronic media and migratory people are the crucial linkage between modernity and globalization (Appadurai, 1996). As people migrate and media becomes increasingly available, the interplay—between messages received, images communicated and hybridizations formed—flourishes. The transformed self, reimagined in the everyday circumstances of life through electronic mediation, both individually and collectively, is reshaping a global culture while simultaneously creating a new form of politics that requires attention to micronarratives of mobile populations, those who have migrated and clustered elsewhere and seek recognition in that new space. These ruptures, Appadurai contends, make the nation-state increasingly obsolete as power shifts away from strong, institutional forms and moves towards mediation, imagination and reconstituting oneself in light of these changes.

Not all analyses of globalization impact are nearly as positive about its creative capacity, however. The notion of globalization as a rupture, or a fundamental alteration of world society, has been challenged by those such as Gayatari Chakravorty Spivak who argue that the liberalization of world financial markets, as in the Bretton Woods Conference agreements, represents a fundamental shift from previous, state-bound economies. Yet, the repetition of hegemonic colonialism is present in all points of change as well. She explores the case against Osama bin Laden to stand trial under international law, for example, demonstrating how the rupture of adjudicating international law related to terroristic acts is "still culled from various older axiomatics – here, the juridico-legal" (Spivak, 2004). The prideful assertion often uttered in the North about triumphal globalization chooses to disregard the ways that identities and institutions are bound within post-colonial ways of perceiving and acting in the world.

The residues of colonialism in the contemporary global era can also be illustrated in Barack Obama's Administration, which has been plagued by trumped-up claims about his legitimacy to be president. Conspiracies about his birth surrounded his first term and linger through his second. Detractors claimed that his *bona fides* as a US citizen, born in Hawaii, were faked and that he was in fact born in Kenya. Even after counter-evidence was presented over and over again, many activists, media personalities and public officials continued to make unfounded assertions otherwise. Perhaps more unsettling is the refrain heard at Tea Party events in the 2010 healthcare debate that "We want our country back!" The irony of this statement, that a black president had somehow stolen the US from itself, is difficult to sort out rationally, yet it revealed a deeper dynamic of how race was being interpreted in light of the Obama presidency. Despite claims by many who voted against Obama in 2012 that race was not a factor in their decision, it is difficult to disentangle the demands to take a country back from assertions that the US was post-racial. The evidence of just how racialized the American electorate remains was written all over the results of 2012. While Obama carried over 51 percent of the vote nationally, for example, he received just 14 percent of white male and 16 percent of white female voters in Alabama (NBC, 2012). Race continues to cast a long shadow over US politics, as one might expect, despite full-throated claims to have wiped the slate clean. These sentiments mirror the claims made about post-national, post-colonial globalization starting afresh when the turmoil of the colonial era and its neocolonial offspring are evident in many places.

Spivak troubles the way that culture is typically engaged in globalization discourse, challenging the facile construction of culture to "a place where different explanations always collide, not just by races and classes, but by genders and generations. Culture is its own explanations" (Spivak, 2012, p. 121). The implication of this critique, that culture is tautological, demonstrates the looseness of culture as an analytic term. Culture is a ground for assertion, or what people within a culture believe, think or feel about something, a categorical way of thinking that obfuscates the diversity of perspective inherent in all social groupings and among individuals. Thinking about culture and globalization with dissensus challenges simple explanations to why events unfold as they do or superficial efforts to theorize choices as simply part of culture, as in why those engaged in suicide bombings do what they do, for example. Culture is thus viewed as a straightjacket, a disembodied force that compels certain others to think and act in certain ways. This too is an inheritance from the ancient Greeks, who dubbed *ethnos* as "one's own kind of people" and *ethnikos* as "other people" with all of its pejorative power (Spivak, 2012, p. 150). The current, globally inspired division of us/them has an additional layer, however, as Spivak notes, an inheritance from colonialist discourse that privileges the West and makes suspect the rest. She illustrates this layer with this best-case scenario of liberal multiculturalism's enactment:

> On a given day we are reading a text from one national origin…. People from other national origins in the classroom (other, that is, than Anglo) relate sympathetically but superficially, in an aura of same difference. The Anglo relates benevolently to everything, "knowing about other cultures" in a relativist glow.
>
> (Spivak, 2012, p.142)

Perhaps the main point of contrast among those who see globalization as a rupture in identity and those who view it as a repetition is the implied sense of agency. Do people have the ability to freely and of their own will make choices about their lives? Those like Spivak who argue for globalization as a repetition are inclined to say no, that free will and choice are really "deeply imbricated with capitalism disguised as a pursuit of happiness" (Spivak, 2012, p. 130); whereas those like Appadurai and Appiah praise "contamination" as it abides by the golden rule of cosmopolitanism, or "I am human: nothing human is alien to me" (Appiah, 2006, p. 111). For Appiah, globalization has unleashed profound changes that affect people economically and culturally, and yet they retain the ability to choose what to wear, eat, believe, debate, think and do. And like Appadurai, larger social and technological changes have set the table for this multicultural smorgasbord in a way quite unlike the past, allowing a wider degree of choice for an increasing number of people than had previously been possible.

A number of controversies surround a cosmopolitan subjectivity, however, particularly as the concept has increasingly been deployed to illustrate ongoing renovations with respect to the meanings of citizenship. Will Kymlicka and Kathryn Walker (2012) offer *rooted cosmopolitanism* as a way of thinking through the dilemmas that inhere in the concept while drawing on the work of Appiah. Rootedness points up the limitations of earlier versions of cosmopolitanism that equated it with Western knowledge, language and dispositions, perhaps a *post hoc* justification for European colonialism. Kymlicka and Walker's notion of rootedness recognizes the possibilities to be worldly and not of that particular world, however. They consider Canada as a nation grounded in a conceptualization of rooted cosmopolitanism and see this subjectivity as one that does not replace national subjectivity with a global one but coordinates these identities as mutually reinforcing.

> This is the promise of rooted cosmopolitanism: that the very same national identities that bind people deeply to their own particular national community and territory can also mobilize moral commitment to distant others, and that inculcating and affirming a sense of Swedishness or Canadianness among co-nationals can simultaneously inculcate and affirm a sense of global citizenship.
>
> (Kymlicka & Walker, 2012, p. 6)

Their book illustrates the ways that certain nation-states—such as Canada and Sweden—have incorporated a global outlook that seeks diverse perspectives and honors difference into their conception of what it means to be Canadian and Swedish. Wing-Wah Law's research in Taiwan and Hong Kong suggest a similar effort to balance subjectivity and civic identity—local, national/regional and global.

Environment, or How Do We Think and Act in Relation to the Biosphere?

Environment is an impossibly broad topic that raises a myriad of issues with significant effect on global citizenship discourse. Two particular areas of interest include sustainable development and degrowth. Sustainable development is widely considered desirable and might be described as mainstream with regard to government policies and attention. Degrowth, however, is a relatively small yet significant strand of discourse that calls for a more fundamental shift in thinking about people's relationship to the biosphere. While the former is more congruent with the perspectives of those studied herein, the latter presents an alternative way to think about problems of development.

Sustainable development coalesced as a result of the World Commission on Environment and Development's call to create "A Common Agenda for Change." This call resulted in the Brundtland Report (1987), named for the former Norwegian prime minister who led the Commission, Gro Harlem Brundtland. The core of the Report involved balancing environment, development and equity:

> Many critical survival issues are related to uneven development, poverty, and population growth. They all place unprecedented pressures on the planet's lands, waters, forests, and other natural resources, not least in the developing countries. The downward spiral of poverty and environmental degradation is a waste of opportunities and of resources. In particular, it is a waste of human resources. These links between poverty, inequality, and environmental degradation formed a major theme in our analysis and recommendations. What is needed now is a new era of economic growth – growth that is forceful and at the same time socially and environmentally sustainable.
>
> (*Our Common Future*, 1987, p. 2)

A major contribution of the Brundtland Commission was its ability to raise awareness that the environment was not simply a resource to be exploitatively used but rather an integral part of human development now and in the future. Furthermore, links to social issues demonstrated the need for accounting for social development not as an economic drag but ultimately as a contributor to future social development. The notion of "interlocking crises" was foundational to the Report. The aim was to develop human societies in such ways to meet the needs of the present generation without compromising the ability of future generations to meet their needs.

Sustainable development over the past three decades increasingly became the basis of global governance structures, including the International Monetary Fund (IMF) and World Bank projects, along with state governments, international governmental (IGO) and non-governmental organizations (NGOs). Environment and development conferences, such as the Rio Earth Summit 1992, Johannesburg Earth Summit 2002 and Rio+20 Earth Summit 2012 offered opportunities for delegates from cooperative sectors around the world to discuss efforts, share insights and revamp goals. The Millennium Development Goals benchmark of 2015, established in 2000, has generated a good deal of discussion about accomplishments, problems and new direction. These goals are undertaken with the full cooperation of all stakeholders, from private corporations, NGOs and IGOs, governments, universities and think-tanks, to UN agencies and global institutions (e.g. IMF) and private citizens. The new Sustainable Development Goals, 2015–2030 build on these efforts while promoting discourse and policies towards those ends. The goals reveal the maturation of sustainable development over the past three decades, while broad principles have been refined and operationalized into a problematic yet operative global system.

Additional friction points for sustainable development emerge from how sustainability names and reifies practices that might otherwise not be viewed as either *sustainable* or *development*. As Timothy Luke (2005) examines, sustainable development is increasingly used to paper over activities that are ecologically harmful and do not serve social development but employ the category as a way of rhetorically branding their activity in politically amenable ways. The recent British Petroleum (BP) campaign in the wake of the disastrous and grossly negligent oil spill in the Gulf of Mexico illustrates Luke's point. The polluting, carbon-dedicated industry, following the spill and their cleanup efforts, can embrace the mantle of being *sustainable developers* ironically as they commodify and proliferate fossil fuel consumption, the most unsustainable of resources. What's more, BP and other petroleum companies actively lobbied to continue deep-water drilling, the high-risk variety that led to the massive blowout in the Gulf while growing profits in the aftermath of the Deepwater Horizon spill at a rate unseen before in this economic sector. Green ad campaigns by carbon polluters like these paradoxically reinscribe the "cash commodity nexus (in which) the objects (were) produced all in the name of developing sustainably" (Luke, 2005, p. 235).

An interesting point of analysis about the original Brundtland Commission Report *Our Common Future* is the way in which education is discussed. Education is the focus of section 3.2 in that document but mainly from a policy perspective of providing universal access to primary and eventually secondary education, increasing literacy rates, developing access for girls' education and creating curricula that are locally relevant (e.g. agricultural education in farming regions). Curiously missing, however, is attention to global learning itself, save a call for environmental education "at every level" and "teacher training… encouraging contacts among teachers from different countries" (*Our Common Future: Report of the World Commission on Environment and Development*, 1987, p. 96). This way of thinking about education, where it is positioned as an institution to transmit knowledge and therefore improve social development but not as a laboratory to engage students and teachers in learning about and acting on problems, is common. Interesting too is that civics is only mentioned twice in a 300-page document and no attention is given to global citizenship, a phrase that lacked currency in that era. This illustrates a predilection on the part of policymakers to view educators and students as being directed to carry out the work of development without full knowledge and participation in the nature of the problem of development itself.

This may seem like a minor issue but it points to a deeper problem in how we typically think about education, which tends to be rooted in an industrial/productivity model that ironically views students as part of the process of production but not part of the creation of that process; or, education as something done to or for young people but not with them. This germinates a certain degree of alienation in education, leading students and teachers to think of their work as "not real" for in a sense they are correct, the "reality" has been distilled out leaving only mandates for knowledge transmission behind.

This points to a conundrum in developing ecological sensibility since while students might be taught this "at every level", if they live in an urban or suburban community completely surrounded by the human-built environment, they too develop a sense of isolation, if not alienation from the very contact that would make environmental education "real." Richard Louv illustrates this problem in light of what he has termed "nature-deficit disorder" or how contemporary youth in the US are consumed by digital devices and mediated experience rather than first-hand experiences in and of nature. Louv posits five dimensions of the current age, including: (1) a severance from food's origins, (2) a disappearing line between machines, humans and other animals, (3) an intellectual understanding of our relationship with animals, (4) the invasion of cities by wild animals and (5) the rise of new suburban, interiorized, forms (Louv, 2008, p. 19). While Louv admits that these patterns are not all intuitively linked as a group, they illustrate the nonlinear nature of epochal change. In sum they all point to a dislocation of young people from their natural environments and towards the mediated experience of a digital device.

Concerns about the isolated way of thinking about childhood in the US resonate with the concerns of some early progressives at the turn of the last century. As John Dewey argued, the shift from an agricultural to an industrial society marked a significant break between learning about life on a farm, where the sustenance and labor of each day were necessarily intertwined, to life in a factory, where the experience of raising food was gone, replaced by the mediation of hourly wages used at a local market selling food from farther and farther reaches. This change experienced by so many in the period of rapid industrialization, immigration and urbanization led to a similar break in how students learned. Learning was removed from the immediacy of experience in the child's life and turned into an academic affair of rehearsing alien symbols and abstract concepts. Dewey's most telling anecdote about this problem involves his visit near the turn of the last century to the river town of Moline, Illinois. The students did not realize that the Mississippi River described in their book was the very same river that flowed through the western part of their town (Dewey, 1969).

The increasing disassociation caused by modernity, reaching an apex in the digital age, has attracted the attention of many thinkers of the past century. Yet, few have challenged the basic premise of Western society now exported virtually everywhere: that development is a synonym for growth, that the environment offers both resources and dumping grounds for that growth and that development will be unequal. Sustainable development principles in fact do not challenge the premise of development being equated with economic growth; indeed, the foundation of sustainability is to maintain the current system and extend growth to more places. Recently, however, a growing movement of scholars, intellectuals and citizens, has begun to coalesce around the principle of degrowth to reorient thinking about what constitutes development.

Richard Heinberg, a senior fellow at the Post-Carbon Institute, argues that economic growth as we have known it ended in the global financial crisis of 2008 as the world economy bumped up against permanent limits including depleted resources, declining industrial output, growing human population, increased food scarcity and increased pollution (Heinberg, 2011, p. 5). The advent of Peak Oil, or the time when oil production reaches its maximum rate before beginning "an inevitable decline," estimated currently to be sometime before 2035, is elemental to his thesis (p. 111). This will likely trigger a cascade of problems, including territorial conflicts over remaining oil supplies, price spikes and decreasing rates of exports to import-dependent states and fundamentally an alteration in oil-dependency, which permeates so much of modern life. This is not the sole source of the problem, however, as Heinberg explains.

Water, food and minerals face post-peak conditions wherein prices are increasing due to a decrease in productivity in the past few decades, decreases that point to exhaustion of certain resources or severe scarcity on the near horizon. Fresh water, for example, is steadily declining in access such that the UN predicts 1.8 billion people will be living in areas of absolute water scarcity by 2025 (Heinberg, 2011, p. 125), not unlike the increasingly dire situation in California in 2015. This accounts for the degradation of supplies that is exacerbated by decreases in snowpack due to global warming affecting colder climes. With regard to food, price spikes mirror those in petroleum due to the coincident challenge of producing food (with water, of course) and then transporting it for distribution, which uses energy and increases those costs. Coupled with human population growth, the bottom line is that food production is being slowly outstripped by demand. Minerals pose a similar challenge as many have reached their production threshold and face decline in availability, rising prices and eventual exhaustion. Given current usage, for example, antimony, gold, indium, lead, silver, tin and zinc have between 25 and 50 years until full exhaustion (Heinberg, 2011, p. 142). If the consumption of these and other minerals reaches US rates, as more people globally seek a convenience lifestyle of consumption like that in the West, these time horizons shrink to between 5 and 20 years.

Environmental challenges are daunting yet there is still an opportunity to consider alternatives. Transition initiatives are under way globally. One such example is Totnes in the southwest of England. As they note in their website, "Transition Town Totnes (TTT) is a dynamic, community-led charity that is strengthening the local economy, reducing the cost of living and preparing for a future with less oil and a changing climate" (Totnes). Their focus includes rebuilding local food production, localizing energy, reconsidering building materials and healthcare, and rethinking waste management (Heinberg, 2011, p. 271). The principle at work in this town, and many like it that are part of a transition effort, is that governments and individuals are incapable of mounting such major changes in the relatively short time frame needed but communities have the possibility of experimenting with these changes and eventually serving as exemplars of degrowth that are workable and satisfactory.

Other challenges to sustainable development norms have been raised from the global South, particularly around the hypocrisy of calls for sustainable development emanating from the global North, countries that created societies that were neither environmentally sustainable nor socially inclusive. The argument might best be summarized as follows: the North's rapacious and wanton development of the 19th and 20th centuries created much of the historic environmental mess that we are in as Western development held no regard for the environment other than as a trove of resources and a place to locate waste. And yet now, having achieved economic vitality and a measure of social inclusion, the North turns to the South as if to say, "you must not develop in the same way." Vandana Shiva (1997) wittily captures this critique in the following scathing rebuke:

> The moral framework of the global reach is quite the opposite. There are no reflexive relationships. The G-7 can demand a forest convention that imposes international obligations on the Third World [sic] to plant trees. But the Third World [sic] cannot demand that the industrialized countries reduce the use of fossil fuels and energy. The "global" has been so structured, that the North (as the globalized local) has all rights and no responsibility and the South has no rights, but all responsibility. "Global ecology" at this level becomes a moralization of immorality. It is devoid of any ethics for planetary living; and is based on concepts not of universal brotherhood but of universal bullying.
>
> (Shiva, 1997, p. 234)

This is perhaps the most daunting conundrum of global citizenship, the view that it is yet again an imposition of North upon South in a manner that serves to reinscribe rather than ameliorate social inequalities. There is no simple solution for this dilemma though I contend throughout that as global citizenship discursively takes shape over the next century and beyond, these issues must be addressed in the discursive space of GCE.

Moving Ahead

I set out in this chapter to establish a context for global citizenship, one that will continue to be informed and shaped by the illustrations of educational practice discussed herein. This overview is limited in that some important domains could reasonably constitute whole sections, if not chapters themselves, such as the status of women, media, civil society, arts and aesthetics, engineering and design, to name a few. An important subtext of the overview is that of urgency. The situation in which we find ourselves in the early 21st century suggests that the enormity of global challenges, not the least of which is global warming, coupled with the relative incapacity of our world to address these challenges, is a dire situation that begs changes.

Citizenship and global, both problematic terms commingled in this neologism, are under renovation conceptually as the discourse moves to account for myriad changes. The issue of scale coupled with the openness of who belongs to such descriptions is a vital piece of how that conversation is unfolding, evidenced in borderlands and what were once borders across the world. Relatedly, the flow of capital, information and ideologies like human rights has created significant tensions in the world, ones that can be read as undermining the sovereignty of states coupled with a reconfigured, not yet imagined political, social and legal framework. And as changes in power—economic, political and legal—emerge, understandings of what it means to be a person, both individually and collectively, are too on the move. Culture as a concept seems to have lost its explicatory luster as people harvest other landscapes—such as media, digital interaction and institutions—to answer questions about who they are and what it means to be of those fluid communities. All of this is occurring amid an increasingly demanding backdrop that deserves attention in the foreground, one of a deteriorating biosphere. Shared agreement about the value of the environment, not diminutively as a warehouse of resources or a dump, but an integral dimension of what it means to be human, is emerging; an insight that has propelled and will propel many changes.

This introduction points towards a decisive next-step in this inquiry—What is the nature of global citizenship education? The motivation for education springs from a recognition that a handful of experts having knowledge of these weighty issues will not suffice. Rather, there must be a communicative space, a truly educational opportunity, that opens up possibilities of knowing the world more intimately, in a way that conjures the limitless sense of being human that seeks transcendence while deeply grounded in the temporal and material realities of a day in life. That is what lies ahead.

2

GLOBAL CITIZENSHIP EDUCATION

One of my first encounters with the breadth of what it means to say *global education* occurred about 20 years ago as I was presenting a new research project on global learning. I began by saying that I was going to talk about a study I engaged of how young people learned about the world, and immediately five people stood up and left the room. This was somewhat surprising to a neophyte academic but I later realized that while the session to which I was assigned was entitled *global education*, others on the panel interpreted their work and the field as being about international comparisons between school systems, not analyses of what global learning goes on in those schools. What made their work global was the locations and contexts in which the research was conducted rather than curricula or happenings at schools and in learning spaces, which was and remains the focus of my work.

This episode led me to pull back from academic circles that solely focused on international comparisons and policies if only to gain a sharper sense of what I really wanted to do. But a tension lingered in my thinking around the question of why these fields—global learning/curriculum and international/comparative education—were so disparate as not to be in conversation. And I also began to wonder why other fields—such as innovations in schools and multilingual/multicultural students—were also having separate conversations about how globalization affects education.

The intention of this chapter is to briefly put these strands into the same conversation while exploring more deeply what it means to engage in GCE. I then offer a heuristic of what is meant when GCE is referenced throughout the book while considering discourses that created this way of thinking about teaching and learning. But first I take on a brief overview of globalization and education through three separate discourses—comparative policy/research, educational innovations and multilingual/multicultural students—and how each of these three largely separate conversations about globalization and education takes shape and is interrelated to the others and GCE. Next I move on to consider GCE by looking at various frameworks for global learning that points towards engagement as a citizen, namely those frameworks offered by Oxfam, the Maastricht Convention and the United Nations Educational, Scientific and Cultural Organization (UNESCO). I close the chapter by offering my own, *bricolage* version of GCE that points to both the everyday and transformative, mundane and existential questions that meaningful GCE can raise with students, teachers, schools and, arguably, society and how that way of thinking can form into a habit of thought.

Comparative Research and Policymaking in a Global Era

Education as a field is a relatively late-arrival to the changes brought about by globalization—broadly understood as the integration of world societies that has roots in the movement of early hominids hundreds of thousands of years ago, the quickening and deepening of that integration with the rise of modernity (~1500CE) alongside the hyper-digitized and mediated connectivity of the past six decades. One might also say that education as we know it—with schools, organized in classroom units with one teacher and multiple pupils engaging a prescribed course of study—is a fundamentally Western phenomenon that spread from Europe to the world as a direct result of colonial enterprises over the past 400 years. In a sense both claims are true: education in its Western form is a centuries-old, global movement while researching and refining, or comparing educations, is a comparatively new one.

Comparative education has existed as a field for the better part of the 20th century though the use of international comparisons in schools has only very recently become mainstream conversation about education (Darling-Hammond, 2010; Spring, 2009). Many regard Marc-Antoine Jullien's call in 1817 for governments to collect and share statistical data about schools so that policymakers can "deduce true principles…an almost positive science" as the earliest systematic efforts in comparative education (Fraser, 1964, p. 20). The move to study others became increasingly pronounced in the 20th century as societies were organized, university courses were established and long-distance travel became more routinized such that knowledge about other forms of education shifted from happenstance and anecdotal accounts towards a systematic field of study. The establishment of the World Council of Comparative Education Societies (WCCES) in 1970—an NGO that cooperates with UNESCO to support comparative education research—brought together over 30 national/regional organizations to engage in this cooperative, comparative inquiry. The aim of WCCES is to promote the study of comparative and international education throughout the world and enhance the academic status of this field and to bring comparative education to bear on the major educational problems of the day by fostering co-operative action by specialists from different parts of the world.

(Societies, 2015)

Organizations like WCCES demonstrate how thinking globally about education has gained traction in the past 50 years.

Nadine Dolby and Aliyah Rahman (2008) provide a useful typology of the various strands of international education and research, identifying six elements of scholarly discourse and practice, including: (1) comparative, (2) internationalization of higher education, (3) international schools, (4) international research on teaching and teacher education, (5) internationalization of K-12 education and (6) globalization of education. Each of these strands represents a discourse/research/practice community in its own right and has contributed to an emerging, if incomplete, understanding of what it means to engage in education in a globally interdependent world. The presence of these various types suggests an emerging consensus that *something else* related to how we understand schools is needed, though that something is highly variable depending on the particularities of subfields. As Mary Hayden (2011) notes,

> Even for those school-age students today who will never in adulthood leave their native shores, the future is certain to be so heavily influenced by international developments and their lives within national boundaries so affected by factors emanating from outside those boundaries that they will be hugely disadvantaged by an education that has not raised their awareness of, sensitivity to and facility with issues arising from beyond a national "home" context.
>
> (Hayden, 2011, p. 212)

The use of the term international as compared to global among comparativists like those in Dolby and Rahman (2008) suggests an important difference. *International* is typically preferred when the unit of analysis, the nation, is prominent as in matters related to ministries of education; while *global* references dimensions of interdependence, flows and networks that may or may not have policy ramifications.

Another missing element in Dolby and Rahman (2008) is how much economic competition dominates the conversation of what globalization and education have to do with each other. Global economic competition undergirds most of their identified strands because it serves as the most significant and typically singular rationale for global engagement by policymakers. Policymakers tightly couple educational success with economic development and generally bound their successes in national containers. While global economic competition has grown remarkably in the past three decades concomitant with neoliberal global reforms, educational competition has emerged with it (Spring, 2009).

Also, education itself has gradually shifted from being purely within the state/ social sector to a mixed entrepreneurial space of start-ups and venture capital, such that the global market in educational services is approximately US $111 billion annually (Spring, 2009, p. 84). Thus, having *globally competitive* schools, or ones that reference an international standard of what quality education constitutes coupled with the inclusion of schools as supposedly legitimate venues for capital investment, has become a significant aspect of what education in a global era has come to mean within policy circles. I am not advocating either international school benchmarking or capital investment in what ought to be a social investment as both changes are deeply problematic. Yet, that these factors describe the terrain of what is happening globally with respect to schools is unmistakable.

The ability to draw attention to different choices made in other societies and subsequent economic gains has become an especially significant dimension of policy debates that now have global moorings and resonance. Linda Darling-Hammond (2010) illustrates how the US has lagged in comparison to other societies in expenditures for education, for example, shining an especially glaring light on the underinvestment of the US in communities of historically marginalized youth and those living with significant poverty (Darling-Hammond, 2010, p. 14). The proportional decline in commitment of resources in the US and particularly with respect to geographic areas of greatest need has produced a rapid deterioration of US standing vis-à-vis other countries. She notes:

> In the space of one generation, South Korea moved from a nation that educated less than a quarter of its citizens through high school to one that now ranks third in college-educated adults, with most young people now completing postsecondary education.
>
> (Darling-Hammond, 2010, p. 5)

Education policy discourse, thus, strategically offers counter-examples and contrasts from various parts of the world as to say, *Why can't we do this?* in a way that is pointed and likely persuasive to a national audience.

A driving force in the apparent convergence of educational policy is an imagined yet powerful concept of *world-class standards*, or an assumption that there is an expert-endorsed education that rises to a certain level of quality, though the very concept of such an elusive standard has been vigorously critiqued (Silova & Steiner-Khamsi, 2008; Steiner-Khamsi, 2004). Political actors within borrowing nations strategically deploy this imagined reference to *world-class standards* to gain legitimacy (Steiner-Khamsi, 2004). "Thinking metaphorically, we may imagine references to elsewhere as screens onto which positive images – the ideal school, the model system of education – can be projected" (Waldow, 2012, p. 419).

Borrowers, therefore, typically have designs for purposeful extraction of educational policy. And their motivations tend to be economic and political ones.

This aspect of educational comparison has energized the spread of educational policies beyond local origins. These include a host of neoliberal, market-oriented reforms, including attacks on university-based teacher education and the concomitant creation of alternative pathways to teacher licensure; the rise of charter schools in urban areas often designed for minority students and financially supported by non-state entities such as corporations and nonprofits; and performance pay for teachers to introduce market and reward principles to the profession—just to name a few—all illustrative of how changes in one location quickly become taken up elsewhere in the world (Apple, 2011, p. 223). These reforms indeed have a *US/West-to-the-world* volition as many of the reforms such as charter schools, online learning and rapid teacher certification (e.g. *Teach for America/All*) began in the US. Such reforms are often pressed by global elites, among them ministers of education, corporate heads and those with a national and/or corporate interest in having their educational systems viewed favorably in global comparisons while serving private interests.

The phenomenon of *curriculum-from-elsewhere* has generated many responses, not the least of which is a recalibration of curriculum discourse in the US in light of a wider, global discussion. Ongoing debates between structuralist and reconceptualist curricula, for example, have been redirected by a growing conversation outside the US about the nature of curricula, particularly as comparative test scores shine the spotlight on high-achieving countries/regions such as Finland, Singapore and Shanghai, China; one that has touched off a re-examination of the global moorings, or lack thereof, in the US. Janet Miller (2005) illustrates the intersections and possibilities arising from this new worldly terrain for curricula, a field that has traditionally been organized around the US:

> The worldliness of US curriculum studies implies an understanding of how it, as a field, is implicated in a range of both national and international social, cultural, and political educational relations as well as discursive practices that produce both existing power relations and forms of subjectivity. We must work to understand how we are implicated in that worldliness and its attendant relations and practices—implicated not only in the sense of our vested interests but also in how US curriculum studies folds in, on and around (in a Deleuzian way) other cultures, knowledges, and identities, and how those, in turn, enfold US curriculum content and practices.
>
> (Miller, 2005, p. 22)

Miller reminds readers that efforts to nostalgically retreat to neatened structural/reconceptualist debates are not congruent with the current moment, one that is shot through with conversations happening at many different nodes in an expanding network of educational discourse that no longer presupposes a US-center to curriculum discourse.

Another node within the education discourse network is student movements. Student-led movements, such as opposition to standardized testing and protests against poor-quality schools, periodically demonstrate how global mediascapes allow for a multifaceted flow of ideas, critiques and actions. And this is not an insignificant point since the channels for these flows are just as riven with possibilities as they are inscribed by dominant voices. The fact that Darling-Hammond—an educational researcher with wide-reach who was a key advisor to candidate Obama in 2008—uses the same tools for engagement as students who protest winnowing educational funding is significant as it shows that the contents of global conversations about education are not fixed. Savvy use of media tools can create lasting effects, as demonstrated recently by students in Newark, New Jersey who organized a protest of thousands of young people to call attention to the deteriorating quality of their education ("Thousands of Newark Students…", May 22, 2015). This event, among other things, precipitated the resignation of conservative reformer Superintendent Cami Anderson less than a month later.

The dynamism surrounding global discourses about education, media and a widening array of actors matters insofar as conversations around global practices in education, particularly in the policy discourse of the US, often presume an abstract, hard to pin down standard of *world-class education* along with an evaluative yardstick used to ostensibly show deterioration in certain systems/regions and growth in others. This claim does not discount the value of comparative study of education, but rather suggests caution regarding sweeping generalizations about educational quality of a universal sort along with claims of relative quality in a global era of education.

Innovations, Education and a Global Era

Educational innovations broadly conceived occupy a significant share of bandwidth in the emergent conversation of globalization and education. What might be called innovative is disputed, though, since the category may include *instructional practices* like online and blended online/face-to-face learning and game-based learning; *tools*, such as iPads/iPhones, Smartboards and other commercial products; *multimedia platforms*, such as wikis, social media sites and presentation software; or *conceptual changes*, such as project-based learning, experiential education, student personalized learning and shared-governance within schools. Educational innovations of the past decade like these draw deeply from global processes and metaphors to motivate and engage. These innovations tend to be tightly coupled with technological hardware and software that are rooted in connectivity, thus the global aspects of educational innovations are typically comingled. Globalization is infrequently talked about without reference to digital technology's affordance of constant and distant connectivity.

Citizenship, too, has become deeply intertwined with digital technology as illustrated by the prevalence of media in social and political domains and the use of digital networking among activists. There is an interesting relationship between technological innovations and diverse places—e.g. Singapore, Silicon Valley and Shanghai—where these changes have been tried that has contributed to the otherness, or global character, of the reforms.

Those who write in the area of information and communication technology (ICT) see the compatibility of global connectivity and new ways of learning as foundational to an ongoing shift of when, how and why people learn. These shifts are often articulated in light of global economic competition and opening access to education.

> The *future prosperity of countries* around the world depends on how their education systems can be designed to foster economic development. If the United States is going to compete successfully in a global economy, it will have to rethink many of its assumptions about education.
>
> (Collins & Halverson, 2009, p. 128, emphasis added)

The conflation of ICT and global is evident here, though the global appears in this iteration as economic competition among nations and the need to "keep up with *the Singapores*." ICT is often talked about in terms of being a non-negotiable since it is ubiquitous and therefore a necessary tool in education. The fact that these tools are constantly in flux by dint of a global marketplace that pushes instruments towards ever-faster obsolescence is rarely part of the same dialog; however, this condition serves as the deep substructure of how technical innovations shape education.

Not all who write about innovation emphasize the technical nature of what it means to learn and think differently about education. As Andy Hargreaves and Dennis Shirley (2012) contend, living in an "age of techne" educators can fall too easily into a trap of thinking the next form of digital technology will be a long-sought elixir for all that ails education. They suggest that harmonizing innovations with sound pedagogical practices is a desired path, drawn from their study of robotics education in Singapore and adaptive technologies for special education students in Ontario, a heuristic they summarize as "switch on; switch off; stay balanced" (Hargreaves & Shirley, 2012, p. 199). But it would be a misrepresentation to suggest that the innovation/global nexus is solely based around technology, as the human dimensions, at least in terms of organization and management if not emotional aspects, are equally prized and sought after in the global quest for innovative excellence. As Michael Barber (2012) notes in his review of innovative, ostensibly high-performing global schools:

> The fundamental message...is: set high standards; monitor whether they are being achieved; provide excellent teachers who improve their teaching

throughout their careers; ensure well-trained, well-selected principals or head-teachers; and then reorganise the system's structure so that it becomes a dynamic driver of change rather than a static bureaucracy – a driver of quality rather than an enforcer of compliance.

(Barber, 2012, p. 59)

Still others writing about the age of connectivity and how this global/technical moment is an opportunity for thinking differently about education and learning have considered the disordered character of the current moment. As Michalinos Zembylas and Charalambos Vrasidis suggest, there is discordance between the metaphor of the global village as a small, interconnected community and the stark realities that speak to the contested and hegemonic nature of ICT domination. They propose a counter metaphor, that of the global nomad, who is "to live with the discomfort of uncertainty and the complexity of change" (Zembylas & Vrasidis, 2006, p. 71) and who has critical emotional literacy, engages in collective witnessing and participates through collective intelligence, all of which can be nurtured within an ICT space that employs the tools of an era of global connectivity, while at the same time using those tools in the service of its critique.

Educational innovation is unmistakably global both in the rhetoric and enactment of initiatives. Globalization serves as the priming context that creates conditions for global awareness around educational system comparisons, which then leads to educational gamesmanship, along with cooperation, around insights derived from those comparisons. Furthermore, the focus of innovation typically involves the deployment of technologies that lead to greater connectivity across time and space. At core, then, the move towards educational innovation is part and parcel of the current global moment in education.

Multilingual and Multicultural Immigration

Still another aspect of the interaction between education and globalization is the increasing flow of migration. The changing demographics of communities, particularly with South to North flows globally, calls upon teachers and schools to be more responsive to diversity in multiple forms. Michael Apple (2011) notes, however, that this is more than developing linguistic sensitivity alone since it requires a much deeper knowledge of the circumstances of those societies.

Superficial knowledge may not be much better than no knowledge at all. It may also paint a picture of parents and youth as passive "victims" of global forces, rather than as people who are active agents continually struggling both in their original nations and regions and here in the United States to build a better life for themselves, their communities, and their children. Thus, teachers and teacher educators need to know much more about the home countries—and about the movements, politics, and *multiple* cultural traditions and conflicts from where diasporic populations come.

(Apple, 2011, p. 223)

The broad recognition of language diversity in schools, for example, is a welcome social change in many societies, though recognition alone does not make schools necessarily hospitable to new arrivals.

The North's interest in welcoming diverse immigrants, primarily for the labor provided, couples oddly with a "feel-good" sense that having others around to embody difference is of value, perhaps as a way of compensating for collective guilt related to colonialism's long shadow and how these patterns now manifest in expanding global inequality and subsequent migration patterns. The tenor of conversation has been well-noted in the literature related to migration and educa-tion. Yet, as indicated by some, the disciplining of diversity that goes on in schools is indeed paradoxical. As Anne Rios-Rojas (2014) indicates from her research in a secondary school in the Catalan region of Spain, an area known for its embrace of ethnic diversity generally, the "feel-good" is complicated by explicit efforts to dis-cipline and control immigrant others vis-à-vis the dominant, here Catalan, culture.

> Whether framed in positive or negative terms, diversity needed to be dis-tributed in carefully measured doses so as not to upset the balance of the sys-tem. These local management concerns can be further understood in terms of their entanglements with national interests. Within a nation imagining itself as tolerant and progressive, too little diversity within a school might be problematic and could be seen as an indicator of segregation and intoler-ance. However, too much diversity concentrated within one school was just as disconcerting, threatening the balance of the nation and challenging modern conceptions of tolerance. As it stood, diversity was indeed some-thing that could not be left to its own devices; unattended it was prone to concentrating and growing to potentially alarming proportions.
>
> (Rios-Rojas, 2014, p. 12)

The presupposition about the static/balanced nature of regions or nations is reveal-ing as it positions diversity as tolerable only to the degree that it does not upend the norms of a particular area, those norms determined by empowered "locals" or "nationals." One can readily imagine a very similar dynamic as described in Barcelona occurring in Brooklyn or Brussels. Diversity—yes, so long as it "adds color" without disturbing the settled state of the local/regional/national culture, as imagined and reified.

The increased presence of language minority populations has also been cor-related with an increase in religious diversity, particularly in European societies.

Reva Jaffe-Walter (2013) found in her study of Muslim youth in Denmark that well-intended schools create "technologies of concern" that attempt to enfold immigrant students into dominant cultural norms that ironically exacerbate the otherness of Muslim youth. She describes a lesson about impossible love among adolescents, a classic theme in Western literature, that a teacher deploys as a way of normalizing romantic love as something more universal than culturally determined. Teachers in this study believed that part of their task as educators was to cultivate in immigrant students a sense of national belonging that abided by certain values and discarded others, or as one of the students interpreted their teachers actions, "Muslim students have to behave like Danish students" (Jaffe-Walter, 2013, p. 628).

The intersections of civic identity and legal dimensions of citizenship often appears as a point of friction in Northern schools engaged with Southern immigrants. Like Jaffe-Walter, Thea Renda Abu El-Haj (2010) explores the post-9/11 situation of a Palestinian community in a Pennsylvania high school. Students of Palestinian descent, though fully US citizens, were treated by faculty and administrators as foreigners or resident others, subtly denying them the full identity of national citizenship. Despite claims by teachers that they viewed all students individually, itself a Western presupposition, they would frequently make comments that positioned Palestinians as cultural captives in contrast to the freedom of individuality and choice afforded US students.

Tensions associated with immigration and education animate similar problems in the preceding educational borrowing and lending discussion. The normalized power dynamic—be it the immigrant who comes North for economic reasons and is burdened by unwanted social demands or the educational ministry of the global South that is beholden to economic development narratives not of their choosing—is working in both phenomena. The normativity thus presumed is part of what makes globalization and global education so controversial as otherwise well-intended educators may employ these normative values unwittingly in ways that exacerbate the challenges inherent in migration.

Illustrations of GCE

A forerunner to GCE is global education, which emerged in the late 1960s at the peak of the Cold War, in the context of various emancipatory movements throughout the world and with growing awareness about environmental concerns. Robert Hanvey's (1975) conceptualization is typically cited as the elemental core of global education, which includes five domains: perspective consciousness, state of the planet awareness, cross-cultural awareness, knowledge of global dynamics and awareness of human choices.

Global education has been critiqued as lacking a coherent conception, having been invoked as a slogan system rather than a way of organizing curriculum (Kirkwood, 2001; Lamy, 1987; Pike, 2013; Popkewitz, 1980). Some have argued that the ambiguity of global study allows for greater flexibility in developing

	Intended antecedents	Intended transactions	Intended outcomes
Political	Mainstream 'cosmopolitan democracy' perspective; not prevalent	Mainstream 'cosmopolitan democracy' perspective; not prevalent	Mainstream 'cosmopolitan democracy' perspective; not prevalent
Moral	Focus on human rights and responsibilities, strong cosmopolitan ideals; fairly prevalent	Some indication of 'new cosmopolitan' perspective, focus on human rights and responsibilities; fairly prevalent	Some indication of 'new cosmopolitan' perspective, focus on human rights, obligations and empathy; fairly prevalent
Economic	Focus on international development perspectives; not prevalent	International development perspectives but some discussion of fair trade; fairly prevalent	Focus on the benefits of global trade and technology for international development; fairly prevalent
Cultural	Focus on globalisation of arts, media, languages, sciences and technologies; positive features of multiculturalism; highly prevalent	Strong focus on multicultural awareness-raising; very highly prevalent	Strong focus on multicultural awareness; very highly prevalent
Social	Focus on ideas of global community and enhancing communications between peoples; fairly prevalent	Focus on relationship-building between schools and pupils in different countries and cultures; very highly prevalent	Strong focus on co-operation and inclusion; very highly prevalent
Critical	Focus on ideas about bias and stereotyping; fairly prevalent	Focus on challenging stereotypes and mainstream perceptions of subaltern populations; not prevalent	Focus on challenging stereotypes and changing perspectives regarding subaltern populations; fairly prevalent
Environmental	Focus on 'sustainable development' policies and principles; anthropocentric perspective; not prevalent	Focus on managing the environment sustainably; fairly prevalent	Focus on anthropocentric concerns regarding the human condition in relation to the environment; not prevalent
Spiritual	Focus on belief systems as cohesive units; not prevalent	Focus on exploring the belief systems of major religions; fairly prevalent	Focus on exploring identities in relation to belief systems; not prevalent

FIGURE 2.1 Oxley and Morris Global Citizenship Typology

Key: dark solid shading, very highly prevalent; dark hatched shading, highly prevalent; light hatched shading, fairly prevalent; no shading, not prevalent.

educational programs, not unlike a claim made herein towards expanding GCE (Case, 1993; Davies et al., 2005; Gaudelli, 2003; Kirkwood, 2001). The openness of global education, however, might also explain why it has been so strongly criticized for being an "anything goes" area of study that allegedly promotes relativistic, anti-US thinking (Burack, 2003).

Global education in the US has origins deeply rooted in the Cold War. Much of the earliest literature refers to this orientation, evident in a focus on denuclearization, war/peace studies and third-generation human rights like adequate living standards and food/shelter, as these were all issues on which the US–Soviet conflict was centered (Gaudelli & Wylie, 2012). By the early 1990s, however, the shift in global learning away from international, bipolar world politics towards multiculturalism and diversity began to appear in the literature and various forms of practice (Merryfield, 2000). In the past decade, global learning has increasingly been renamed to emphasize activism and social justice while highlighting civic duties and belonging, thus the inclusion of citizenship. As Lynn Davies (2006, p. 6) notes, "What seems to happen with global citizenship education is a confirmation of the direct concern with social justice and not just the more minimalist interpretations of global education which are about 'international awareness' or being a more rounded person." The apparent consolidation of the field around a central concept, one that couples global awareness with acting in the world as a result of that awareness, offers some clarity. Yet, GCE remains a diverse field of study and practice.

The various streams of discourse around globalization and education—from international comparisons to innovations to multilingual youth—all contribute to a wider context for interpreting various declarations and actions related to GCE. I outline briefly some of those calls, turning them over to understand how they might be appealing to various communities while responding to the contextual factors at play in education and globalization generally. My intent in this section is not to cover all the bases related to various GCE articulations, of which there are many, but rather, to provide a purposeful overview that will give readers a sense of the landscape coupled with an analytic grasp of what's going on. This will be followed by my bricolage on GCE and a preferred direction for the field.

A useful typology introduced by Laura Oxley and Paul Morris (2013) provides an analysis of curriculum efforts related to GCE. They begin from the problem that GCE is contested ground, summarized eloquently here:

> GC[E] is distinctive because of the polarity of opinion it engenders: for some it implies universality and a deep commitment to a broader moral purpose, while for others it cannot feasibly be a valid concept due to the perceived absence of a ruling authority (e.g. a world government) on which to base such an idea of citizenship.
>
> (Oxley & Morris, 2013, p. 303)

They proceed from this starting point to outline the discursiveness of the field, emphasizing the various types that appear in scholarly literature, while recognizing the inherent limitations of any categorical summary.

The top-line of the graphic, including *intended antecedents, intended transactions* and *intended outcomes* can be restated as current conditions, interventions offered and desired outcomes. They then shade the various typologies, not categorically as a sum but on each of these axes, to identify the prevalence of these ideas and practices. So, for example, the cultural domain of GCE, which addresses cultural diversity and expression, is highly prevalent in schools both as responding to current conditions and in articulating certain outcomes; but the spiritual aspects of global connections are much less prevalent both in what is currently offered and the expression of desired outcomes related to this domain. They have created a heat-map of the field based on discourse and practices in England, weighing the various positions that people inhabit in relation to GCE and how these are more or less prevalent. The first four species of GCE exist within the overarching category of cosmopolitanism and include: *political, moral, economic* and *cultural*. The latter four are included as advocacy positions that articulate a stance about the world and how we are oriented towards it, including *social, critical, environmental* and *spiritual*.

As to the first set of cosmopolitan perspectives, each begins from the presumption of the plurality of differences within a fundamental sameness. *Political* refers to the support of existing transnational organizations, like the United Nations and its affiliate bodies, coupled with the possibility of creating a world federation of state and non-state actors. The *moral* perspective draws substantially on human rights discourse and seeks fair treatment and justice under a cosmopolitanism based on a shared moral outlook about people and their social organization. Unlike the political, the moral perspective affirms the local manifestations of these attributes and sees strong congruence between acting in a particular community and sharing in global communitarianism. *Economic* cosmopolitanism refers to the creation of business norms that are spread globally by virtue of economic relationships, the same force that arguably began the process of globalization in the first place. Corporations, for example, engage in humanitarian efforts that demonstrate the possibility of economic types of global citizenship. Last, *cultural* suggests the spread of images and narratives through media and art as a symbolic location of global citizenship coupled with the ability to read and interpret this "global language," one that opens up possibilities of increasingly shared understanding of our commonness.

The four advocacy positions, including *social, critical, environmental* and *spiritual*, abide by a less universalistic ethic and are more communitarian in organization while also showing some overlap with the previous cosmopolitan varieties. The *social* orientation addresses affiliations that symbolize a person's belonging to particular identities, what might be thought of as multicultural discourse, coupled with the fluid interplay of those groups within a larger societal context. The *critical* stance draws from the vast inequalities that are structured into the world system and employs diverse theories from postmodernism, poststructuralism and postcolonialism to critique hegemonic, global institutions and thought (e.g. the World Trade Organization). The *environmental* advocacy position articulates in its more radical version the preservation of a non-sentient entity, the Earth, as the foundation for all forms of known social life and thus superseding all others. This derivative is perhaps most complicated in comparison to the others since it can be interpreted as being anti-human given its predilection to privilege ecosystems and nonhuman animals as compared to human development. The last advocacy position is *spiritual*, wherein the love of humanity and the planet provides an orientation as efforts are aimed at seeking transcendence beyond strict rationality and towards a more holistic, spiritually centered worldview, a view well illustrated in Pope Francis' recent encyclical on global warming, *Laudato Si'* (Francis, 2015). These eight domains of GCE suggest a terrain of wide-ranging views within the field while simultaneously suggesting many points of connectivity to the wider landscape of education, schools and society. In short, the days of global learning being a specialized subfield within social studies education or housed by a university's international programs office are largely in the past, as the future suggests a more expansive conceptualization befitting the contemporary scene.

The next three sections outline widely promulgated conceptual frameworks for GCE—including Oxfam, the Maastricht Convention and UNESCO. These offer a sense about how GCE has emerged in the past two decades, what has changed and what those changes mean for the field. Each has strengths and occlusions which I suggest along the way before making a claim in my *bricolage* about where I think the field of GCE should be headed.

Oxfam

Oxfam began as the Oxford Committee for Famine Relief in Oxford, England during World War II in 1942. Oxfam shifted their focus after the War to becoming an organization that provided food and supplies for those suffering from conflict particularly refugees globally. Currently Oxfam is organized by 17 affiliate offices with operations in 90 countries with the aim of eradicating poverty and six inter-related goals: civic engagement, equal rights for women, save lives in emergencies, promote food security, promote economic justice and increase funding for basic services (Oxfam, 2015). Oxfam promotes empowerment of communities to help themselves rather than a charity-model, even though a charity orientation was present in its origins.

Like most aid organizations, Oxfam has an education office that promotes a version of global learning. They have been outspoken advocates in this arena for two decades, with one of the earliest published school-based frameworks for global citizenship dating back to 1997.

Education for global citizenship is not an additional subject, it is an ethos. It is best implemented through a whole-school approach, involving everyone from learners themselves to the wider community. It can also be promoted in class through teaching the existing curriculum in a way that highlights aspects such as social justice, the appreciation of diversity and the import-ance of sustainable development.

(Oxfam, 2015)

Oxfam's concept of GCE springs to life in schools by engaging in an ongoing learn-think-act process that is meant to permeate a school.

- *Learn*: Exploring the issue, considering it from different viewpoints and try-ing to understand causes and consequences.
- *Think*: Considering critically what can be done about the issue, and relating this to values and worldviews and trying to understand the nature of power and action.
- *Act*: Thinking about and taking action on the issue as an active global citizen, both individually and collectively.

The process of learning, thinking and acting is recursive as it is assumed that students will develop increasingly more sophisticated insights about how glo-bal issues are interwoven, thereby making connections between what otherwise might be treated as separate concerns, say, water access and violent conflict.

Oxfam organizes a range of activities each year that invite student and teacher engagement. In 2015, Oxfam coordinated a "Send my friend to schools" week to raise attention of world leaders about the fact that some 58 million children around the world do not have access to education. This was coupled with a "Water" week that encouraged students to raise money and awareness while con-tributing to a joint fund to provide sustainable, potable water solutions around the world. Oxfam also offers teacher materials that provide hands-on, minds-on activities intended to engage students across all grade levels in learning about glo-bal issues that point towards avenues for social engagement. GCE from Oxfam's perspective is more a way of being and thinking in the world than a prescribed set of curriculum activities, though the latter are provided for teachers. Implicit in Oxfam's work is the hope that GCE catches on in a particular school, that teach-ers and students adopt this way of thinking about the world, such that it eventually becomes embedded in the culture of a school.

There are significant challenges with Oxfam's approach to GCE. The school-wide ethos, while highly desirable, is somewhat unrealistic in many schools particularly those in middle and secondary grades when specialization and separ-ation is preferred over what might be described as generalization and collaboration. This view of schools is highly congruent with thinking in the 1990s about school reform. There was and remains a widely held belief that whole-school reform was the best way to move the needle in terms of learning goals and improving school quality. This emphasis has shifted somewhat in the intervening years, however, as a classroom-focused orientation, which highlights micro-processes and instructional practices, as opposed to a macro focus, has emerged. This change is perhaps most evident in the consequent shift from school-based curricula as a discourse and practice in education to a small-frame orientation—one that emphasizes instructional practices and "evidence-based research" practices (Biesta, 2013). Big picture work in schools, once the domain of curriculum scholars, has increasingly lost its connection to the core work of schools, a decline well documented for a variety of reasons (Pinar, 2013).

Oxfam's recent strategic adjustment to developing after-school programming and special initiatives, or drives, has the advantage of moving into the relatively unencumbered space outside of state-governed curriculum requirements. Yet, the development of after-school programming is also a reaction to the crowding out of curricula caused somewhat ironically by global educational competition that has translated into more attention to numeracy and literacy, or the burgeoning of science, technology and mathematics education (STEM). GCE in the space of after-school programming is more likely to be taken up as auxiliary rather than integral to learning in school. And a related dynamic of Oxfam's approach is that when GCE sits outside or tangentially within existing curricula, it is likely that it will not be owned by the entire faculty but by just a few inspired teachers who have a particular interest in promoting GCE. This pattern is generally quite common in GCE, although challenging, since a set-aside status belies the importance and holistic way of thinking that GCE strives towards, one that ideally reaches all students.

Maastricht Global Education Declaration

In the early years of the 21st century and soon after the attacks on September 11, 2001, mounting calls were issued for increased attention to global education, particularly emanating from the North and specifically in western Europe. Some of this attention was no doubt related to the belligerent stance of the US, namely President George W. Bush's bifurcated *with or against us* international policy precipitated by the attacks. Also, there was considerable attention to the UN's Millennium Development Goals, articulated prior to 2000 with the intention of achieving those by 2015. The MDGs include: eradicating extreme poverty and hunger, providing universal primary education, promoting gender equality, reducing child mortality, improving maternal health, combating communicable diseases, promoting environmental sustainability and cooperating to support development (UN Millennium Development Goals, 2000). As the US embraced an aggressive, militaristic stance towards world affairs in the shadow of 9/11, an opposing current among institutions such as the UN and governmental organizations affiliated with the European Union saw the 9/11 attacks as an opportunity to promote a more globally minded agenda in schools and society. There was a palpable sense of a new world emerging, one less starry-eyed than the previous decade's "end of history" and "new world order" proclamations, but globally interconnected and sharply discordant nonetheless.

A European conference in Maastricht, Netherlands in 2002 solidified a European conception of global education called the Maastricht Declaration on Global Education (O'Loughlin & Wegimont, 2002). The report from the conference offered this broad vision:

> Global Education [GE] is education that opens people's eyes and minds to the realities of the world, and awakens them to bring about a world of greater justice, equity and human rights for all. GE is understood to encompass Development Education, Human Rights Education, Education for Sustainability, Education for Peace and Conflict Prevention and Intercultural Education; being the global dimensions of Education for Citizenship.
>
> (O'Loughlin & Wegimont, 2002)

The Maastricht Declaration illustrates the desire to amalgamate global learning, or to unify the multiplicity of *educations* into a cohesive statement of the whole, a singular version of education that was needed to support the UN Millennium Development Goals. The effort to conjoin the various species of globally focused curricula—such as development, sustainability, peace and human rights education—also made Maastricht uniquely well positioned to adjoin these allied communities. The founders were attempting to create pockets of educators that shared much in common but had previously staked out separate domains. Each group had and has integrity to stand individually but was also inextricably woven into the fabric of what constitutes global learning. The inclusion of "citizenship" in the final phrase illustrates the orientation of global learning broadly since 2000—towards greater community engagement and political activism. Maastricht also interestingly avoids claiming the whole of citizenship, traditionally viewed from within a national boundary, to only its "global dimensions."

The conference report references the desire to integrate global education within existing curricular frameworks, expressing concern about the auxiliary status of the field and the need to move it to center. This, coupled with a desire to coordinate among ministries of education, led to the creation of GENE, or the Global Education Network of Europe. GENE emphasizes policy sharing through periodic peer reviews wherein delegations of global educators visit and develop a national profile of a country. These are used to share information within and beyond the network about how best to proceed in implementing global learning.

An ongoing concern addressed at Maastricht and the work that proceeded from the conference was the relationship of South to North around what it means to be globally educated. The South Caucus on Global Education, though not part of Europe geographically yet deeply woven into its history, was part of the initial conference and remains in the orbit of this work. Naty Bernardino, of the Resource Center for the Peoples Development in the Philippines, offered the following remarks about the North–South tensions that often surface in GCE:

> I will not deny that before coming here, some of us have been apprehensive as to whether or not the space given to South participants in this Congress would indeed result into a meaningful engagement. Such sentiment is not surprising because our past experience in many intergovernmental meetings including those of the UN has not been so encouraging. Despite the formal recognition given to the role of civil society in many UN summits for example, there is an observable trend that this role is being diminished or has become tokenistic, reducing our presence to an adjunct of the official process albeit necessary so as to project a semblance of participatory democracy. It is therefore our fervent hope that this meeting would prove otherwise and indeed lead to a constructive debate and meaningful engagement.
> (O'Loughlin & Wegimont, 2002, p. 37)

By the conclusion of the Maastricht Conference, the South Caucus issued a Statement of Invitees from the South:

> There has been insufficient analysis and dialogue in conceptualising and problematising Global Education, from a global and specifically a Southern perspective, resulting in inadequate contextualisation of the global crisis.
> (O'Loughlin & Wegimont, 2002, p. 129)

At issue is how neoliberal thinking about economic growth and development is viewed as a foundational assumption in contemporary education coupled with the fact that the continued reverberations of colonialism are often excised from conversations about development, poverty and human rights. The Maastricht Declaration sheds light on a rift in GCE around North–South concerns, a tension that remains to the present. GCE is widely and accurately viewed as coming from the North. Exacerbating this tension have been the efforts by some in GCE to couple the work with development goals that have a decidedly Western orientation.

The Maastricht Declaration offers important insights about GCE. The consolidated statement provides a way of thinking about the field as unified rather than disaggregated into smaller realms. The advantage of this approach is that it allows for broad constituencies while it befits the interconnectedness of global learning generally. Yet, it can also contribute to the fuzziness of amalgamation, losing the conceptual clarity offered by categories such as *human rights* and *development education*, specializations that some scholars and practitioners prefer. Combining various foci, too, may provide a unifying image but in fact lead to even greater dissensus about the nature of what it means to learn globally. And in light of the consolidating tendency of Maastricht, the presumed stance of GCE as universal is called into question by the deep dissent that was voiced therein and thereafter, by delegates from the South, some of whom feel that GCE is yet another instance of imposition from the North which further solidifies a singular notion of education as producing economic development.

UNESCO

The United Nations Educational, Scientific and Cultural Organization (UNESCO) developed a statement on GCE (2014). I provide a graphic summary of some key elements of UNESCO's document here:

UNESCO's conception is articulated in a broad and inclusive manner, similar to the Maastricht Declaration, such that justice, peace, tolerance, inclusivity, security and sustainability are explicit. The modes suggest attitudes, like empathy, caring and openness while the foundations note topics like human rights, diversity and democracy as core elements of GCE. A key element of UNESCO's articulation is the idea of generating social action and engagement.

UNESCO's version of GCE is very much rooted in contemporary education conversations in that it views school systems not as singular educational institutions but one among many educative agencies, including the wide and growing civil sector of NGOs and nonprofits. The authors point to the importance of sports competitions, digital media, art and music exhibitions

Global Citizenship Education
UNESCO (2014)

Global citizenship education aims to empower learners to engage and assume active roles both locally and globally to face and resolve global challenges and ultimately to become proactive contributors to a more just, peaceful, tolerant, inclusive, secure and sustainable world.

Conception

Modes

multimodal and lifelong   participatory

dispositions of openness, caring, empathic   critical, creative and innovative thinking

Respect for human rights, democracy, non-discrimination, diversity and sustainability   Sense of belonging (not legal)

Foundations

Psychosocial framework of connectedness   Generates action and engagement

FIGURE 2.2 UNESCO Conception of Global Citizenship Education

and youth-led efforts to engage with their communities in light of issues that have global resonance. UNESCO's GCE aims to embed lifelong learning that is not solely focused on schools. This is a fairly significant change from the Maastrict Declaration of some 15 years prior, because that document assumes that schools driven by Ministry of Education policy are the forum for GCE. UNESCO is also somewhat contiguous with Oxfam's approach in the deployment of after-school programming space as a primary, strategic means of getting GCE included in formal education. UNESCO's GCE also suggests a degree of fatigue with the slow pace of change in schools and, by extension, a desire to seek other educative spaces that are unregulated since these groups often act independently of a national agenda.

UNESCO also seems to be responding to the North–South friction around GCE of the past 15 years. The prevailing notion that GCE was a universal, one-size-fits-all model that exists despite local currents and concerns is evident throughout the text. The need for GCE to be more reflective of local circumstances is made explicit, such that the wide berth of concerns allows for certain issues to override others based on temporal and regional salience. Peace education, for example, will likely take on greater prominence in war-torn regions, whereas post-authoritarian states may focus more on participatory rights, while societies that experience extreme intercultural conflict may address marginalization and diversity (UNESCO, 2014, p. 18).

Perhaps the most telling aspect of UNESCO's connection to the current moment in education is the focus on metrics and measurement. UNESCO entered into a partnership with Brookings Institution and the Youth Advocacy Group of the UN General Secretary Ban Ki-moon's Global Education First Initiative (GEFI). The growth in measurement, evaluation and accountability in education has no doubt contributed to this focus. Interesting, too, the metrics themselves are not solely based on GCE but expand to include issues of access, literacy and numeracy, harkening back to the UN Millennium Goals. The Brookings Institution focuses on three primary questions that generally speak to matters of access and quality: (1) What learning is important globally? (2) How should it be measured? (3) How can measurement of learning improve education quality? (Learning Metrics Task Force 2.0, 2015). The group intends to create a heuristic, single measure statistic that will allow a convenient summary of access and quality. Though this work is informed by the UNESCO conception, the Learning Metrics Task Force's concern with access, literacy, numeracy and the like put it into a broader policy space than that constituted by GCE alone. But it is worth noting that the elements of GCE included in the UNESCO framework are subsumed as part of a conception of what is being offered as robust education for the 21st century. Also, the updated Sustainable Development Goals agreed in September, 2015 for 2015–2030 articulate a commitment to educational quality, not only educational access:

By 2030, ensure that all learners acquire the knowledge and skills needed to promote sustainable development, including, among others, through education for sustainable development and sustainable lifestyles, human rights, gender equality, promotion of a culture of peace and non-violence, global citizenship and appreciation of cultural diversity and of culture's contribution to sustainable development.

(Sustainable Development Goals, Goal 4)

UNESCO's GCE framework is laudable in that it provides a comprehensive conception that is not limited to schools but begins to think of society broadly as educative. The emphasis on the dispositional aspects of learning, such as openness, creativity and empathy, are also noteworthy since these dimensions were not present in previous conceptions. But there are challenges in this statement of principles as there would be with any such articulation. The most significant challenge is the sense of otherness/vastness connoted in the statement. The phrase "face and resolve global challenges" is often a point of humor in courses that I teach when I read it aloud to students, as they remark on the implausibility of such an aim in education despite its desirability. The document also reads as though it was written by insiders for outsiders, or by those who have spent a career thinking about, teaching and formulating these programs, such that it could deflect many criticisms and invite a variety of adherents. Yet, the document also feels unattainably lofty and perhaps unapproachable, as if GCE occupies a mythic space that may make people feel good but be almost wholly aspirational. This may have to do with the weightiness of the subject matter and the breadth of issues necessarily raised by GCE.

Summing up the three illustrative GCE frameworks—Oxfam, Maastricht and UNESCO—certain patterns emerge. First, each demonstrates a nonlinear effort to locate GCE in a particular learning space: Where does it fit, as a school-wide program or as an after-school programming or in community-based education? This pattern is indicative of a larger trend affecting education, or how global economic/educational competition has ironically led to a winnowed curriculum. Second, these various conceptions of GCE vacillate around the deeply problematic North–South gap within GCE, particularly resonant as school systems grow more focused on economic growth at the direction of governments and policy bodies. GCE might look very different if it incorporated Southern views of economic development, human/collective rights and place-based learning, but there has only been a recent shift away from education given in the North for the South towards a position of working in solidarity across those asymmetrical differences. Third, examining these three in concert, the shift towards social action and engagement is the most pronounced. Earlier forms of global education were oriented towards raising awareness about global issues, appreciating cultural diversity and recognizing one's perspective in the wider, global system (Hanvey, 1975). The shift of the past two decades has clearly moved attention to learning that is focused on doing in a social sense. And while there is a long way for GCE to go in addressing embedded North–South tensions and what it means to act in the world, these are important concerns that need to be attended to. In the final section, I examine this challenge in particular, or how those who work in GCE can begin to move it from silos into open fields; from auxiliary education to the main event.

GCE as Everyday and Transcendent

I once gave a talk about GCE with this book's subtitle—everyday and transcendent—as the focus. As I introduced my emphasis for the hour, there were more than a few titters and laughs, to the effect of saying "*Everyday*…sounds quite interesting!" Everyday connotes something run-of-the-mill, unspectacular and mundane, hardly aspirational it seems. I use this phrase, however, precisely for the regularity it connotes. If a broad vision of GCE is to be developed in schools and society, then it needs to be done with the taken-for-granted quality presumed in everydayness. The simple fact that we inhabit an extraordinary planet, that we are a singular species living within and sharing a thin biosphere of limited capacity is a composite insight that, whether we choose to acknowledge it or not, is a persistent, daily reality. I have a good deal of optimism that this way of thinking can become habitualized, in a Deweyan sense, as part of the fabric of daily life. I could list examples to fill pages—from the US electing an African American president to the acceptance of gay marriage to the proportional decline of war in many regions. The salient point is simply that societies change continually and improvements have occurred and will continue to occur.

At the other end of the spectrum from the everyday or mundane is the transcendent. This way of thinking also must be wound into GCE since as a curriculum it runs counter to much of what our species has experienced. Human history has witnessed more war than peace, more intercultural discord than accord, more environmental degradation than preservation. GCE's normative value premise, then, is one that invites people to literally *think and be in the world differently*, in a way that is neither rewarded monetarily nor valued socially. Consider how much a community organizer or social worker is paid compared to a hedge fund manager or an investment banker and it becomes readily apparent that GCE's volition is different. GCE's alterity begs a transformation, one that transcends the patterns of human history that up to this point have become taken for granted. Thus, the shift represented by GCE is to think the world differently in such a way that everyday thinking is refashioned.

One might say this is all too idealistic, perhaps even dangerous, in that GCE sounds like a mindset that all must adopt, a rigid imposition of a narrow script. I have a similar sense of caution as I'm skeptical of grand designs that have utopic undertones. Yet, in the ways GCE has been articulated I see both limitations as noted above along with wide discursive possibilities that will iterate differently over time and in different areas. And to a degree, the everydayness of global thinking is already well under way. Take, for instance, the prevalence of human rights discourse today as compared to 50 or 100 years ago. The notion that people have inalienable sovereign rights to dignity, respect and equal treatment, while not a daily reality, is increasingly a normative principle. The number of political deaths caused by the horrors associated with the early 20th century, numbers in the tens of millions of people, are fortunately nearly impossible to imagine in the contemporary context. What has changed in this relatively short span of time is the recognition of the sanctity of each life, a trend that I attribute in part to the repeated affirmation of human rights over many decades by a wide and growing chorus of voices. Of course there are grave injustices in the world but the change is that acts of violence and violation are increasingly unacceptable whereas previously they were accepted as *how things are*. Given the context of transformation and everyday, I offer six interrelated questions that are simple and approachable—everyday let's suppose—while each speaks to profound possibilities. The questions will be briefly considered to demonstrate the range of possibilities that each invites.

Who am I? Subjectivity

Who am I is perhaps the philosophical question of the ages. Our ability to think of ourselves as being is integral to this question and elemental to human experience since it suggests our fundamental subjectivity. Who we are and how we think ourselves in the world is a simple yet potentially profound orientation to GCE. James Gee (2000) offers a useful heuristic for thinking about identity, categorizing those as "nature," affinity, discourse and institutional. "Nature"[1] refers to how identity is embodied in a physical being, attributes such as skin color, personality and gender. Institutional identity includes things such as one's profession, religion or political identity that contribute a sense of oneself. Affinity identifies those belongings that people choose, like a hobby or activity that creates a sense of group, while discourse refers to political orientations, beliefs or ideas that unify a sense of oneself. These categories are overlapping at times, since one's discursive connection to being Jewish, for example, can also include, or not include, an institutional identity, say belonging to a particular synagogue. Gee's framework is useful in that it does not diminish those attributes, like political orientation or sense of belonging to a state, from others that are more socially recognizable, such as ethnicity/race, class and gender. But as noted, the framework inheres historical baggage in associating race and gender with people's "natures."

Research and scholarship on how identity matters in GCE is perhaps the most robust aspect of the field, particularly since contemporary global education arose in the period 1960–2000 at a time when diversity and multicultural discourses were most prominent in education. This work includes studies about how various ethnic/racial populations interpret global learning (Asher & Crocco, 2001; Gay, 2000; Subedi, 2008), the various ways that cultural difference is encountered (Merryfield, 2001; Wilson, 1998) and how racism, colonialism and historical marginalization continue to cast a long shadow on schools and society (Merryfield & Subedi, 2001; Subedi, 2010; Subedi & Daza, 2008). Subjectivity is a critical dimension of what constitutes a meaningful education for children, coming to know themselves emergently and socially. That young people come to understand themselves as parts of various social groups for a variety of reasons; that their identities are mainly static in certain ways, somewhat mutable in others and contextually derived; that identity has and ought to be cause for celebration, joy and introspection while too often it has been used as a justification for horrific violence—for these reasons the significance of subjectivity cannot be overstated. It is the prima facie way that we as bipedal apes come to find ourselves in the world and understand how others understand us. Yet, GCE would be too limiting if it confined itself to identity, as it too often has, leaving aside other salient concerns.

When is it? Temporality

GCE can also be examined through a grasp of when it is, or temporality. Time is a long-standing mystery in that there is no easy way to define it other than by measurement, which in and of itself tells us very little about its quality or what constitutes time. One might say that time is equivalent to experience or the stuff that seems to fill it, but in this way it is strictly an absence, or the tableau upon which experiences are written. Is that sufficient? Noting and leaving aside the metaphysical question of the nature of time, the issue remains how temporality can inform GCE. There have been limited forays in the GCE literature into this question. Elise Boulding's (1990) brief discussion on the 200 year present, an ever forward-moving epoch measured by the existence of someone 100 years old in near proximity to people being born today who will be alive 100 years from now, offers a sense of what she meant. The interdependence of people's being demonstrates that these two people are connected and therefore we too are all connected to that ever-moving epoch. This heuristic device is useful in that it helps to orient thinking towards what has occurred that shapes the contemporary while pointing to what may occur as a result of our present actions. Challenging though this view of time may be because it calls upon GCE learners and teachers to imagine what is not yet, attention here is warranted.

The rise of Big History discourse in the past two decades suggests a substantially more expansive, and therefore an even more unimaginable, stretch of time, as the focus is on eons rather than mere centuries or millennia (Christian & McNeill, 2011). Big History attempts to situate human history within universe history, such that the age of humans is vastly dwarfed yet intensified. In the vastness of this time horizon one can readily witness the substantial impact that humans, particularly modern ones, have had on the world. Focusing on broad trends and wide patterns, such as agrarianism and urbanization with periodic attention to illustrations of these patterns, helps to illuminate the big picture of human history in the oceanic relief of universe history. This pedagogical approach, of tightening and broadening the lens, mirrors what temporality can mean in GCE. The particularistic universalism, if such a solipsism can be permitted, gives a sense of the temporal bellows, from close-up to pulled-back, invited by a Big History approach.

Where is it? Spatiality

Michel Foucault remarked in the early 1980s that history was receding in importance and space and networks were becoming the analytic terrain of the new epoch.

> The great obsession of the nineteenth century was…history: with its themes of development and of suspension, of crisis and cycle, themes of the ever-accumulating past, with its great preponderance of dead men and the menacing glaciation of the world.…The present epoch will perhaps be above all the epoch of space. We are in the epoch of simultaneity; we are in the epoch of juxtaposition, the epoch of the near and far, of the side-by-side, of the dispersed. We are at a moment, I believe, when our experience of the world is less that of a long life developing through time than that of a network that connects points and intersects with its own skein.
>
> (Foucault, 1986, p. 22)

Foucault's assertion of an epochal shift is evident through globalization. The synchronicity and speed of media and capital flows increasing at ever-hastening rates has created an odd contrast. What was once wholly tangible and embodied, say a classroom or a conversation, has become increasingly dislocated and dispersed, via networked tools that concomitantly bridge and pronounce those spaces. The omnipresence of these networks too creates a puzzle of nostalgic longing and strident nomadism (Zembylas & Vrasidas, 2006). Thus where we are has increasingly morphed from a singular, embodied presence towards a multiplicity of presences manifest in emails, Twitter, Facebook and whatever else is on the horizon that disperses our sense of location and our presence through connection. People have become, and increasingly choose to become, dislocated through mediation and multiplicity in a digitally networked society (Castells, 2009).

Assertions about the apparent escape of embodied and immediate space are often wound into a technological utopic narrative that is itself a form of escapism from the significant hazards in other dimensions of space—namely the biosphere. The Industrial Revolution and rise of urban spaces has contributed to myriad problems, chief among them emissions of atmospheric carbon from fossil fuels, along with water scarcity/pollution, soil degradation/erosion, deforestation and desertification and the catastrophic loss of nonhuman animal species as we experience the most rapid era of mass extinction since the Mesozoic Era some 66 million years ago (Mosley, 2010). Increases in carbon outputs since the Industrial Revolution, perhaps the most significant driver of ecological damage, are truly stunning:

> Coal production increased 500-fold between 1810 and 1990, from 10 million to 5 billion tonnes. Oil extraction rose around 300-fold in the century after 1890, from less than 10 million to more than 3 billion tonnes… (thereby) humankind released huge quantities of carbon dioxide that had been securely locked up underground, profoundly altering the global carbon cycle.
>
> (Mosley, 2010, p. 9)

Perhaps it is more than happenstance that visions of digital networks creating new spaces, not to mention planned voyages to Mars, have become more prominent in the cultural imagination as the status of the biosphere has become more beleaguered. People's desire for placeless-ness is similar to the claim made by the chemist Clemens Winkler in 1901, who asserted that coal "disappeared without a trace" (Mosley, 2010, p. 98). The era of digital communication, for all the possibilities that it creates, is parasitic on the desire to exist without being implicated in the tangible circumstances that surround us. Similar to the young child who hides her head under the blanket believing that if she cannot see others she cannot be seen by them, people at times relish magical disappearances and anonymity. The recent app phenomenon of Yik Yak demonstrates this tendency as it allows college students to gossip about each other in anonymous fashion, making for an unusually nasty, degrading slice of cyberspace. The question *Where am I?* reminds people of the plurality of space that is the contemporary digital moment but always in light of the inescapable bonds of inhabiting space particularly and in the biosphere.

What Matters? What can be Done? Significance

GCE, unlike global education of an earlier variety, foregrounds the civic aspects of global learning. Simply knowing about the increasing release of carbon and its potentially cataclysmic implications is not enough: knowing begs action and engagement. But civic action with a global orientation introduces a host of problems, including scale, or how people can affect events or problems so broad; and breadth, or how to act on a breadth of problems; and efficacy, or how doing something actually matters. An important dimension of GCE is engaging in dialog about what to act upon along with what it means and how it matters to act.

At root, significance is a social question. People communicate and learn about an issue—say violations of human rights through extrajudicial killings or the extinction of charismatic megafauna like white rhinos or the inaccessibility of potable water for hundreds of millions of people—and the very process of becoming aware elevates its significance in the mind of the learner. When teaching about human rights principles, codification and violations in high school in the 1990s, most of my students were completely unaware of the Argentinian state-sponsored terrorism of the 1970s or the global use of torture methods in judicial systems, such that my raising the issue and students exploring it elevated their sense of its significance. Yet, our discussions often considered the deeper question as to *why human rights violations matter*, which led to interesting conversations about the principle of inviolability and interconnectedness. I recall a colleague and friend who served as a guidance counselor saying at the time, "Why should they be interested in this stuff, they have enough problems of their own," a challenge related to significance that I was not yet ready to encounter.

In talking about significance I am brought back to thinking about John Dewey's conception of interest. Dewey explores the etymology of the term in its conjugated version, something of inter-esse, *esse* being the world. "The word interest suggests, etymologically, what is between—that which connects two things otherwise distant" (Dewey, 1916/1944, p. 130). He suggests that literally anything is potentially of *interest*, or connected between people and the world, since we are of the world in every sense. The challenge of pedagogues is not to begin and end with the interest of the child—immediate, myopic and fleeting—and follow their whiplashing tendencies alone. Rather, a skilled teacher guides students from the immediate, felt circumstances to draw out, or *educate*, from that event, object or phenomenon to something linked up and connected to myriad other social things. Some have referred to this as rippling or chaining, a way of seeing the fundamentally social connectivity of being in the relief of one's situatedness.

So thinking back to my dumbfounded nonresponse to my colleague about our students learning about human rights, I should have responded quite differently. I might have suggested that the feelings of teen angst they experience about being controlled by parents and teachers have parallels throughout the social world, as we are all constrained by institutions and structures that we accede to belong to, whether implicitly or otherwise. And I might have then engaged them in inquiry about how various institutions constrain differently at times, such as prior restraint on free speech demonstrations that may lead to violence or confidentiality agreements that corporations compel employees to sign or any other number of constraints. I then might encourage them to study coercive and violent denials of rights, for instance when a government agent engages in torture against a supposed enemy with information. I would need to exercise caution so as not to equate the anger of adolescents with human rights atrocities as this potentially trivializes the severity of the latter, which are indeed crimes against humanity. But this line of thinking would help move students towards not *locking in* solely to the immediate situation of their lives and focusing simultaneously on the numerous ways their experiences manifest, albeit differently, in other contexts.

Setting aside the issue of significance, then, what does it mean to act on matters of concern beyond one's immediate circumstances? The multiplicity of ways to act is an important principle to guide GCE inquiries. Educating oneself and others is an action, echoing the thinking of Paulo Freire (1993/1970): "There is no true word that at the same time is not a praxis [reflection and action]. Thus, to speak a true word is to transform the world." To communicate truly with others, therefore, is a form of action. Freire's thinking is confounded somewhat in an era of instant messaging via social media like Twitter, Facebook and Instagram. Put another way, does a "true meme" transform the world? What does it mean to communicate via these mediaspaces meaningfully and in the spirit of GCE? The potential superficial and ephemeral nature of an online post, for example, troubles what it means to transform the world.

Tools or activities of engagement in GCE are too often the focus rather than the experiences these tools may permit. Davies contends from her work in the UK, for example, that if GCE is to be more than an empty slogan it needs to manifest as engagement in school democracy as well as community service (Davies, 2006, p. 16). Regarding school democracy, learning about human rights in light of rights and responsibilities within the immediate community of school is a vital way to act. As to community service, the value of these forms of engagement is related to how much people are working—hearts, hands and minds—in the activity, such that it is not random behavior but thoughtful engagement on why homelessness and hunger exist and how these issues are socially webbed. Issues of significance and meaningful action in GCE suggest another critical dimension: what it means to work in solidarity with others globally as opposed to working for charity.

A consideration of how gift-recipients may feel humiliated by gift-giving is rarely part of the conversation among donors (Korf et al., 2010). A significant scholarly literature surrounding the 2004 South Asian tsunami has revealed the messiness of gift activity in an economically disparate globe. As Korf et al. note, "What started as an otherworldly practice in the global North – as a 'pure' gift – ended in a chain of relations, obligations, and reciprocal expectations and the dirty world of politics and patronage" (Korf et al., 2010, p. S71). The cases drawn from three ravaged communities in Sri Lanka demonstrate how donors competed with each other for the most photogenic aid opportunities, or those that would reveal to the givers the outcomes of their giving regardless of the real impact on Sri Lankans in these communities. As Gabay (2008) notes, as the gift-giver expects an emotional, often photogenic response to their gift, the practice of generosity reinscribes power relations.

Such practice is in fact based at least as much upon the psychological needs of comparatively resource-rich individuals as it is on the material needs of distant sufferers. In effect, such practices reinforce the existing socio-economic hierarchies and differentials in power which drive many of the problems such campaigns seek to address.

(Gabay, 2008, p. 201)

Who acts globally, for whom and about what are vitally important questions to raise in order to avoid mindlessly perpetuating injustice despite one's best intentions.

What do Others Think? Experience? Feel? Positionality and Empathy

The final question I introduce in this nonlinear set of GCE queries raises issues of positionality, or the socialized meanings of subjectivity, along with empathy, or our ability/limitation for getting inside of another person's lifeworld. In positionality I am referring to how one is situated vis-à-vis one's social location. As a white man living in the New York metropolitan area who is middle aged, formally educated and affiliated with a prominent university though coming from working-class roots as a child, these aspects inform and shape, though do not determine, how I see the world and how others see me. This was never more apparent to me than when I was giving a talk to educators in Poland and I focused at some length on the challenges of global warming and the need to educate for an imperiled climate. The next speaker, a good friend, joked with the audience about the irony of someone from the US teaching the world about global warming since we had been the source of so much of the problem. This episode helped remind me of the position that I embody even though I do not think of myself as a carbon glutton nor a loyal patriot. Regardless, I symbolize those identities to others I encounter due to my national affiliation.

Naming one's social location in the world has been an ongoing, iterative conversation in global discourse and one that must be reckoned within GCE. The older binary of First/Third World, contemporary in the 1960s, '70s and '80s, has been displaced by other dichotomies, including Developing/Underdeveloped, North/South, North/West and South/East, Western/non-Western and One-third/Two-thirds World. Each of these is troubled by the desire to capture the variability and fluidity of social spaces over time, a point eloquently developed by Chandra Talpade Mohanty (1988) as she exposed the diminution of "Third World Women." She considers how the category was consistently deployed in social science scholarship as a generic, totalizing mass in what is now considered a landmark essay. I use North/South throughout the book to signal a variety of distinctions, roughly between where transnational capital does and does not flow, to signal that have/have not dimensions of the world exist in all geographic areas, but also to preserve decidedly geographic dimensions of a North-dominated globe (see Mohanty, 2003, pp. 505–6).

In such understandings of the world, the North carries a substantial amount of baggage given the serious global problems perpetrated by countries of the G8 (Canada, France, Germany, Italy, Japan, Russia, UK and US) and multinational corporations headquartered in the North with long, complex reach throughout the world. As Shiva notes, global is a misnomer since the global that is most typically discussed today is a *globalized local*, or, "a particular dominant local [who] seeks global control" (Shiva, 1997, p. 231). The *global* in this sense is really not representative of the planet, biosphere and all inhabitants but the privileged few people of the global North, and in particular, those with extraordinary power within those societies. The global is a singular form and a peculiar type of local but this version of the global often stands in for what can be a totalizing category. The global elite who perpetuate this *globalized local*, many of whom live only briefly in one particular location as they have multiple places that shifting constitute a domicile, wield most of the power in the world and thereby set the agenda. Shiva notes quite accurately that this global elite enforces regimes of economic development through institutions like the IMF and World Bank. They globalize their local by imposing those versions of existence throughout the global South—and indeed in the Souths that exist within the North—such that the possibility for a democratic or communitarian ethic to emerge globally is choked off by an obsessive adherence to economic growth with only a faint nod to sustainability. Global in this elite sense has come to mean rigid adherence to standards set by this small, powerful group of people coupled with the active reinscription of norms that benefit very few and marginalize many others.

Others have raised similar concerns regarding peace education. Ilan Gur-Ze'ev (2010) argues that peace education is based on hegemonic Northern values, such as capitalism and individualism, and fails to teach students to be critical, or even aware of the normativity of such values. Thus, students unmindfully reproduce those values while replicating a moral sensibility to concretize and impose this worldview. Those engaged in peace education of an a-critical variety would hardly think of their work as ethically akin to the IMF or World Bank. Yet, the tendency to be uncritical about the epistemological foundations of Western-style education will continue to be a daunting challenge to those with the best intentions, people who imagine the world otherwise but may not be circumspect of their own values, privilege; and global position. This move can open up space for dialogic possibility and hope; however, it needs to be done with a sense of equity and solidarity rather than imposition. But this is complexly frustrating work since, as Akomolafe (2014) notes, well-intentioned peace and environmental activists from the North tromp off into the forests of Brazil to ironically teach indigenous people how to value their land and resources. Similar to Gur-Ze-ev, Akomolafe struggles with how to engage the world in such a way that does not promote the dominant logic behind those same actions.

I think part of the answer may reside in the ability to think empathetically, or to put someone else into the position of another. This is complicated work and at some level, an impossibility, since it is not fully possible to experience the world as another person does. Recognizing that condition is a necessary first step in being empathetic, in listening and observing with the intention of understanding someone's lifeworld, not to coopt or manipulate but to understand and thereby honor them. I recently visited a school in the Netherlands where it showed a cartoon of two students, one with his head pressed inside the torso of another. I found the image disturbing at first and was not sure I was seeing it correctly as it appeared invasive. Yet, I think this captures some of what is problematic about "getting inside" someone else's worldview. The spirit of the image is quite generous in that it tries to approximate what life is like inside another person, a way of seeing resonant with GCE.

Matters of positionality invite GCE learners to see themselves as inheriting a social location, positioned by the world and in relation to the vast inequalities structured therein along with a capacity and desire to be empathetic, to see and feel the world as another person does. And, as disconcerting as this awareness might be, to recognize that the dominant logic of being in the world is often reanimated and reproduced in one's best efforts. Yet, this interrogative space opens up the possibility of conversation, openness and learning that comes from listening to others across all boundaries and borders. This question, unlike "*Who am I?*", encourages educators and learners to see themselves socially rather than individually, to imagine possibilities of working together in solidarity on issues that matter in the full light of the intrusion of global capital in communities the world over.

Moving Ahead

My *bricolage* about GCE draws on the work of Deborah Meier at the Central Park East schools, Graham Pike and David Selby's conception of domains in global learning, Bill Bigelow and Bob Peterson's critical perspective on global learning and Grant Wiggins and Jay McTighe's discussion of essential questions and backward design (Bigelow & Peterson, 2002; Meier, 1995; Pike & Selby, 1999; Wiggins & McTighe, 2005). My experiences as a teacher, researcher and writer in global education for over 25 years have contributed substantially to this framework, particularly in teaching and working with masters and doctoral students at Teachers College, Columbia University and in numerous public talks over the past ten years, audiences to which I am deeply indebted for challenging and shaping my thinking (Gaudelli, 2003). I pose these questions to signal a pedagogical orientation of inquiry, exploration and wonderment. And they are intended only as broad starting points and way-stations as the inquiry that inheres in any singular concern that might be called a global issue—from the status of women to the state of global warming to the exploitation of minors in the contemporary global slave trade—warrants a lifetime of study.

One of the many challenges associated with GCE and evident from these questions is the breadth of subject matter. In the research I have engaged, I have yet to find a comprehensive approach to GCE that addresses the breadth of the field in a substantial way. The tendency, rather, is for programs, courses or emphases that focus on one dimension, such as human rights, sustainability, cultural diversity or some other foci. The questions I am posing herein, however, suggest that while the content or issues of GCE are important to some degree, the process of engaging the study, using the frameworks articulated and/or the questions I offered, is substantially more important than the content, per se.

The next four chapters detail some of the studies I have engaged, both acting alone as a researcher and in the company of two of my doctoral students, Ching-Fu Lan and Scott Wylie. The cases themselves were selected to push the envelope about what this work means variously and how it is enacted. Rather than hold these up as exemplars (though I believe there are exemplary aspects of each) *to learn from*, I see the profiles of educational programming as illustrations *to think with*. The foci of each chapter—from human rights/citizenship to environment/sustainability to identity to teacher education for GCE—help round out conceptually what GCE can be in schools, through after-school programs, in universities and with nonprofit/community-based organizations. In addition, these illustrations are purposefully drawn from a variety of global locales to illustrate, though not comprehensively, a range of contexts that intersect with GCE diversely. How GCE is understood and enacted variously will become increasingly clear, though by no means foreclosed, by those who led such efforts.

Note

1   I use quotes around nature to call the readers' attention to the problems associated with this terminology, as it was used historically to categorize and subjugate people based on their "nature." Moreover, the notation gestures towards the mutability and social dimensions of categories like gender and ethnicity that were previously viewed as immutable.

3

HUMAN RIGHTS AND CITIZENSHIP EDUCATION

Human rights education is often a vehicle for GCE as it affirms the dignity of all people regardless of legal standing. As citizenship centers on the relationships of individuals to each other and the larger society, bodies of law and constitutions are a typical starting point. But human rights education (HRE) is somewhat different than civic education from a legal/national frame, since the latter presumes a sovereign, state-based jurisdiction and HRE has a transcendent ethos related to personhood that is not necessarily confined to a national entity. In this way HRE intentionally orients outwards, beyond the legal entity that most typically grounds a person's identity as a citizen. HRE is therefore a useful venue for GCE and one that makes it fairly prevalent in fields of practice (Oxley & Morris, 2013).

But it is this inherent otherness and transcendent quality that makes HRE problematic in teaching and classrooms. As HRE often deals with events and principles in a distant place, it is all too easy for teachers and students to disassociate from these concerns, seeing them as someone else's problem. When I taught a nine-week unit about global human rights in high school, this was a common reaction of students, particularly when they felt implicated by the issue. We would investigate, for example, how clothing and material objects of their lives were wound up in an economic trade system that supported horrendous working conditions in factories throughout the South. Students, feeling implicated by their economic choices, would quickly say that labor conditions were national problems, or that factory workers should simply take up another occupation, or that nothing could be done about such injustices since there was no way to enforce universal standards of human rights protections for labor.

Students would often focus their responses on national politics and the inability of nations to solve their own problems. So as a class we would then pivot to look at enforcement mechanisms, such as the previous regime of annual reporting before the United Nations Human Rights Committee and the long-standing pressure of moral suasion in the global community, often led by groups such as Amnesty International and Human Rights Watch and broadcast through global media outlets. But these procedures, as students would quickly come to realize, were typically unable to prevent or mitigate human rights violations themselves. Raising awareness, though, does help and has helped to build a global discourse of human rights, which has been a significant achievement of the 20th century. My approach was to inquire with students about how these seemingly distant concerns were directly connected to their life experiences, as many teachers have done and continue to do. Labor conditions in Bangladesh, for example, are a product of interdependent choices that the students were engaged in, such as clothes shopping.

Despite these efforts to think about the larger implications, students defaulted to relying on national legal systems as a preferred means of addressing human rights abuses. Students quickly came to realize how human rights principles typically recede as *real politicks* ascends, or that human rights was an aspirational way of thinking the world that often lacked a firm grounding in current political realities that are more directly governed by national and legal frameworks (save those situations where legal principles happen to overlap with human rights guarantees). In fairness to these students, they were articulating what they came to learn about citizenship in prior schooling and throughout so many points of experience: that is, nations matter, civic engagement is defined by these parameters and human rights concerns happen beyond the water's edge. Audrey Osler (2011) has noted this same tendency in the context of the European Union because there is a tension between viewing citizenship as developing a national character and the aims of promoting in students a sense of global solidarity. This is particularly the case with respect to minority groups within nations of the global North, as bringing others into alignment with national identity is typically the basis for citizenship education, rather than promoting a sense of personhood that transcends national boundaries.

The coupling of HRE and citizenship education is well established in the scholarly literature, despite various tensions of scale that this connection introduces (Banks, 2009; Hung, 2012; Osler & Vincent, 2002). Dina Kiwan's (2005) typology, which includes five conceptions of citizenship—moral, legal, identity, participatory and cosmopolitan—demonstrates points of friction for citizenship and HRE. She argues that human rights are founded on moral and cosmopolitan principles; or, in other words, a basis that does not presume a legal/state apparatus. Yet, allowing for participatory rights, for example, presumes a legal system in which those rights can be exercised, which suggests a logical conundrum: Can one have a moral imperative that has no legal correspondence?

The dilemma that inheres in HRE and citizenship education involves coupling a transcendent idea such as human rights with the deep-rooted resonance of concepts of citizenship. Part of this tension lies in affiliation, or how one comes to be identified as part of a group, or one's status as belonging to a group. Human rights necessarily assumes an affiliation that is as broad as could possibly be imagined, reaching out to every person. Citizenship, however, connotes belonging that tends towards exclusion rather than inclusion, or matters of *who is one of us*. Can these conceptualizations work together, or reinforce each other, given this tension?

Conceptualizations of citizenship typically conjoin status, affinity and engagement—or *being, feeling* and *doing*—into a composite of what constitutes ideal civic character. A person may be considered a citizen to the extent the law establishes their identity as such. And by the same standard, a person is a citizen because of their legal status alone rather than their belonging in a fundamental, human sense. Osler (2011) reads the citizenship curriculum of the UK, for example, as being largely focused on status and practice, or the legal standing and engagement of that citizen in schools and local communities that point towards national citizenship. She found that teachers in the eight schools in England she studied tended to conceptualize citizenship as a merger of knowing and doing while believing that doing was often limited to the immediate community or regional context. Though teachers in her study reported efforts to engage HRE through the Convention on the Rights of the Child (1989), their pedagogical interpretation leaned towards a local and national rather than global focus. And when teachers did engage students in global learning, such as in a school's global partner program with a school in Gambia, "overt political objectives seem to fade, and the project focus appears to become charitable" (Osler, 2011, p. 15). Some versions of HRE address local acts of engagement that connect to global issues but are less likely to be taught in light of global circumstances.

There are three dilemmas that emerge from the two cases examined herein, ones that will shape the conversation at the chapter's end. First, the scale dilemma, or the conundrum of how one studies the local, national and global considering each other and at the same time, surfaced in both Ontario and Mumbai. Second, the problem of how human rights advocacy organizations, particularly in the North, often employ stereotypic images of others to fundraise in ways that reinforce global charity scripts and fail to point towards possibilities of working in solidarity across difference and in commonality. This problem is unique to the Canadian case presented here although it does resonate with activities described in the case from Mumbai. And last, the presence of historically marginalized people within the HRE work described here, both as subjects in Canada and as participants in the case of Mumbai, typifies how otherwise marginalized people can and must be engaged in what it means to live globally and be a global citizen.

Children's Rights in Canada

The Child Rights Project (CRP) is organized by the International Committee for Human Rights Protection (ICHRP) in Canada.[1] ICHRP-Canada is an International Governmental Organization (IGO) dedicated to promoting the rights of women and children throughout the world while operating on a global scale. One division of the organization is dedicated to educational outreach, focusing on development concerns in Canada by promoting rights-based education in local schools. The CRP aims to energize local communities to work collaboratively to promote global awareness, specifically around the rights of children so that they can draw out from the immediate concerns about rights in the context of schools towards its wider dimensions.

Patricia, a project leader, explained that she was a teacher for ten years in east Toronto and worked in a predominantly immigrant population school. She taught English, geography and world history and was drawn to the caring community embodied in her high school. When she left the classroom, she initially worked in education and community outreach on sustainability issues. She shared that while working on sustainability, she sensed that students were not fully engaged as it didn't matter in an immediate way. Sustainability was something they *should* be doing rather than something they *wanted* to do. Patricia commented,

> How do you get young people engaged? How do you get them caring about the future? How do you help them to collaborate with each other and feel like they can make a difference? The CRP brought it all together for me, all of these issues that I had been working on all came together and it was like *this is all about rights*…that all of these young people need an opportunity to engage with their communities. These aren't a bonus or an extra in schools, but they need to be embedded in the culture of the school and help teachers understand how a rights-focus will make their classroom a better place. Where do you have the most opportunity to reach children and young people, right?! Teachers reach thousands of students, so working with teachers and how they teach, you can really make a big difference in the world.

The pitch that ICHRP employed with school boards, teachers and students derived from the value of immediacy and engagement; that human rights issues as played out in a school were meaningful to adolescents and helped them to become active in their community.

ICHRP educators were sensitive about CRP becoming obsolete, aware as educators of the many wonderful initiatives that preceded their work and now sat on teachers' bookshelves collecting dust. This led ICHRP to make the work seem doable for teachers, cognizant of the challenges that teachers face daily and constantly vigilant that even teachers with the best of intentions would jettison initiatives that were seen as added-on. "It's more about how you can be an aware, concerned and empathetic citizen of the world in *everyday* life, that it's really all interconnected." Patricia was also sensitive to being an outsider when working with teachers, administrators and other school personnel, frequently reminding them in workshops that "this is your community so you have to make it fit here." Patricia's reckoning of the immediate concerns of teachers and communities was doubled in the sense that the contents of children's rights connected to particularities of students' lives while the process of enacting the curriculum would embody those same contents.

ICHRP addressed the local-fit dynamic through an intake process designed to select only those school boards (or jurisdiction of schools) that had a high degree of administrative, teacher and staff buy-in coupled with a multi-year commitment to integrating CRP. Once a board signs on to the project, they assemble 25–40 stakeholders from throughout the district to participate in a two-day ICHRP training around the *Children's Rights Convention* (1989) and how it interfaces with local CRP projects. I attended one of these sessions to get a grounded sense of how the CRP is enacted with staff. A curious omission from the two-day workshop, somewhat ironic given the focus, was student participation. When I asked Patricia about this she indicated that this decision lies with the board though most choose not to invite students.

Patricia, along with other educators within ICHRP, understood the problem of scale as one directly related to student and teacher engagement with the material. Studying children's rights in a distant way, or from the vantage point of global others in situations far removed from Canada, would lead most students and teachers towards disinterest, a feeling of irrelevance, and ultimately, to HRE not being taught. Furthermore, the focus on local aspects of scale was thought to be a strategic means of getting school boards involved. ICHRP believed that the best way to get buy-in from schools was to invest them in improving the immediate situation, focusing on student behavior, building a stronger sense of community and deploying children's rights towards these ends. Sonya, a program officer based in Vancouver who engages with schools in western Canada, discussed this approach.

> I think the local dimension is crucial. From my perspective of having done youth work, which requires voluntary participation, unless the issues are made relevant to the individual's personal life it's just not going to go very far. I ask kids in my workshop, *so what's going on?* and they will say I'm concerned about what job I'm going to get, I've got family issues, or there's drugs in the area, or it's about sex and then we use that as a starting point to look at global issues, drug trade, sex trade, whatever it may be. So from my perspective in youth work, the personal has to really factor in, working out from the local, to regional and to the global out there.

Sonya previously worked on a similar initiative in England and encountered some of the same obstacles she had previously, of teaching young people about faraway places while they were so intently interested in the immediacy of their lives. However, the educators in ICHRP did not address how to move beyond or ways that not only showed connections but oriented students and teachers outwards, to other global situations. Their implicit assumption, a problematic one, is that if students and teachers are encouraged to make local–global connections they will necessarily come to value those concerns and issues and seek out the perspectives of others in all future inquiries. The trouble with an inside–outside formulation of pedagogy is that the other or external illustration can be read as tacked on or auxiliary to the primary concerns, say the immediate ones of drugs, relationships and family problems. How to scaffold that connectivity into learning was an unexamined assumption in the work that begged explanation and development, a point of pedagogical controversy unexamined.

The *gestalt* of teaching children's rights through embodying their practice and study was very attractive to participants at a theoretical level, but the translation of these principles was not readily accepted by all educators. As one principal in the workshop noted, "If the Children's Rights Convention [CRC] focuses on what is in the best interest of the child, there will be debate, since kids trying out for a sports team and being cut denies them an opportunity to play, so how does that become a part of it?" to which Patricia replied, "Yes, it's complicated and it's a big conversation." I asked Patricia later in the day about this exchange and she explained that it was a typical concern, about how a right implies entitlements, which will always leave room for interpretation. Her resolution of this was to avoid imposing a solution but to encourage educators teaching about and through children's rights to have complicated conversations like these.

In an activity later in the same day, participants discussed the possibility of having students, parents and community members involved in hiring panels for new faculty. Some thought it would be a beneficial change for the school board and one that would resonate with a rights discourse, while others maintained that such decisions were best left to professional judgment. There was an echo in this conversation of the human rights/children's rights conundrum, or whether children ought to be entitled to rights in a way that approximates adults'. Participants in the forum, some of whom were not yet persuaded about CRP, raised concerns that students lacked a comprehensive understanding of what being an educator requires and would therefore not be able to contribute meaningfully to a hiring decision. Still, others held that a student voice was significant as they could best offer perspective of how students might respond to a particular teacher.

These conversations interrupted the flow of learning about children's rights in the workshop, in a productive if tangential way. Almost instantly, attendees began troubling the notion of children's rights in light of their everyday practices. Kit, a social worker, began sharing stories about the friction experienced by Canadian immigrants from sub-Saharan Africa and the Caribbean. She argued that girls from certain immigrant communities receive starkly different messages at home about their rights as young women, a discourse which Kit described as being largely absent from their home, replaced with talk about duty and obligation rather than entitlement. She believed that this situation could lead parents to remove children, particularly girls, from school for fear of the messages they would receive about children indeed having rights. Kit claimed that precisely this had happened during a previous situation where school social workers intervened on behalf of children who they believed were abused. Tara, a social worker in the group, also noted that when children begin to confront their parents, they will soon disappear from the school district. As she said, "It's all fine and dandy to fight for children's rights, but not for the child who disappears." There was tension among participants who feared that children's rights might serve to further alienate already vulnerable populations, such as female immigrant students.

These three vignettes from the CRP workshop suggest a problematic dynamic in GCE. In both situations the overarching principle of access to educational (sports) activity, participation in school governance and the treatment of girls with dignity are generally agreeable in the abstract. But when viewed in a particular situation they take on a much more complicated and historically derived character that belies facile decisions. So the dilemma of scale is not simply a matter of student engagement, local–global connections or facilitating work already being done in schools with a new lens, but also a question of how existing local practices are reckoned against a new frame of reference, such as global children's rights. Few educators would deny the value of participation, either in sports or decision making, or treatment with dignity in theory, but within the complicated terrain of *our school* or *these kids*, these principles imply actions that are dramatically more difficult to resolve.

The second dilemma that surfaced related to HRE in a global citizenship frame is that of the image of others. I mean here images in the literal sense of the word but in the figurative manner too, or how conversations animate particular images of other people, typically people with whom students and teachers have no direct contact. At one point in the workshop participants were asked: *What is the most significant issue affecting children?* Participants did this individually and then were asked to join with a partner to try to convince them that their issue was more important. Joan and Susan partnered and shared answers: Joan's being teen stress and Susan's being access to water. The images connoted by each, the former of an adolescent student in Canada working to manage a hectic life and the latter of a young child in a poor country struggling to find clean water as part of their daily existence, couldn't have been more different. Joan promptly said, "We will definitely pick yours as it's much more global." When they shared responses with the larger group most had an otherness about them, with issues such as hunger, clean water and lack of resources trumping stress, college admission procedures and peer pressure.

The pattern of response was fascinating as many pairs had similar, dyadic local–global issues and the pairs consistently selected the typically global one as being more important, likely due to the context of the workshop. The local–global contrasts appeared throughout the activity, with those offering typically Canadian problems (e.g. teen stress in a hyper-modern society) having a "silly me!" response to their counterparts who raised wider concerns, such as lacking clean water. The prioritization activity also forced participants to choose between two options, but in reality the two are deeply interwoven. One plausible path of connection might be that adolescent stress in Canada is a by-product of the drive at school to achieve premier university admission, which eventually leads to a stressful position working for a transnational corporation that is imbricated in a global capital network. The global capital network forces national leaders, particularly in the South, to create pro-investment policies, ones that generally undermine public funding for improved infrastructure, like water treatment facilities. The focus on building communities to support industry rather than on the communities themselves creates conditions where the needs of daily life are trumped by the imperatives of global economic competition. Economically marginalized people are often compelled to relocate to urban centers for proximity to economic activity to improve their financial situation. But then they are forced to locate and transport clean water since the government does not provide or maintain infrastructure.

The water access/teen stress moment demonstrates a conundrum of GCE: How do educators address issues such as clean water that are wrenching, daily concerns for some on the planet and taken for granted by others as a commonplace? And, can that be done in such a way that does not fundamentally other those in need of water? I discussed this conundrum with another ICHRP staffer in education, Sonia, as she encounters this dilemma frequently in her work—what she refers to as the *pitiful other* problem. She said that in global learning, particularly from the situation of Canada, there is a nearly automatic response among students to feel pity for poor people around the world, falling into the deep groove of the global North as donor and the global South as recipient. As she noted,

> It's so easy for teachers to fall into the trap of teaching the pity perspective, *oh those people are so poor.* So you need some pretty intense, critical reflection by teachers and students around the question, *How do you want to work in the world?* It's really tricky, isn't it? What you do want is for people to feel empathy and get fired up to do something. For example, what they buy intricately involves them in that web of interconnections. It's quite a challenge to explore that with students. Some will save up to send soccer balls overseas, when they learn that children do not have equipment and they want to support the right to play but then to question, *Is that the best thing to be doing?* What's most important is that the student wants to take action, so you don't want to squash that.

Sonia articulates a foundational element of GCE in that student engagement with the world is an important end-in-view. ICHRP's approach is to have students learn about their personal experiences in a social manner, link those to wider concerns, develop empathy for the situation of others and then act. The difficult element is moving students to problematize their actions, often the ones that they will choose by default, like charitable participation. This is counter-cultural, however, in the sense that Canadian students, like those throughout the North, live within a broader culture that positions the South as being in need of charity. GCE educators must then confront the awkward situation when students want to help in ways that implicitly reinscribe their privilege as the "giver."

I recall a similar event in my town when I was invited to visit an elementary school and read a short-story. After reading Mem Fox's *Whoever You Are* to a group of third graders, the teacher began asking questions about a recent trip I had taken to India. She said, "Did they have any books like that one? Did the children have any materials for learning?" and I began to realize that she was setting me up to articulate a well-worn narrative about *poor, deprived children of India*. I gently refused to participate in this way, offering students a more nuanced portrait of the very limited India I have come to know in my work there. While there are schools desperate for materials in India, there are also ones far better equipped than those in our community. In a sense, I tried to leave them with the understanding that "it's complicated." As I left the class, I could hear the teacher saying to her students, "Do you see how lucky you are that you have books to read not like the kids in India?" While I understand that this approach may come from a hope that students in the North will better appreciate what they so often take for granted, a worthy goal, to do so by portraying a country of over 1 billion people as solely in need of charity is a dramatically simplistic and misleading yet all-too-familiar stance among North educators.

The activist and othering dimensions of children's rights work were a sensitive, internal challenge for ICHRP staff. Sheila, an Ontario-based field officer who had written much of the Child Rights Project teacher and school leader curriculum, talked at some length about this concern. She explained that being both the original curriculum author and now doing implementation in Ontario, she was able to see areas that needed revision.

> The organization [ICHRP], as an international development organization, is dedicated to funding programing around the world. There are proven techniques and strategies that work to go out to the general public in Canada and encourage them to make a donation. So there are certain images that we use and stories that we tell about the global South. As an educator it's challenging at times to know that those stories are going out en masse with a lot of capacity behind them and you as an educator with little capacity, and you find yourself questioning, *Is this an accurate picture of the global South? Is this a full picture of the global South?* That's what we like

to talk about at ICHRP, closing that loop, not just teaching it in a flash to give money but to really develop empathy so that when they act they are doing it because they want to help…not out of a sense of guilt or pity or obligation. So there's that creative tension and in the mass media we don't have the time to unpack it to help people understand.

Educators within ICHRP were unable to alter this pattern, however, since fundraising within Canada was a higher priority than educating Canadians about the world in a deep and nuanced way. The staff talked frequently about this tension though they viewed it as a productive one within the organization, while serving as a reminder that the primary work of ICHRP is not education in Canada, per se, but improving the economic and social conditions of economically disadvantaged people in the global South while helping people to see how these two societies parts of the world are interrelated. My larger concern around this issue emanates from the shift in GCE going on, as NGOs and IGOs increasingly participate in global education. Since these organizations all share the need for external fundraising, they will likely continue to reinscribe the *pitiful other* image in their campaigns.

That the *pitiful other* image is recirculated by the same groups that would seek to eradicate the conditions which produce misery is not the most confounding aspect of the dilemma. Rather, some charitable acts may only serve as a palliative for the donor rather than a meaningful contribution to recipients, deployed as a means of deflecting Northern guilt over vast and vastly growing global inequities. Furthermore, ICHRP materials have a recursive flow as teachers use ICHRP donor-oriented materials from the website along with the classroom-prepared materials to support instruction. Among the donor-oriented images are those of children walking in untreated sewage and living on top of waste dumps. Sheila shared that some teachers and parents of elementary students, when learning about the Children's Rights Convention (1989), felt that their children were too young to engage in a study of poverty and its social dimensions in other parts of the world. Thus, the ironic takeaway is that a South toddler can live in a dump but elementary school children in the North should not have to see such things.

Slum Schools and Civic Action in Mumbai

The Darpali Group is a Mumbai-based NGO that was created when Sunali, the daughter of a wealthy banker, was alarmed by the sight of begging children on the streets of Mumbai. Sunali decided to do something, organizing English classes and other sports and enrichment activities during the evenings in unused office spaces. She recruited students from nearby colleges to teach teens who lived in the slums of Mumbai. This effort started in the early 1990s and has flourished over the past two decades to become an organization involving hundreds of teachers and staff working with the most economically vulnerable youth in Mumbai and Pune. The civic action programs to support slum-dwelling youth organized by Darpali include: (1) an after-school/weekend program for those attending Ministry schools and (2) a school-based program within charter schools.

Darpali began largely as a program to augment existing schools and recently morphed into one that runs charter schools and enhances programming within these new charters. Paavai, the educational director for Darpali, explains the shift under way:

> Our programming had been geared towards providing 2.5 hours of instruction for these students over the course of a five-day week. The focus was on English language skills, mathematical skills and values education. At first English was the focus because we thought that would give our students an edge, because a lot of students went to public schools in their home language – in Hindi, Urdu, Gujarati, Mahrati – and English was just a subject taught. So the students and parents from poor families wanted English-medium schools and programs so they would have college opportunities since English is the language in most colleges. That's how Darpali started and that was the focus area, an after-school program.

The shift from after-school programming towards full-day charter school was somewhat strategic as Darpali capitalized on an opportunity provided by the provincial government to encourage charter schools, an idea taken from the increasingly global discourse about school reform discussed in Chapter 2, part of a larger initiative to prepare students for an increasingly global marketplace. This was interpreted by Darpali as better preparing students in English to provide more opportunities for postsecondary education.

Darpali's emphasis on college-preparation and English-language learning illustrates a Western orientation to the work; however, there is a sense that the best way to prepare students for success that will lift them out of poverty is to adopt to global changes. There was consensus among staff around this direction with a relative absence of critique about how this path could undermine Marathi and other cultures and language groups in Mumbai and Pune, especially given the spiritual focus in the region. The absence of internal critique about the Western overtones of Darpali's program may speak to the location and urban concentration of the work, since Mumbai in particular prides itself on being a city that blends and hybridizes many spiritual, linguistic and cultural traditions. And the dire economic situation of Darpali's students positions the critique of dominant norms as a luxury, when English speaking provides access to economic opportunity.

There is an ironic aspect of including Darpali's work in a chapter about GCE with a human rights orientation. The students served by Darpali, most of whom live in slums, might reasonably be viewed as those most adversely affected by the rampant capitalism of the global era and themselves sufferers of human rights violations—notably the lack of access to adequate living standards such as drinking water, nutrition and healthcare. The double-quality of the illustration is one part of my rationale for inclusion of this case since the program aims to support young people who live in slums, but also because of the outwardly focused citizenship action project they organize. Darpali's efforts open up a way of examining the knowledge/power relationship about who acts in regard to HRE, similar to Appadurai's (2013) detailing of civic organizations operating among the most destitute in Mumbai. That the work on HRE and citizenship education is happening within a globally and historically marginalized group of the global South is also significant because it provides a counter to the typical way that HRE is conceptualized and enacted in the North, as illustrated by the previous case.

Darpali staff are committed to showcasing the impressive talent of young people who live in slums and sharing those expressions with a wider audience. I interviewed Barsha, the director of art education for Darpali, who explained why the artwork had become a signature aspect of the organization. Students create artwork for external fundraising and to build awareness of Darpali's efforts. Barsha explained that when students are engaged in learning about and making art, they develop a stronger sense of self and accomplishment, particularly for those students who may struggle academically. "Students saying 'I know how to paint' gives them a huge boost of knowledge and the power that comes with that, building social capital." She also explained how important the artwork is for the public face of the NGO since it helps the wider public reconfigure what they think of kids who live in slums. Barsha noted, "I've heard people say when coming across a piece of art, 'I can't believe a kid from the slum did this!' which is sad actually that they think this, but it gives people a chance to think differently about our kids." The art projects, however, had a Western orientation as students were learning and mimicking the styles of the impressionists and cubism of Europe.

The Service Learning Program (SLP) organized by Darpali has an emphasis on learning about civic action and human rights through social inquiry. The SLP was the original effort by Darpali to provide enhanced learning experiences for adolescents that they might not otherwise receive. As Darpali's internal curriculum documents explain,

> The Service Learning Program focuses on the following issues: governance, public administration, human rights and citizenship; the education system and related issues; discrimination—gender, class, caste, ethnicity, sexuality, physical disability; health and related subjects; child rights and child sexual abuse; environment and related issues; rural–urban divide, migration issues; and understanding agriculture.

The intention of Darpali is that as students engage in social inquiry around these topics they will not only learn about global issues but will develop dispositions and skills such as self-regulation, problem-solving, inquiring and community building.

Raj, the Darpali staff member who leads SLP, offered the following overview of the program:

The students are studying things that affect them directly through local surveys and by them asking people, *What is the biggest problem that you experience?* Students study rights issues like discrimination, classism, sexual abuse, corruption and governance. The underlying philosophy is using a head, heart and hand approach. So what is it that's burning, that you *feel?* Then, to think intellectually, and last to go ahead and do work. We are trying to develop a multi-perspective understanding about that issue. And then the students do something about it with an organization working on that issue. So if you think the biggest problem is child sexual abuse then you will go work with an organization working on that issue for an entire summer.

The SLP meets three times per month during the academic year (July through April) following a selection process in June. Programs are held on weekends and holidays at over 40 centers around Mumbai and Pune. There are special programs such as a Service Jam, which is a two-day workshop that students attend for skill development that builds towards choosing an internship. The internship, as Raj noted, is designed to place students with NGOs and similar civic sector organizations who are engaged in the work that students identify as issues of concern. I attended special sessions of Darpali's SLP on Republic Day, a national holiday in January to honor the establishment of the Indian Constitution. Students participated on a Sunday for six to eight hours on what was otherwise a national holiday, meaning that schools were closed. Darpali staff members commented that student attendance on what would have been an opportunity to make money for their families was a sure indication of the value that students and their families assign to SLP. Programs such as Darpali's offerings are positioned as an opportunity to escape poverty even though they require an economic sacrifice for these families.

The first portion of the day included short presentations while students gathered from throughout the Darpali network to present poetry that related to their understanding of India's current situation and place in the world. This was the culmination of a three-week activity as students came together over the previous month to prepare and rehearse their Republic Day poetry. Raj mentioned that it was a learning opportunity for them as it developed their public speaking while developing a sense of belonging as Indians. Many of the students wore Darpali shirts adorned with artwork and the Gandhi-inspired phrase "Be the change." Students delivered their poems in front of an improvised flag, with green, white and orange silk cloths draped over a wall which served as a makeshift stage.

The students shared strong views about public issues affecting India and shared these openly in the forum, somewhat surprising given the context of a national day of celebration.

- India is my country, we are divided into different castes. India is for everyone, where people talk so many different languages. We have such freedom and we have heroes like Gandhi. I'm proud to be Indian and I love my country.

- India, a country with unity and with corruption and bribes. We have potential, the question remains how we can change. It's the responsibility of every citizen to change.
- My country, our country has so much pollution and corruption and people cheat. But India is our mother. We should take care of nature. We can't hide from the children anymore. You ride like an Indian tiger. You have imagination now you need education.
- People there are a lot, but there is a scam, deposits in Swiss banks, people have hunger, the world is angry, no beast will survive, she is raped. Look…here there is a crime, there there is a crime!! My eyes are shut my legs are tied in frustration, but deep down inside my heart aches. I see some rays of hope, showing me a brighter side and I know there is a hope for India.
- I have a dream to make India as delicious as a chocolate ice cream.

As the poems were being read, the Darpali staff beamed with pride, with raucous applause among audience members, suggesting that the activity was what participants and staff imagined in their weeks of planning. There was a measure of positive embrace of what India is and the spiritual heritage for which it is recognized. But students also expressed critical love about what needs to be done and problems that remain: specifically corruption, pollution, discrimination, perpetuation of caste and violence against women. There was a palpable sense of *being real* rather than abiding national cover stories given that these young people live in slums and regularly witness many of the problems expressed.

I also noted a pattern over the course of the three hours of poetry related to gender and language. Most of the 80 participants were girls, with approximately 15 boys and 65 girls. All of the boys spoke in Hindi while most of the girls used English. It was interesting to see that one of the students asked the same question, though not in reference to gender, about why so many students spoke in languages other than English. Raj responded:

> It's important to know who you are, to stand up for who you are and be firm in that belief, in that language because that is who you are [long pause]. It's good to know other languages, like English, Gujarati, Bengali, but you also need to know who you are [long pause, ~20 seconds].

I spoke to Raj about the gender disproportionality and language differences and he offered an explanation:

> For the Republic Day poetry project, many students had joined from Darpali schools…the young ones if you noticed were in school dress, and most of those children were girls. The schools' students, since they are encouraged to speak in English most of the time, do so in most formal conversational opportunities. The SLP students, however, are encouraged

to use a language that they are most comfortable with and hence choose to speak in Hindi/Marathi at times and in this group there was a more equal gender distribution.

An insight that resonates again in this HRE program is the explicit effort to abide where students are, rather than to assume and coerce something that is not yet developed. The SLP is oriented this way, both in student choice of a social inquiry and the language used to express themselves, as this pedagogical choice issues from the belief that the content and process of the work must connect in order to be meaningful. In addition, there is a degree of incongruence on this point with the English-medium schools, the younger group of girls that Raj notes, since English is unlikely to be their home language and yet they use it for informal, educational settings.

Following a short break for lunch, about three-quarters (~60) of the students, the pre-teen group, were released due to the mature nature of the afternoon session. Raj invited a group of daughters of sex workers who had organized an NGO to engage a panel discussion for the students about their experiences of their mothers' involvement in the sex industry. Raj purposely did not explain to the SLP students what the panel was about as he planned a learning activity that would reveal their identity only after an initial discussion. He started by having the remaining 20 students rate how much various occupations contributed to India's growth, raising hands to vote on the various professions: doctor (all hands), sweeper (some hands), teacher (most hands), film maker (most hands), housewife (a few hands), taxi driver (more hands than housewife though not most), plumber (most hands), businessman (all hands), software engineer (most hands), politician (some hands), sex worker (no hands except representatives from the group of sex workers' daughters). Raj then inquired about the student rationale for the various rankings, saving sex worker for last. The teen boys were the most outspoken about this group, with a few expressing the view that sex workers help the economy because of their availability for international visitors, though most of their comments focused on the social stigmatization of the group generally.

Raj then pointed students' attention to the group of eight young women and explained that they were teenage daughters of sex workers, who had formed an NGO to educate people about the plight of their moms and families. The students were noticeably shaken by Raj's disclosure and it took them a bit of time and a few questions to be sure that they had accurately heard what he said. Some sat in stunned silence. At this point, *nearly all* of the dialog shifted to Hindi, with periodic English code-switching, perhaps due to the intimacy of the subject, and so my notes are drawn from a Darpali staff member who sat next to me and translated comments over a wide-ranging, two-hour conversation. Again, much of the talk focused on the teens' negative reactions to sex work. One girl, among the most outspoken of the group, said, "according to you, sex is a bad thing and that's why you don't want to become a sex worker, because society has taught us that."

The girls talked about sex as not being a taboo but a normal part of human relations. Another offered her mom's rationale for her choice: "My mom got involved in sex work because she wanted me to have a better education, but she didn't have the money, so she did this so I would have money to go to school."

The students were listening raptly as the panelists described how their moms have to pay bribes to police to engage in their work, the fact that women are at risk of sexually transmitted diseases and of being beaten by clients while engaged in their work, and the stigmatization that hangs over their families as a result of the economic conditions that force them into this work. The girls explained that the boys where they live know what their moms do and so the young girls get harassed even though they are not engaged in sex work. One of the older boys at one point said, somewhat incredulously, "What do sex workers contribute to the growth of India?!" At this point the conversation veered to examine how caste and traditional marriage choices may be an explanation for why sex work is prevalent. "Some adults are forced to marry but may not be sexually attracted to each other, so they get their needs met by a sex worker and that keeps families together which helps the economy." Students then discussed whether sex work was in a way different than what other professions demanded, meaning time and labor for pay in return. The panel of sex-worker daughters clearly indicated that their mom's occupation was no different than any other profession while most of the boys in the SLP group said that other professions were fundamentally different than a sex–money exchange.

The relativity argument enunciated by the sex-worker daughters rang somewhat hollow, albeit, given the frequent refrain that their moms' were forced into this work. Being compelled to do something suggests their moms might choose otherwise, which further implies something undesirable about the work, including the significant physical and emotional trauma that can be caused by such employment.

Darpali was also engaged in HRE which was quite risky, as they attempted to raise awareness about degrading treatment of a socially stigmatized group by putting young people in direct conversation with relatives of stigmatized sex workers. This approach would be challenging in any context but in India, which tends to be socially conservative, it is all the more perilous. But the staff were quite pleased when asked to reflect on the activity. Raj indicated that it "helped to raise awareness about an issue they would not otherwise have an opportunity to learn about in a setting like this one."

Darpali educational staff's choice to confront this reality so directly is integral to what SLP is designed to do: to enact inquiries from the real situations around students rather than from afar or in an academically detached fashion. This was a ground-level view of human rights discourse in practice, not an academic conversation about conventions and protocols. Many of the students formed their inquiries around the sex trade since it is a major human rights issue that affects Mumbai, for example, and one that is globally implicated. As students were developing their civic thinking around this issue, Darpali wished to connect them to NGOs currently engaged in the issue. Darpali's SLP focuses on developing student civic capacity while studying human rights in a grounded way. They invite students to engage with problems of their immediate communities in ways that open them to the otherness of perspective nearby while helping them to address the grave social injustices that exist in the lives of these young people. The doubleness of this experience—engaging in civic practices about human rights topics while living in the ruins of global capital's excesses—is particularly poignant in this case, an insight not lost on the students themselves who talk openly about their economic situation. While these sorts of programs cannot resolve problems that course through a global city such as Mumbai, experiences like those offered by Darpali provide students with learning about human rights and civic education in an immediate manner that is inquiry based, opportunities they are highly unlikely to have without a program such as SLP.

A tension in doing HRE work in a local way, as SLP and in the previous case in Canada, is the tendency for students to avoid looking beyond their immediate situation, a move that runs counter to GCE. Raj addressed these concerns in a subsequent interview:

> As you would know Bombay, or Mumbai, is known as a city of migrants. Most of us, or our ancestors, have migrated into this city from some other part of India. Especially for our students, who definitely have this history and are still connected to their village roots, migration is a part of our conversations. We also have planned conversations, discussions and modules around rural–urban migration, identities we assume from our origins and native tongues, understood in a global context. We discuss the pros, cons and myths of globalization along with the impact of global issues on local communities and vice versa. We also do a summer book-reading program while students are in their internships. The books are generally a work of fiction on related issues but not necessarily set in an Indian context. That gives a connection to the issues from a larger perspective. We encourage students to engage in pre-internship research, such as online research, reading additional articles and meeting people, which helps them to develop a holistic understanding of how the wider world understands a chosen issue.

And while Darpali's mission includes promoting global citizenship among program participants, priority is given to civic capacity development and human rights study that is closest to home with an eye to the wider world, not unlike ICHRP-Canada's CRP program.

Darpali, given its status as an NGO, may too intently focus on this social mechanism as a cure-all to address systemic problems. The freedom of NGO space is indeed a tremendous asset, yet this approach also incurs the limitations of reaching fewer people than a mass organization, such as a school, coupled with the problem of maintaining sustainability in efforts. Barsha, for example, who was an energetic force within this organization, left her position with Darpali a year following the completion of this study, a common dynamic in the sector.

Moving Ahead

The cases presented herein suggest that it is a tall order to expect students and teachers to fully engage with human rights and otherness at a distance. An issue such as the assurance of an adequate living standard in the CRC (1989), for example, is so contextually dependent that understanding and evaluating the extent to which living circumstances are *adequate* is problematic. Even a focus on the basics of life, such as access to clean water, is so variant as to belie a simple reading by students. What is more likely to happen, then, is a focus on how global human rights issues present in particular communities, for example the operation of schools in New Brunswick or Ontario and gender issues and sex workers in Mumbai and Pune.

Both programs started HRE close to home. The SLP in Mumbai initiates student inquiry with a survey of people in the surrounding community. Students identify an issue of concern, such as child labor or access to clean water, and begin by exploring what other people in their community know about it and their thoughts about what might be done to address a problem. This was followed up with an introduction to NGOs in Mumbai or Pune who engaged in civil society organizing around students' chosen issues, allowing them to learn about human rights locally and beyond. The CRP in Canada similarly focused students and teachers on learning about the situation of others, though their orientation had a more distant locus. While learning about children's rights was grounded in the situation of the school board and processes within schools, the CRC (1989) served as a broad umbrella for articulating and interpreting children's rights. The curriculum materials introduced in the CRP teacher workshop explicitly addressed human rights violations on a global scale while drawing connections to the lives of adolescents in Canada.

The ICHRP education staff had to grapple with the fact that their department relied on funding by the main agency, which is primarily concerned with relief efforts in the South rather than education in the North. This created certain tension around how to balance stereotypic depictions of others that typically yield large donations, while nuanced and fine-grained analyses that educators aim to develop among young people and the wider public are not prioritized. The public face of ICHRP, widely recognized in Canada, has far greater capacity than educators working with school boards on the development of the Child Rights Project. The resolution of this dilemma was to abide the different faces of the organization and to name, describe and converse about the challenge. Staff viewed this as a creative tension, one that had a recursive quality in their work and urged them to rethink how they represented others in teacher workshops and curriculum. Changing the marketing strategy for ICHRP, however, was never on the table since stereotypic renderings of *pitiful others* generate funding, despite the adverse stereotyping it ironically perpetuates.

The representational problem is not altogether different from what teachers face in classrooms, what curriculum developers confront in designing GCE experiences or what other NGOs face as they draw pointed narratives about the world. The consciousness that is brought to the images of others, literal images and those emerging from texts, is a crucial piece of understanding of what it means to learn about others. GCE educators in these two HRE cases invited students, teachers and participants to accept uncertainty inherent in engaging in study and action around human rights issues.

But the presumed audience of HRE was somewhat different in each case, as Darpali focused on historically marginalized slum dwellers and CRP had typical Canadian youth in mind. HRE engaged by Darpali suggests that the issues of historical marginalization can and should be addressed by the very same people who are most directly affected by these onerous social processes. Teaching impoverished youth to engage in social inquiry about human rights issues in their community in ways that resonate with the wider, global discourse is not typical slum school programming. Yet, SLP does precisely that, motivating students who might otherwise be marginalized to engage with their community, to learn about it while learning to address broader social concerns collectively in the NGO space. CRP in Canada, however, chose to work with typical adolescents, not necessarily those affected by human rights violations but who might not be aware of violations at all. While HRE has a universal quality that applies to everyone regardless of their legal, citizenship status (Hung, 2012), the two cases here illustrate how audiences and subsequent approaches to HRE can be quite variant.

These points of divergence might best be captured by positionality, or how people's positions in the world (e.g. North/South, woman/man, abled/disabled) orient the way in which they see the world. Positionality is a crucial matter to explore as it opens up a conversation about the egregious inequalities that exist today. This dynamic is highlighted by HRE as this approach inheres a discrepant way of thinking, either what rights are not being upheld or what violations are currently occurring. Thus, students are predisposed by HRE to examine the problematic and inequitable terrain that is the contemporary, global world.

This contrast was made remarkably clear in the teen stress and clean water access distinction during the CRP workshop in Canada. It was also evident in the Darpali staff recounting for me a "getting to know you activity" they had developed for incoming participants to the program. They asked the students a bit of a set-up question to which the staff anticipated the students' replies—*Do you have access to clean water?* The answer they were given surprised the staff since all of the students answered affirmatively. When the educators probed further, since they knew that students indeed did not have access to clean water, the staff realized students had interpreted the question as having access *at some point during the day* to clean water, which the students do, for about two hours each afternoon. This contrast illustrates succinctly the differences about how others think, feel and know about an issue based on their position, in this case being a slum dweller in Mumbai and living in another part of the city.

The CRP case in Canada centered on embodying the rights of children in the operation and governance of the school. There were opportunities for teachers and students to organize activities for social outreach within CRP curricula, though these tend to focus on communities in Canada and the school as a community through a universalizing framework in the CRC. The ethos of the project was clearly to focus on the local and to act in the daily life of the school in a way that was congruent with universal norms. The SLP in Mumbai, however, focused on active engagement in the community, learning about existing human rights challenges and how they were being addressed. The emphasis was not centered on a school since most SLP participants attended a variety of schools, making the venue for action Mumbai itself. Darpali educators held to a belief that since Mumbai and Pune are global cities, the human rights issues addressed in SLP were deeply connected to the world beyond the community that these students knew best. Thus, similar to the SLP in Canada, the engagement focus was oriented towards the local with overtones of regional and global concerns.

Note

1   All proper nouns and personal names are pseudonyms when drawn from the data of this study, and all other place names and institutions are actual (e.g. Teachers College, Columbia University).

4

SELF, SOCIETY, AND OTHERS

Written with Scott Wylie[1]

This chapter examines the development of identity in relation to oneself, others, society and how these fundamentals inform GCE. At root, this chapter is about identity and society, specifically conceptions of self and others and how those take shape in different learning contexts. A sense of oneself is a matter of being, both in a micro and macro way of what it means to be. One's self is made intelligible through an inside–outside conversation, such that the internal grasp of who one is or how one understands reality is co-determined through the outside sense of what it means to belong to people like that. A sense of self is a means to make the world socially intelligible, as it brings together people's capacity to grasp difference among groups of others coupled with the desire to name and claim various identities in a way that makes sense individually and socially.

The chapter is also about the social milieu of learning or the ways in which what is learned in schools is connected to and drawn from material of the wider society. This too is a micro and macro analysis, in this case of how the school is constituted by the society in which it exists and how society creates conditions for certain schools to exist in particular ways. The interactivity of school and society, borrowing from Dewey's (1969) famous title, is vital to what GCE looks like. Despite the universal overtones of GCE, the premise of this chapter and indeed the book is that this broad curricular stance always emerges in a particular time and place and that necessarily colors its hue and shapes it texture.

The cases explored herein—one in Bangkok and the other in New York City—serve as particularly compelling counterpoints since the former school is more focused on the internal dimensions of self and the latter is oriented towards its external features. Yet both are connected to the cities and cultures from which they emerge in interesting ways. One cautionary note in reading this chapter—for the authors and the reader—is to avoid over-reading the comparison such that it takes on a deterministic quality, or that an internal way of thinking about oneself is the sole province of the East and an external locus is unique to the West. Both nodes on the internal–external continuum are constantly interacting regardless of how or where identity work is engaged.

In addition to this caution I also want to offer two grounding issues related to identity. The first is about simplification and automaticity, or how people tend to group others according to superficial observances; a tendency that is rooted in our evolutionary predisposition to perceive subtle differences to identify those of the in-group and all others. The second contextual idea is about the social meanings of identity, or how people group and are grouped according to similarity, perceived or otherwise, and how those identifications take on particular meanings at given times and places.

I want to begin with how we see ourselves, or what elements of that elusive sense of who we are strike us in particular places and moments as especially relevant. Not too long ago my family visited the Feast of San Gennaro in New York City, something that I recall hearing about as a child frequently and occasionally visiting. I do not often think of myself as Italian American though all of my relatives originated in Italy some 90 to 130 years ago. But on this sunny day, walking in the Little Italy that is a showpiece of nostalgic ethnic culture, I somehow felt more Italian. Perhaps it was the food, the smells, the conversations of passersby and their memorable expressions ("y' know that sausage and peppers thing, ma sista invented that"), the recollections of my childhood and the imagining of how my grandparents walked across the Manhattan Bridge, as they so often recounted, to shop for groceries on these same streets. We can all conjure similar moments—when due to the place we were in, the moments in those places and the experience of those moments—when we felt one aspect of our identity radiate.

But identity too has a necessarily social dimension, or how others view social groups and how those impressions shape perceptions and interactions. And of course who one is in a social sense can be problematic as some identities are more vulnerable to hostility and social exclusion than others. I was never, for example, passed by numerous empty taxis as Cornel West recounts happened to him in New York City (1993/2001). As a white person in the US, I have not experienced the sting of the social exclusion of racism. Some identities afford nostalgia while others generate brutality, as the depressing year of police violence in US cities in 2014–15 bitterly reminds us.

Stereotypes are often the only mis/information that we have of the countless others we encounter on a daily basis in a large metropolitan area. And while the disturbing outliers of this way of knowing are all too commonly experienced, the flipside of how one sees the world seeing us is also an important part of identity calculus. Claude Steele (2010) elaborates on these identity contingencies as the way that we navigate social situations in light of our perception of how others view people like us. Among those contingencies is stereotype threat, or the tendency to internalize negative presumptions that society has about a group to which one belongs. Steele's research along with his colleagues in social psychology demonstrates insidious ways that these self-perceptions filter into people's ability to perform or engage in what are considered a-typical activities for social groups.

The reductive tendency of people to see others not as individuals but as representative of larger groups, and the subsequent way that we see ourselves in light of others' view of us, is seemingly connected to the categorical way we are wired to think about the world. George Lakoff's (1987/2008) seminal work, *Women, Fire and Dangerous Things*, considers the prototype effect within categorical thought. As a cognitive linguist, he explores how categories operate within languages to illustrate deeper modes of apprehension in human thought. He argues that humans tend to think of best representations of categories, adding an evaluative dimension to their groupings, while implying that there are degrees of membership, gradations of what constitutes a superb, or somewhat less than exemplary, illustration of a category (Lakoff, 1987/2008, p. 56). A robin or blue jay more aptly fits the linguistic category of a bird than, say, a penguin or ostrich. Similarly, people view others both superficially and automatically, according to well-worn grooves in cognition about how certain people fit into a social landscape. The tendency to view people, nonhuman animals and objects in categorical ways is referred to as the principle of least effort: "To consider every member of a group as endowed with the same traits, saving us the pains of dealing with them as individuals" (p. 173). Such categorization tends to be automatic and superficial and yet can be the source of significant and harmful social interactions. Daniel Kahneman (2011) refers to the slow/fast difference as System 1, automatic and System 2, effortful. As the former is the intuitive response, the latter is the thinking awareness that accompanies the initial impression or instant cognitive formation (see pp. 28–30).

It is too facile to suggest that people view each other as superficially as they might see other animals. Yet, the tendency for people to focus on subtle differences in other people is part of our evolutionary inheritance and perhaps among the most salient aspects of identity. The fact that people view groups to which they belong favorably/automatically while conforming to those groups and viewing others, or out-groups, unfavorably and requiring slow thought to develop affinity is a remarkably consistent finding of social psychologists (Brewer, 2007). Yet social psychology research does not show that in-group positivity correlates with out-group hostility, despite a common belief that these are mirror conditions. As early hominids grouped to survive, and the more successful of these groupings were best able to collectively manage their environment for survival, individuals within those groupings were attuned to the collective aspects of their behavior (Brewer, 2007, p. 730). A more powerful force in the binding of a group identity is loyalty to the group and the distinctiveness of the group vis-à-vis other groupings rather than aggressive hatred for out-groups (p. 732).

The constitution of groups is among the most easily recognizable social behavior of people. I recently attended a professional gathering of 100 people for two weeks that included those on similar career paths. Within two days, the large group had reorganized into smaller groups as people shared activities which developed loyalty to those newly formed clusters by region, ethnicity and interest. This apparently universal behavior develops when groups share common characteristics, perceive themselves as unique and share a sense of positive interdependence within the group (Deutsch et al., 2012, p. 300). This foundational dynamic to how people interact casts doubt on efforts for people to see themselves as part of one very large group; say, all of humanity. But GCE holds the notion of a transcendent human identity that may emerge from the amalgamated other senses of self, as elemental to the work.

However, on the opposite end of the spectrum—the micro—discourse has shifted away from singularizing people in particular groups towards considering the intersectionality of identity. The understanding that all people are multiple and that these differences cross-cut internally and externally in divergent ways has shifted identity conversation in the direction of intersectionality, or how the particularities of ethnicity/race, class, gender, sexual orientation and numerous other social groupings manifest differently in various social contexts (Gopaldas, 2013). While this may be a truer expression of what identity means to people and in society, intersectionality may undermine the political volition of identity as singular while supporting competition for recognition among oppressed social groups. Intersectionality is compounded within a networked, hybrid global culture that permits people to affiliate with diverse others across what were once wide boundaries. Cultural hybridity creates even more indeterminacy of singular groups allowing for even greater plasticity of who one is and how those identities constitute meaning (Appadurai, 2013).

The cases examined in this chapter focus on how two different schools, one in Bangkok and the other in New York City, frame issues of identity within GCE. Both schools share a commitment to helping students understand themselves, their identities, in light of the society where they find themselves, yet the different ways they enact these commitments generate important insights about how GCE is divergently enacted.

Marjoon School, Bangkok, Thailand

A colleague put me in touch with a nonprofit that supports educational reforms in Thailand and I explained the study that I was conducting. She shared that she knew of two schools that fit my description of GCE in Thailand and so she reached out to their heads. On my first visit to Thailand I spent a few days at both of these schools, one of which, Prathom, housed an elementary school, and the second, Marjoon, was primary through secondary with an affiliated institution in teacher education. I chose to focus on one, Marjoon, since it offered a more diverse education across a wider expanse of ages, from early childhood to postsecondary/ teacher education. Marjoon houses both a primary, secondary and teacher education facility along with an architectural faculty on a shared campus. Prathom was oriented towards promoting career readiness and acceptance at prestigious universities on the part of students, certainly a part of what it means to be global in education, though one not highlighted herein. That it exists as a GCE-identified school in Thailand is an important reminder, serving as a counter-balance to the case highlighted in this book.

Marjoon, located about 15 km southwest of central Bangkok, is nestled in a park-like setting with small wood-frame buildings hewn from local hardwoods built around a series of small ponds. I met Sarap, a middle-aged Thai man who works as a teacher educator at Marjoon and is an assistant to the director of the college that sits adjacent to the school. Sarap explained that he is engaged in meditative practice as a part of teacher education.

> Many of our beginning teachers struggle when they work with children to put aside their ego, their attachment to ego, rather than to look at the child. Everything we think, see and hear is a part of our emotional state. So teachers must develop mindfulness about their attachment to ego. The child not wanting to work or acting out, this is not about the teacher but about the child. Teacher mindfulness comes from the point of view that as a teacher they already know what to do, but that they need to be given the opportunity to develop mindfulness in the setting of the classroom. Every Friday [today] all the college students and faculty gather independently for a few hours of meditative practice followed by open reflection. In this setting they talk about some difficulty in their work and about themselves. They do not critically talk about something else or someone else, some problem outside of oneself or some other person, not talking critically about society...this type of talk is useful, but you need to look at yourself first. When we bring difficulties out, we start with you. What do you feel? What did you forget to think about? What do you need to solve this? If we start from this type of self-reflection, this develops mindfulness in their practice. When you share your experiences, then others share and get insights through comparison.

Marjoon is based on Buddhist principles, which could be readily noticed on campus as there are representations of Buddha and stupas situated in various parts of the school. Yet, it did not feel like a religious school, more like a spiritual environment that focused abundantly on the children themselves and the lush, immediate surroundings. Karen, an ex-pat teacher from the US who has taught English at the school for 16 years, talked about this subtle distinction. "While most of our students consider themselves Buddhist, as a religion it is very open to others so that you can be Buddhist while being something else. The principles of respecting life, mindfulness and process are what's most important." She related to me that the three Buddhas located around the school are an attempt to embody the learning practices and principles of Buddhism. Art teachers made the statues themselves with students, learning how to build the molds, filling them with material, decorating the statues and bringing them to India to be blessed. This process captures an organizing principle in the school, an orientation towards inquiry and reflective process embodied by the teachers themselves and engaged by students.

Sarap shared that there is a fair amount of tension between the type of contemplative practice he and his colleagues embrace and what the Ministry of Education seeks with a national curriculum. While there is space to have a school like this, as Marjoon has been in existence since 1996 with a large student body and many parents eager to send their children there, tensions with dominant norms of Thai schooling exist.

> Centralized authority tries to apply the national curriculum to every school but they need to leave space for local curriculum. We solve the problem by turning it upside down as we start with curriculum that is resonant with the local context and the paper [for government regulators] is a formality. We write down core curriculum to present to the ministry from the administration but we choose to do what is locally meaningful.

Teachers sought out topics that would connect to the experiences of students while meeting ministry requirements to benchmark learning. I observed during one visit a student presentation about various flood prevention schemes that had been developed in Bangkok given its low-lying topography, the overdevelopment of the urban core coupled with the frequency of intense, tropical rains. Students in this case were dually meeting ministry requirements for content acquisition (e.g. water management) while using multimedia platforms to represent the results of collective inquiries. The research being focused on Bangkok added to the sense of place importance among students.

But the local focus of Marjoon does not preclude faculty from looking elsewhere to cultivate new thinking about teaching and learning in an experiential framework. Soon after my second visit a group of Marjoon faculty undertook an extensive visit to Finland to learn about teacher development, peer coaching and school leadership. They shared with me their excitement about "learning from the best school system," as Sarap noted, though with an eye towards making the practices of teacher development resonate in a Thai context. I asked Sarap why they had not chosen to visit a school system nearby, such as Singapore or Shanghai, as these are also regarded as high-performing systems. He was somewhat hesitant about this question but it became clear through my interactions with him that he was concerned that "global thinking" was too often equated with consumerism and economic growth rather than spiritual and ecological dimensions embraced by Marjoon. So his and Marjoon's outward orientation was framed decidedly by those ways of engaging learning that privilege a humanistic and environmental rather than economic version of global interaction, one that began and was sustained within oneself.

A humanistic understanding permeates the ethos of Marjoon; that the most authentic expression of identity was one that came from within and developed in light of meditative practice that recognizes one's attachments to ego and others. Karen elaborated on the sense of mindfulness that was actively practised and taught to teachers through professional development.

> What we're trying to focus on is staying in the moment, and the director [Ms. Pathum] always says whatever model the teacher brings, if the teacher is in the moment, not thinking ahead or in the past, then the children pick up on that as well. It is okay that the water spilled. It is okay that it's raining. It is what it is. By our reaction, or actually our non-reaction, the children do pick up on it and manage to stay in the moment.

One's sense of identity in this context is more fluid and less fixed than what one would assume in a typical Western school. In this particular school, and arguably in the wider culture in which Marjoon is situated, one has the capacity to develop an aware self through a practice of being mindful, engaging in meditation and being open to the emotions that carry through each event.

Developing an awareness of self through questions such as "Why does this concern me?" or "Why does this make me angry?" leads to an inquiring disposition about the world. I interviewed two students currently studying teaching at Arava Manda, the affiliated teacher education institute of Marjoon, and they talked about how an inquiring way of teaching contrasts sharply with what they experienced at ministry schools in Thailand while being secondary students. Payat, a young woman who previously studied art at a Swedish university, noted that she never considered being a teacher until she studied abroad and experienced the respect teachers at the university had for their students. "What I love about education at Arava Manda is that as students we learn the purpose of learning by ourselves, how to get knowledge and to use it, compared with conventional education that just follows the teacher without reason." Onto, a young man studying music education, offered a related perspective: "Conventional education is static and this is not right because everything in the world is dynamic, so education should be like this. Teachers and education should not be afraid of the way the world is changing." One concern that occurred to me while engaging with students and faculty at Marjoon was the potential for such a strong self-focus to lead to narcissism, ironic given the stated aim of opening outwards to the wider world. Onto responded to this question:

> I had a very interesting experience in the past that made me realize what a good teacher can be. I wanted to get admission to the university and a

teacher came to advise me about what to do and took an interest in me as a person. I thought, "this should be the real education," having a mind to be considerate of others to value who they were and their humanity.

While I had the concern of self-focus leading to self-involvement, faculty and students at Marjoon shared the opposite view, or the sense that they would lose students if they did not have a strong connection with their developing selves. Sarap shared that his mantra developed from his meditative practice is "change yourself, not others, change yourself."

Change is a touchstone in how Marjoon faculty and students understand themselves and society. In all of my interviews, observations, conversation and emails with faculty, not once did someone refer to social group membership, either of themselves or their peers, which contrasts markedly with the New York City case in this chapter. One way of understanding this difference is the assumed plasticity/rigidity of identity in the two contexts. In Marjoon, students and faculty had a view of themselves as emerging rather than fixed, in keeping with the process orientation of school. They were themselves undergoing a process within a dynamic context and there is a sense that they will continue to change and develop.

There are forces that create obstacles to the self-discovery and change that Marjoon and Arava Manda promoted. The regulations of the ministry, for example, were frequently pointed out by participants as an institution impervious to change, which translated into the practice of ministry schools that was alienating and stultifying by the accounts of those who previously attended. Payat shared that one of her student-teacher colleagues, a young woman not working at Marjoon, met resistance when she was trying to be an agent of change in a public school. When I queried them if the resistance they encounter gives them pause in continuing down this path, Payat replied, "I think back to Buddhist principles, it is better to change yourself since you cannot change other people. I have a big hope that everything is going to be better. Teachers build humanity so I hope my students grow up and become a good person so they make the world better."

Payat's expressed optimism may be just that; but the core assumption that as people change so does society was undiminished. Sarap, though, was less optimistic longer term about the survival of the holistic way of education embraced at Marjoon. While the ministry had previously been hands-off about what they viewed as an experiment in Marjoon, they were growing increasingly wary.

Recently the heads of the government had a meeting with us personally and said, "everything you put forward about inquiry and self-discovery, it doesn't work. We are going to pass a new law despite your criticism that will insure world-class standards" and when I hear this, I feel that I am the dust of this land.

At the time of this book's publication the school was still functioning as before, but clearly the pressure being experienced during the research was more directly felt by Marjoon. Interestingly the invocation of world-class standards, which Marjoon is seen as being in contradiction with, illustrates the pressure of global educational competition explored in Chapter 2.

The process of inquiry, particularly rooted in the early grades curriculum of Marjoon, was also being reinforced at the secondary school. The pattern of finding robust inquiry pedagogy in elementary school that wanes by secondary when content learning becomes the central focus is quite common. Secondary teachers viewed inquiry as elemental to learning in every context, necessarily rooted in the experiences of students while opening outward to the wider world. I interviewed two secondary science teachers, Pavay and Chas, about the ways that they build out from student experiences through inquiry towards global concerns.

> A big concern is climate change so we try to propose a project about this, a crisis for the world now. Looking at the major crisis of the world each of them will have an avenue to research about it, it might be from physics, chemistry, biology, or some science discipline. We do this approach in order to integrate what we are required to study so then they are developing these projects. When the children are actually learning through hands-on activities, their attention and their interest is very high.

Pavay, a female teacher in her thirties, indicated that while the focus of the inquiry satisfied standards for secondary science teaching, the choice of global warming occurs among the students within the classroom with the intention to catalyze students' civic engagement with the issue.

> This is the main priority in how they organize the projects…as they identify problems the students realize they are implicated in the problem, as in energy usage, so bringing them back into the process of solving the problem but changing their own behavior as well.

Here again the pedagogical aim is dually oriented to moving the students to inquire about the material conditions of their lives while directing them towards participating in meaningful social action.

Marjoon has a vetting process both for the teachers they employ and/or develop at Arava Manda, as well as the families that are chosen to join the school. The strong orientation towards mindfulness, meditation, inquiry, or what they define as holistic education, is a criterion used by existing faculty and leadership to determine who would most benefit from being part of the Marjoon community. Karen explained that they offer a mandatory two-day seminar for parents, getting a sense about their values and home life. "We are more interested in the family than in the child" in terms of making a decision about whom to admit.

Once admitted, parents agree to attend parental development classes in a 30-hour sequence to learn about the nature of children, what constitutes a good environment for children as well as activities and learning processes.

These same attributes are developed among faculty as well. Teachers are assigned to three units within Marjoon, a small school and primary school (roughly equivalent to preschool through grade 6), a middle school (equivalent to grades 7–9), and a secondary school (equivalent to grades 10–12). The focus in the small school, particularly, is building a sense of community among the students, allowing them to play freely with raw materials (e.g. rope, cloth, paper) rather than readymade toys, and inviting them into inquiry through the use of stories. Children were at ease in their surroundings and freely played together, inventing activities while mimicking adult ones. I noted too that the classroom, like the entire facility, was at ease with its natural surroundings as there was no clear separation from what was inside or outside the classroom as windows opened to spaces filled with trees that seemingly grew into the room through large, open windows and corridors. I asked one primary teacher what it is like to teach at Marjoon and she said, "This is like a second home for me, it's so natural, just like the children are coming to my house to play together as I nurture them." Karen described the environment, including the use of basic materials, as avoiding over-determining the workspace of children, giving them a sense of agency about their learning while experiencing joy.

Karen noted that some parents grow concerned that the children are not "learning" while engaged in this way, a sentiment that echoed concerns about a self-focused curriculum. She noted, though, that children were folding cloth in geometric sequence, using this as an illustration of how this particular activity was a forerunner to learning about proportionality, which they will likely encounter in mathematics in the next two years. But she suggested that this approach has the benefit of allowing the students to begin with an experience that is their own and then to draw out understanding in a wider, academic context in a way that does not abstract the activity from the social world from which it springs. This learning ethos permeates the work both with young people and with adults at Arva Manda, as the school prides itself on developing "home-grown" talent from school parents. The current school director, with whom I had an extended conversation about a local understanding of teacher development, was originally a parent in the primary, or what they call *small school*.

Linking the home/family and school/child was a consistent principle at Marjoon, a way of teaching children in concentric circles of scale from immediate to global. The activities of Thai life, for example, are in a sense miniaturized in the curriculum, with various physical centers of activity, from a woodshop to a pottery area to a recycling center to a rice paddy, all under the supervision of students and teachers working collaboratively in small clusters of joint inquiry. Grouping and hands-on inquiry are the primary means of learning at Marjoon, as Sarap explains:

We integrate student learning so there is not one teacher for a single course but a team of teachers who are assigned 20 or 30 people per class (or grade level). Five or six teachers will be working in pairs, each with about seven to ten students, so there are three groups in the class. They develop inquiry after action review, which draws upon their experiences and then develops inquiries or questions about those experiences. They develop common concerns or questions in the group and we give them input about how to inquire.

I saw evidence of this as the students created a rice paddy, having gone on a field trip to visit rice farmers and learned about the challenges and rewards of such a life. They then returned to school and went to work, inquiring about what plot of school land could be used, how best to arrange the planting, how much irrigation would be needed and how often, and lastly, what to do in terms of harvesting and distribution. Faculty are guided by principles undergirding inquiry about framing societal problems, seeking evidence and drawing working conclusions that will invariably lead to more questions. But unlike a Western frame of reference, the culture of learning had a strongly spiritual center, one that situates inquiry within a wider conception of mindfulness and wholeness in the development of one's self.

I asked Sarap about how they deal with the languishing of inquiry that may occur or when the lethargy of being told what to do is more attractive to students than going out and creating an inquiry. His response surprised me:

> That is our golden moment! How do you deal with being adrift? When they tell stories about their experience they start to direct themselves in inquiry. This "after action review" helps them to develop a scientific method of thinking critically. We return to their experience to find things that are happening, things affecting them and that matter to them, to begin the process of inquiry again. Our teaching staff had to train themselves from being lecturers to facilitators of inquiry, in how to make a productive conversation. And when central administration comes to scrutinize the school, they realize that this is a good process when we tell the truth about what we do. Some more conservative person might raise concerns about "is it enough?" but if you think about how students internalize the curriculum, yes they do not learn the core curriculum, but they learn how to learn through inquiry.

The surprising part was his sense of joy about the problem of inquiry. A similar question in a Deweyan school in the West might prompt consternation and anxiety, where a social norm that points towards closure is an important subtext. But for Sarap, it was a joyful moment as it mirrored the reality of life, which is filled with uncertainty, periodic disengagement and occasional lethargy. There was a certain sense of pride that the faculty shared about how they were becoming a school community and that they recognized, even enjoyed, the limits that being human imposed on one's ability to not know.

Faculty seemed to feed on the idea that the school was different, which echoed in their students' recounting of teaching in a public school as well as the paper-chase they engage over documenting the teaching of standards. One concern I had that remains with me is the sense of otherness that Marjoon entails, or the uniqueness of such a setting and therefore the improbability that anything like this could be enacted on a mass scale. The otherness of such experimental spaces like this one is confounding, particularly in light of the next case which is in essence a compulsory public school in New York City.

During the Friday morning reflective conversation with college faculty, participants sat in a circle in a high-ceilinged, wood building and simply had conversation together, talking about their lives and experiences over the past week. Sarap translated summaries of what was being said for those that spoke in Thai, though a few switched to English for my benefit, an adjustment that was graciously offered if embarrassingly accepted. Most memorable was a colleague who was visibly upset, sharing that due to problems in her own relationships she felt that she could no longer be part of this school. She broke down into tears and the group listened and comforted her. We ended with a prayer and then adjourned to the other side of the room for a hot lunch. Over lunch, faculty asked me if this was the type of faculty meeting that we shared at my institution, to which I literally burst out laughing causing them to laugh as well. I explained that such a conversation simply could not happen in our context as the sharp division between what is personal and professional is firmly maintained.

Global Education Academy in New York City

GEA began in 2009 as a school that brought together culturally and linguistically diverse students from throughout New York City (NYC) to support students in receiving a state-mandated curriculum that inflected this learning with global elements: project-inquiry, global field experiences (both in NYC and abroad), language learning and community service. Faculty attempted to realize these aims within a policed environment that undermined students' ability to engage in the necessarily vulnerable work of identity development. This context, at times, deteriorated into a hostile environment wherein students deployed calcified versions of self (e.g. neighborhood, ethnicity, language group) that denied the dignity of others while sitting isolated from the formal space of curriculum.

Like many schools in New York City, the Global Education Academy (GEA) is one of several schools that share a single building. When I arrived for my first observation, I stood in line with a number of students waiting to pass through the metal detectors just inside the door. I watched as some students were instructed to remove shoes, belts and hats in order to undergo additional scanning by the New York City police officers stationed at the school. The officers had a complicated relationship with the students, alternating between levity and seriousness as they processed the students. Mounted on the wall, just to the left of the metal detectors, was a television that displayed a static message: *No hats. No headphones. Cell phones will be confiscated.* The sense that this was a disempowering environment, one in which you were literally processed for entry, was palpable for all who entered.

I passed through the scanner and retrieved my bag from the X-ray machine, then took the stairs to the third floor where the GEA is located. Upon exiting the stairwell, I was surprised by the contrast. The formerly drab gray corridor gave way to a bright and colorful hallway, decorated by several different national flags, examples of student work, and a poster outlining the students' and teachers' expectations for the new semester. The physical space of GEA was in purposeful contrast to the controlling and rigid atmosphere of the intake procedure, though the residues of that coercion were not easy to erase on a daily basis.

Before meeting with the principal, I stopped to examine the poster. The heading on the bulletin board indicated that ideas emerged from a discussion between students and teachers in the last advisory meeting.

Thoughts on our new semester!
We DON'T want these things anymore:

- Kids cutting classes or being late
- Play fighting in the halls
- Hearing, "Yo, my n–a!" [*sic*]
- Crowded hallways
- Kids coming to school on drugs
- Too much sitting down—we need more movement!
- Scanning (we want to bring cell phones and be responsible with them)

We DO want this:

- Science labs and hands-on experiments
- To go out for lunch sometimes
- To choose some of our own classes—electives
- Clubs!—Music, art and more
- Our classes to be more interesting…
- And while we all don't agree on this—a couple of people wanted a school uniform and a student government with president, vice president, secretary, and treasurer.

The use of student advisory as a meeting period for students to touch base and process their social experiences at school was foundational to GEA. There was an explicit message often articulated by teachers in advisory, namely that student voice is valued and faculty trust students to make good decisions.

Despite this empowering strategy, GEA faced significant challenges in implementing its vision of GCE. The school offered strategies and designs of effective GCE—fostering cross-cultural understanding, engaging student voice and learning about others. Yet, to get to this point, students had to be scanned, patted down, and sometimes interrogated by police, a contrast that weighed heavily on GCE aims of the school. The daily prison-style screening posed a challenge to the trust required for GCE community building at best; at worst, it sent a message that students should be fearful of their peers and what they would encounter inside the school while they themselves were suspect.

I met with Sarah, the principal of the GEA, who explained that despite these obstacles, GEA leadership, supporting agencies, and school faculty shared a commitment to fostering a community dedicated to GCE. Students' ideas for improving the school were solicited on a regular basis through advisory meetings and whole-school assemblies. Reflecting on the founding of the school, Sarah noted,

> We were able to basically have the theme of the school be lived out even in the first year, not just because there were flags hanging in the hallway, but because of the classes that we offered in the program and the work that we did through our seminars and our town hall. We were able to truly have global studies be incorporated into the work that the kids were doing even in their first year classes.

Sarah's commitment to infusing global studies throughout the curriculum was shared by the GEA faculty, evidenced in the posters and student-works on bulletin boards, the use of diverse religious symbols and flags along with the attention to multilingual signage in the halls.

Students in New York, like their peers in many other states, are required to pass standardized exams at the end of their core courses. As a result, it can be tempting for educators to "teach to the test," ignoring topics that serve the larger mission of the school to spend more time on material likely to appear in the exam. Teachers at GEA, however, found ways to incorporate GCE into existing curriculum. One teacher I interviewed, Diane, said that while she taught two distinct science curricula, she was able to infuse global themes into both. She explained,

> I have two different curriculums that I'm dealing with. I have three classes of students who are gearing up to take the Living Environment Regents. So, a lot of their work is based on that. Now, that's not necessarily a bad thing. The living environment curriculum these days is very similar to the types of things we're trying to do. It focuses a lot on ecology, on human impact on the environment, and also genetics and evolution, which I feel

is very important for everyone to understand. I have another class that has already taken the Regents, so with them, I'm able to use this class to allow them to generate their own viewpoints, their own work. I'm able to draw their attention to misconceptions that I don't normally get to state, and we're also able to do work with other schools in the building that have their garden, that have their own community resources. We're so new that we're trying to piggyback on other people's things. But the best thing I've found is bridging it with their other classes and their seminar work, which right now is community service based.

The seminar work Diane referenced is part of GEA's mission to provide students with varied opportunities for learning both inside and outside of the classroom. In addition to the state-approved high school curriculum, every teacher engaged students in at least one seminar on a global topic. These seminars were introduced as a way for students to engage in independent inquiry. GEA's approach was to treat this activity as a special block that ran parallel to their regular studies contrasted with Marjoon's attempt to integrate inquiry in all aspects of courses. On Wednesdays students were assigned to advisory for a 90-minute, extended period to focus on their inquiry development through the last five months of the school year. Teachers pitched this activity to students as permitting them maximum freedom to study what they wanted in an effort to enhance their motivation to engage the work. As Rory, a lead teacher and vice-principal in the school, explained, "you get to decide what you will learn and how you will learn it." Despite the energy around the inquiry project as part of how GCE is enacted at GEA, faculty and student attention to the process waned in the first year and it was subsequently removed from the curriculum.

Faculty also developed student trips for globally oriented travel, including summer visits to Peru, China, South Africa and Ecuador in which some students were able to participate. Other students made visits to museums and the United Nations Headquarters in New York City. These global field experiences focused on students' language development, learning about historical places and visiting political and financial institutions. Trips were open to everyone at the GEA, but students with strong attendance records were most likely to join in the field experiences as they were present for all the informational meetings. Upon returning from their travels, students would present what they had learned to their peers at a whole-school assembly. Sarah explained that most students were very receptive to learning from their classmates, though "there were a handful of kids who were surely jealous that they didn't get to go." The experiences were originally intended to be service-oriented learning opportunities in an effort to enact the civic dimensions of the mission, but that has shifted in the past five years since GEA's founding towards an academic focus for students.

Though students were generally receptive to learning about cultural diversity in other parts of the world, they struggled with being open within their local classrooms. Students frequently questioned their classmates' identities and challenged their cultural belonging during informal discussions. Students commuted to the GEA from all across New York City, so students' sense of self was oriented by the borough or neighborhood in which they resided. This identity, or the ability to define what their neighborhood represents, was a common point of contention. I observed the following conversation between two students working on a group project:

> **Martin**: "Yo, I'm about to take Marcus' name off the project. He's not doing anything!"
> **Marcus**: "You better recognize!"
> **Martin**: "Marcus, you're from the East Side."
> **Marcus**: "So? What's that got to do with anything?"
> **Martin**: "Because you acting all tough and you're from the East Side!"
> **Marcus**: [You are from] "Brooklyn? *Really?* It's like the most violent borough!"

A similar exchange involving a student's home borough took place during discussion on literal and figurative descriptions. The teacher wrote the sentence "I'm so happy" on the board and asked the class to rewrite it using figurative language. One student responded, "I'm so happy that I'm gonna fly to Harlem." This led to the following exchange:

> **Taisha**: "Why would you want to fly to Harlem?"
> **Omar**: "I was born in Harlem, you got a problem with that?"
> **Taisha**: "You were born in Harlem?"
> **Omar**: "Yeah, you got a problem with that?"
> **Taisha**: "God, I was just asking."

In both instances, the teachers redirected students back to the lesson while not addressing the content or tone of students' interactions. Given the global focus of the school, it was surprising that these teachable geographic moments were not actively connected to related curricular themes. Students' tendency to territorialize their sense of self was a by-product of the magnet status of GEA in the NYC system as students came to this school from disparate regions of the city. This identity work was part of the immediate, felt aspects of self that clearly resonated with students but did not become interpreted via curriculum. At GEA, thinking about global citizenship was largely an outward facing perspective that was enacted at particular apex moments, such as the student inquiry project, advisory period or on a global field experience. Yet, these values were seldom applied to issues within the school community and on concerns that connected directly to the lives of students.

The outward facing perspective was also evident in my conversation with Diane regarding her science curriculum. She explained:

What we do here [in the US] does affect the farmer in China and what the farmer in China does affects us here. I think in order for everyone to achieve the best for themselves and each other, [the students] need to see that.

Diane's perception of China as largely agricultural is somewhat dated given their growing industrial presence in the production of consumer goods. Diane did, however, recognize the value in connecting her lessons to students' interests. When asked what content she focuses on in order to engage students in GCE, she explained "the best way is to start by picking a comment that was made by one of them on a topic that they happen to be chatting about. If I pick that and join their conversation, it definitely helps." Diane provided an example to illustrate her point:

We had this great assembly yesterday about the environment. This group that is trying to get youth motivated to reducing their carbon footprint. It was an amazing presentation. So they had a little check in of what have you done since yesterday's presentation to reduce your footprint? So we're having the discussion, and somehow—I don't understand how we got there, but that happens sometimes—sexual orientation came up. And I heard a student make a comment, "No no no no…people choose to be gay." And so it was this amazing opportunity that I had to discuss scientific evidence. And the kids were so interested that they actually got involved, I was like I'll bring in the articles I have tomorrow, and they were excited.

Despite the intentions of GEA faculty, these teachable moments were not always developed as I witnessed numerous occasions that were missed, such as the New York City geography-identity discussion previously. Even though the value of this episode was recognized, its connection to the larger curriculum was deferred to a later date and typically left undeveloped.

Though teachers at GEA were committed to engaging with global issues in the outside world, they seemed hesitant to address related issues in their classrooms. Many of the students at GEA were English second-language learners and the use of English was another point of global inflection that manifests in student-to-student interaction but was not brought into the formal learning of the school. During a seminar on developing the inquiry project, one student volunteered to pass out class materials. When he, a Latino, only gave paper to Latino/a students, an African American student accused him of being a racist. The teacher responded, "I wouldn't say racist, I would say irresponsible." She then gave paper to the African American students and continued the lesson without further comment.

The teacher was bilingual, and code-switched instructions between English and Spanish. As the students began working in language-based groups, an African American student interrupted two Latina students who were speaking Spanish. "We don't talk like that here," she said, "welcome to America!" The Latina students were visibly angry about the comment, but five minutes later they were teaching the African American student how to say *I don't speak Spanish* in Spanish. The quick shift from confrontation to collegiality was something that happened quite often in the school. Students were quick to draw boundaries between themselves and others, but at other times open to working through and learning through those differences. The teachers seemed to recognize this pattern and took a less directive approach, assuming that students would eventually work things out for themselves and there was occasional evidence that this was indeed happening.

Not all cross-cultural interactions at the GEA were unproductive, however. In a later lesson, two students were talking about cultural and religious traditions as they worked on an unrelated project:

> **Sytira**: Are you Jewish?
> **Cherise**: Pretty much.
> **Sytira**: Don't you have to be white to be Jewish?
> **Cherise**: My grandma is.
> **Sytira**: Can you have chocolate and stuff?
> **Cherise**: Yeah, we aren't like that.

The assumptions in this brief exchange—regarding the racial dimensions of Judaism and an undeveloped understanding of Kosher dietary laws—presented opportunities for moving beyond superficial identity exchanges. These identity conversations, however, were not a part of the explicit curriculum and occurred tangentially, if parallel to the work of GEA. Students' explorations of identity were largely through examinations of cultures outside the US through international travel, language learning and cultural celebrations and sites they visited in New York City, rather than those that bubbled up in daily life at GEA. Sarah identified this as one of the biggest challenges facing the school, noting that she hoped to find more ways that GCE could "help us connect with the world that my students are really living in on a daily basis."

Moving Ahead

Society, understood at one level as the intersection of self, groups and identities, remains a vitally significant dimension of what GCE must engage. GCE is curriculum space that invites these issues to the fore as identity at all levels of scale and recognition matter, along with how those senses of self have diverse meanings in locations and moments. In the contexts examined herein, teachers and students grappled, at times indelicately and often through subtexts and surroundings of formal curricula, with the inside–outside dynamic—that is, the navigation of one's sense of self as an individual and as a member of social groups and a community.

In Marjoon, these identities were in a continual state of becoming with noticeably less attention to social categories than in New York City. The process in Marjoon centered upon actively self-seeking, or sorting through the events and emotions of everyday experience to understand oneself better and to awaken a greater sense of self-control and direction. The curriculum of Marjoon, however, was decidedly less outwardly focused than GEA as the latter had all of the trappings of global learning such as international field experiences and cultural visits, while the former was more interested in how daily events (e.g. preparing meals) illustrated connectivity and difference. In New York City, students' identities tended towards being fixed and one might go so far as to say defended. Difference was initially encountered with hostility, as students sought to shield their sense of self in light of an individual, context or idea situated as other. This initial hostility, however, often gave way to a sense of community, if a fragile one, as students opened themselves to learning from peers and to some degree about more distant others if not always those seated next to them.

As noted at the outset, there is a danger in over-reading these cases within an East–West frame of identity discourse as internalized–externalized. While the cases do approximate this continuum, there are of course elements of externality in Bangkok as there is internality in New York City. The tendencies notwithstanding, both suggest the need to move GCE curriculum towards the other pole. Amitai Etzioni (2004) offers a way of thinking about identity that is neither untethered nor rigidly conformist, a blending of what he describes as balancing Eastern and Western thought about self and society, the former privileging the collective and the latter the individual. Etzioni seeks greater harmony between these poles rather than a dualistic choice, a hybridity of values wherein East becomes more like West and West becomes more like East. The value in this dialogic approach to identity brushes up against the tendency to view oneself in fixed ways while troubling the neat categorizations we employ to organize an unmanageably vast amount of data about people. It also sets aside the desire for ideal type models of thinking about how best to teach with and about identity. A hybrid orientation is especially important in the context of GCE as it touches upon the development of a new, heightened sense of self, synthesized with all other identity aspects known and unknown, recognized and emergent, of being a global citizen.

Note

1   Scott Wylie served as assistant investigator in the Global Education Academy research in the 2009–10 academic year and jointly authored this section of the chapter. I maintain the use of the personal pronoun "I" for consistency within the book but the reader should note that this refers to the co-author in that section only.

5

SUSTAINABILITY

with Ching-Fu Lan[1]

Sustainable development has achieved broad recognition within many sectors of society, particularly in the North. The codification in the widely cited Brundtland Report (*Our Common Future: Report of the World Commission on Environment and Development*, 1987; see Chapter 1 for a more detailed discussion) served as a catalyst to begin rethinking the logjam between environmental preservation and economic development. Sustainable development, or meeting the needs of the present generation without jeopardizing the ability of future generations to meet their needs, has come to permeate policy documents in international and national venues while being widely adopted as an institutional and educational priority among universities, nonprofit actors, and various human-service institutions. Corporations have also taken up the call, though critics have referred to their participation as juggling "people, planet and profit" with the last category subsuming the first two (see Jickling & Wals, 2008, p. 2). The 1992 Rio Earth Summit introduced sustainable development to a global audience of advocates and policymakers while raising awareness about the need to address mounting environmental concerns. These concerns were compounded by the collapse of state-economic systems of the former Soviet Union, whose demise spawned new national economies in eastern Europe and western Asia. Emerging markets complicated and pressed on an increasingly liberalized global economic sphere, all while China liberalized their economy in the context of a rapidly expanding Asia.

Sustainable development represented a major shift rather than a tweak of the global economic system. It constitutes three interlocking layers—environment, society and economy—specifically: environment, including resources, water and waste streams; society, involving employment, human rights, gender equity, peace and security; and economy, aiming to address poverty, corporate responsibility and accountability (Little & Green, 2003). Education for Sustainable

Development (ESD) emerged from *Our Common Future* (1987) as well as the Rio 1992 Summit as their architects recognized the need for public awareness and generational attention to pressing issues if sustainable development was to be realized. Environmental education, however, was already well established, dating back at least to the 1960s and represented a point of friction with the newcomer ESD (Iyengar & Bajaj, 2011).

Environmental education, like many related educational-modifier movements (e.g. peace education, global education, human rights education), has a diversity of discourses and adherents with various perspectives. One broad conceptualization of environmental education is

> a lifelong teaching/learning approach that has the potential to strengthen people's capacity to address environmental and development issues, to be more aware of and better understand such complexity; to develop knowledge, values and attitudes, life-skills and ethical behaviours consistent with sustainable development, as well as for effective participation in decision making.
>
> (Rose & Bridgewater, 2003, p. 265)

The aggregation of these elements have been consolidated into for what Oren Pizmony-Levy (2011) constitutes a "global script" for environmental education, one that crystallizes discursive heuristics about how to engage environmental education, including environmental knowledge, learning outdoors, awareness of issues, commitment to pro-environmental dispositions and civic engagement with these issues into a singularity (Pizmony-Levy, 2011, pp. 602, 622). These six elements are not fixed, however, but emerge from a complex, recursive interaction that is at once driven by global imperatives while constantly being reconstituted by myriad locals. By the early 1990s, sustainable development education (SDE) had begun coursing through these overlapping channels and by the reckoning of some, crowding out environmental education (EE) along the way.

There has been some discord between EE and SDE communities, with the former sensing that they were replaced by the latter (Jickling, 2010). The debate between SDE and EE advocates and practitioners might also be read as a global–local tension, wherein advocates for SDE tend to align with globalization and continued economic integration and those advocating for EE tend to have a strong local or place-based focus more closely associated with deep ecology or the locavore movement (e.g. those eating food grown with a 100-mile radius). But this dualism is too simple as there are many points of synthesis between the two along with areas of disagreement. In addition, SDE has the privileged position of being the "new brand" in a consumer-infused scholarly landscape wherein the "rebooted" version is typically preferred over earlier iterations. This tension is worth noting, particularly as I situate sustainability in a book about GCE, not in an effort to put these problems aside but to allow them to run through the various issues raised herein.

I vividly recall teaching about sustainable development in a global studies course in 1990. Students' reactions varied though two main responses surfaced in our conversations: first, that SDE incorporated an economic/consumer dimension, which alleviated some of their ecological guilt; and second, that they believed shifting the corporate bottom line to account for the environment was unlikely to occur. Students who already embraced a pro-environmental identity were happy to see the increasing attention among policymakers and elites. What we did not envision 25 years ago, however, was the upcoming era of massive mediation via the internet and social media, one that would allow many people to im/mediately share ideas with many others. This churn of information, now a quarter of a century old, while not necessarily altering the material conditions of society and the environment, has certainly popularized environmental concerns and moved talk about the biosphere into common parlance.

I also recall a strong sense that this issue was finally resonating in a way that promised significant changes on the near horizon, though in hindsight, I think we all suffered a bit of echo-chamber effect in our thinking. Public opinion polls over the last 25 years indicate this was indeed the case. A time-series Gallup poll dating back to the late 1980s posed the following question: "Protection of the environment should be given priority even at the expense of economic growth or economic growth should be given priority, even if the environment suffers to some extent." Two important insights from this longitudinal polling are that a majority of respondents always placed the environment over the economy, with the closest overlap between the two data points being 2003, placing the environment at 47 percent and the economy at 42 percent. Yet, the highest point for the environment on the graph was in 1990, with 71 percent favoring the environment to 19 percent preferring the economy. These polls suggest an ebb and flow of public opinion over time but with a general deterioration of environmental advocacy in those same 25 years, and support for the environment falling demonstrably in times of economic growth (Jones, 2015). An additional finding in Gallup's report indicates that people are much more concerned with water quality, by a spread ranging from 15 to 20 points over time, than they are an issue like global warming.

Concern for water over global warming suggests an important conundrum in sustainable development discourse generally, that being the inability of people to grasp the *global environment*. Even the term itself is somewhat contradictory, since the *environment* connotes a specific place, a particular context or a local surrounding; while *global* has a universal, everywhere denotation, a tension not unlike the SDE and EE debate. "When one thinks of 'the environment' in global terms, social realities are bound to drop out of sight even if physical realities don't" (Sparshott, 1972, p. 17). A worldwide study of textbooks' treatment of environmental issues speaks to this dynamic. The authors found in a review of 484 social studies textbooks from 65 countries that there was a significant increase in environmental coverage in the period 1970 to 2008 along with a strong correlation between the presence of post-national discourses (e.g. human rights education) and robust environmental education (Bromley et al., 2011). They conclude that the global dimensions of the environment outweigh national discourses and parochial interests about local concerns. What the study cannot show, however, is how textbooks are understood by students and teachers in light of particular environmental problems experienced in a local community, such as access to clean water or the presence of toxic dumps. Read in light of the Gallup data, at least in the context of the US, local concerns prevail over global ones.

The immensity and potentially alienating quality of a phrase such as the *global environment* may have value, however, at least insofar as it calls attention to the significant environmental changes we are experiencing in the Anthropocene. The nearly tripling of human population from 2.5 billion to 7.3 billion since 1950, or the fact that there are now two people on Earth for every person in 1950, illustrates the rapidity of population growth with all of its attendant resource/consumption and waste issues, despite a relative decline in the rate of growth over that same period (Engelman & Terefe, 2014). The world now consumes seven-times more meat (including cattle, pigs, chicken, fish) than people did in 1950, a 600 percent increase, for example. This growth trajectory cannot be sustained given the requisite land-use for grazing, additional water for grain crops for feed, increased methane gas production from cows and run-off pollution from all those activities (Guilford & King, 2013). The increase of methane, unfortunately the most efficient of heat-trapping atmospheric gases, has increased 100 percent in the past three centuries coupled with a 40 percent increase in atmospheric carbon dioxide (Crutzen & Stoermer, 2000). As a result, the world has experienced ten of the hottest years in recorded history since 2000, with 2014 being the warmest ever recorded ("NASA, NOAA Find 2014 Warmest Year in Modern Record," 2015). In light of these weighty challenges, it is understandable that most people when surveyed choose to focus on water quality as this issue hits closer to home and has a tangible, immediate quality that seems to be fixable rather than overwhelming. The tangible–intangible dimension of this issue is one that I take up in the case studies of this chapter, both in light of the use of media tools for exploring environmental issues (e.g. *Second Life* and multimedia platforms) and the sense of efficacy derived from keeping efforts local.

A third issue that comes into play in this chapter is the aesthetic dimensions of the biosphere and the extent to which young people are developing such sensitivity. The Earth is overwhelmingly massive to grasp conceptually. But in its widest frame of perspective, the iconic image of Earth from space is remarkably small and wondrously beautiful. Up close, too, the planet is awe-inspiring, from the serenity of a body of water, the majestic rise of mountains to lush tropical rainforests and myriad other landscapes. Pope Francis' (2015) encyclical on global warming, which invokes the Pope's namesake, the mystic St. Francis, illustrates this reverence for nature in his biography.

> If we approach nature and the environment without this openness to awe and wonder, if we no longer speak the language of fraternity and beauty in

our relationship with the world, our attitude will be that of masters, consumers, ruthless exploiters, unable to set limits on their immediate needs. By contrast, if we feel intimately united with all that exists, then sobriety and care will well up spontaneously. The poverty and austerity of Saint Francis were no mere veneer of asceticism, but something much more radical: a refusal to turn reality into an object simply to be used and controlled.

(Francis, 2015, p. 11)

The objectification to which Francis refers stems in part from a failure to see nature as an entity deeply interconnected with humanity; a rigid divide between the human world and nature. This way of thinking about the world often manifests as a making of nature in human terms, a domestication of the sort that diminishes the complex and sometimes harsh reality of predators and prey into a sanitized, made for Hollywood version. Louv (2008) explores this same human tendency to "make the world in its image" by considering nature-deficit disorder, or the raising of a suburban/urban culture of youth in the US who lack direct experience of walking in the woods and seeing nature on its own terms. He argues that instant mediation has created a denatured childhood which begs the need for a back-to-nature movement to meaningfully reconnect with the biosphere on its terms as opposed to ours. The stakes of addressing an anthropocentric state of mind that pervades a global market culture are great indeed. Fumiyo Kagawa and David Selby (2015) detail a "thickening procession of catastrophes". Climatic incidents have increased in intensity and led to great loss and suffering: the 2010 Pakistan floods that affected 18 million people, the 2011 Horn of Africa drought that resulted in 13.3 million people requiring humanitarian assistance, the 2011 Australian floods that affected hundreds of thousands, the 2013 devastating typhoon that swept through the central Philippines and the climate-induced spread of the Zika virus, to mention only a few of the more recent and high-profile examples. These catastrophes demonstrate the urgency that is needed for inhabiting a climate-altered planet and the fundamental nature of environmental concerns. Mutuality in these cases, however, is not a munificent kind since those whose economies are petroleum fixated, as in the global North, visit harms on those of the global South, who too are seeking economic growth through fossil fuel production and consumption. The threat of catastrophe coupled with the sea change needed in people's minds about their relationship to the environment are not separate problems but indeed a unified field. Part of the challenge for educators is drawing a bright line between activities of consumption and ecological damage while promoting the value of the ecosystems to which we belong.

The commodification of spaces and resources, presumes the viewer or remover as valuing the whole, which in many cases is not true. The recent dispute over the Keystone Pipeline project to transport tar sands crude oil from Alberta, Canada to another pipeline in Nebraska, which was eventually vetoed, is illustrative of this point. Advocates of the pipeline did not view the issue as an environmental one primarily, but rather as a commodity, within a context that simply needed mitigation. As F. E. Sparshott notes:

> Someone who looks on the world strictly as an object of exploitation is
> not thinking of it as an environment at all. It is inadequate to say that he is
> blind to aesthetic aspects of his environment; he is blind to all aspects that
> make it an environment. The consumer's view reduces the whole world to
> fodder and feces.
>
> (Sparshott, 1972, 13)

But the problem of an aesthetic valuing of the environment on its terms is not
resolved by identifying those who do not uphold that value. If an aesthetic
response is primarily a visual one that is understood as pleasing to the viewer,
it creates the problem of subjectivity, or who decides what is pleasing, as well
as one of transience, or the mobile visitor "favoring bright facades drained of
meaning" (Sparshott, 1972, p. 15). Imagine a drive through a picturesque moun-
tainside, luxurious and verdant, teeming with life. But this "scene" is literally
that, one digitally recreated for the pleasure of the one visiting. This digitized
version might serve the aesthetic perception but would in fact exacerbate the
problem, as despoiling "behind the scene" could be rapacious. So while aesthetic appreciation is of interest for those that uphold such values—and indeed
we may wish to bring up young people with those appreciations—this alone is
insufficient for the type of ecological sustainability desired. Sparshott concludes
that what is aesthetic about the environment will not be resolved through reasoned analysis but is likely to be formulated by the sway of social convention
and habit (see also Jagodzinski, 1981).

Aesthetic appreciation, while important, cannot alone constitute reason enough
because it opens the possibility for a substitution that has none of the qualities of
nature that the viewer is supposedly valuing. Aesthetics, therefore, runs the risk
of building facades, thus exposing the anthropocentrism wound within the very
concept of aesthetic experience while simultaneously denying the materiality of
the environment itself. To put it more simply, if a tree falls in the woods, and no
one is there to hear it, the tree does indeed fall and there are consequences, known
and otherwise, in that event. To what extent can societies continue perpetual economic growth without causing serious, even cataclysmic environmental harm,
regardless of the inability to perceive these material circumstances?

I do not revisit the growth/degrowth issue here as it was previously addressed
in Chapter 1 but this tension demonstrates the range of discourse that is opening
up around biosphere concerns and societal imperatives. Furthermore, the North/
South dynamic is a major political issue for achieving broad-based resolve to act
on environmental protection. Specifically, the irony of the fossil-fuel-dependent
global North establishing dictates for the South about what kind of development is acceptable while demanding Western-style, unsustainable, infinite economic growth lays bare this tension (Shiva, 1997; Sniegocki, 2008, p. 327). The
rising critique of Western ontology, which is deeply rooted in a Cartesian logic
of categorical dualisms (e.g. people/nature, environment/economy), animates the

possibility of alternative futures that cannot yet be foreseen (de Sousa Santos, 2014, p. 23). Such images and musings are increasingly in circulation after the economic debacle of 2009 raised more fundamental questions about economic development as a singular aim.

Shifting attention to cases of sustainability-related GCE work, they are drawn from two locales, Hawaii and New York City. The first case is a collaborative network of universities and nonprofits in Hawaii that address sustainability, organic agriculture, early childhood education and community action, and the second a New York City-based after-school program that teaches historically marginalized students about sustainability issues through new media and digital film making. These cases will illuminate the issues raised in the introduction while pointing towards the larger argument of the book about GCE being everyday and transcendent.

Hawaii and New Kulanui University

Hawaii is one of the world's most remote islands. Living on such an isolated island, people are predisposed to think about maximum carrying capacity and resource limits, making the state an ideal location for environmental discourse to root. While sustainability is often viewed in light of economic development, sustainability in Hawaii is understood not solely in terms of the environment but also in relation to preservation and development of native Hawaiian language and culture, which are inextricably bound up in traditional Hawaiian cosmology. Deep veneration for Earth and its environs is foundational to this worldview. A conception of being Hawaiian and living according to one's elders involves a reverential abide for the land, at least in a venerated understanding of historical culture.

The case centers upon New Kulanui University, which was recently established as a commuter school for nontraditional, first-generation college students to attend university in Oahu. I interviewed faculty and students while visiting classrooms, observing an online course and speaking to community-based stakeholders who have partnerships with the university. I quickly discovered that my efforts to "neaten the case" or make clear the boundaries of what is part of the university's efforts for sustainability and what is not ran counter to the assumption of integration and collaboration within the culture, both of the campus and Hawaii. As I was told by a faculty participant, "Hawaii in the end is a small set of islands with only one and a half million people so everyone knows everyone else." Thus, in representing the university as the center of the case, the nodal points in that network of activity are equally significant to uncovering the story.

Sustainability is not a new idea in Hawaii as it is and was very much a part of the culture that developed in this remote island chain. Chiana, a native Hawaiian and Native American man in his forties who recently returned to the university to complete his degree, shared this perspective during our interviews, or as he and others called them, talk-stories. Chiana explained that a conservation mindset was elemental to a traditional Hawaiian worldview.

> As a native Hawaiian from a cultural perspective, we learned about the life of the land, taking care of things coming from the last generation. We live on an island and things are limited. So it's the type of living that we used to do and this way [sustainability] is really returning to the past, it's totally not new to me it's just that they frame it in this new way—sustainability. Everything from the type of gardening that they talk about, the old Hawaiian ways to pick these crops in rotation and only at certain times, following the moon, or that only royalty can eat certain items by putting *kapus* [taboos] on those things, there was a reason for that, so that the fish and land could lay fallow. It's no different than what they're doing now but they are talking about it under a different name—sustainability.

Faculty and students incorporated the preservation of cultural identity as part of the concept. Sustainability is understood as both recovering the heritage of conservation and reinvigorating and maintaining Hawaiian cultural identity.

New Kulanui identifies as an indigenous-serving institution, recently completing construction on a Hale Halawai, or a meeting house, to be used for commencement and other significant ceremonies and meetings. The university is developing indigenous degree programs, recruiting indigenous faculty and students and promoting holistic growth among all students in keeping with Hawaiian tradition. There were concerns expressed by faculty, however, not about the direction to develop indigenous knowledge and serve indigenous students but by how these expressions can be symbolized but not fully enacted. As Jennifer, a non-Hawaiian faculty member who takes sustainability seriously, explained, "There are people who take a Western way of doing things, slap a Hawaiian name on it and say they're being culturally sensitive." Jennifer was politically active and worked against early childhood readiness programs that she argued were deeply Western in their orientation and did not include Hawaiian language and cultural values as norms. She spoke about how these values get translated:

> I was looking at the question [on what sustainability means locally] and I kept thinking about *malama aina*, which means taking care of ancestral lands. When we keep reverting to Western ideas [for education programs] we're not connecting to the community and so there's inherently no sustainability, it's just you come in and you do the assessment, or you come in and you make the judgment, or you come in and some outside agency is telling locals what to do and so there's nothing that goes beyond that. I've said it a lot in these meetings, we're making decisions based on a desire for

federal money and that's just a quick fix, but if you write something that's based on native, indigenous ways of knowing it's going to have staying power when you go into the community and get that Western money as well. It's not hard to understand and I think that the indigenous ways of knowing are good for everyone.

Jennifer and Sharon began co-teaching a sustainable development and early childhood education (ECE) course in part to address what she and her colleague believed are hegemonic practices being foisted on indigenous and economically distressed families throughout the islands. The course was offered to students of New Kulanui in the ECE program and centered on the following student-developed questions:

1. What is sustainable development and a sustainable community?
2. How can diversity, cultural perspectives and empowerment contribute to building sustainable communities?
3. What are global perspectives on sustainable development? How does this inform local perspectives? Why is the UN particularly interested in early childhood education and sustainability?
4. How do families, teachers and communities perceive and enact sustainability?

Thirteen students enrolled in the course, ten of whom were completing degree requirements in ECE and three, like Chiana, were community members with some affiliation to local sustainable development efforts, such as organic farming or alternative energy production. Community members were invited into the course to help students make linkages between their studies and local practices while serving as resources to support research about topics in the course.

Of the ten regular students, most were 19–25-year-old women who were either currently teaching in early childhood centers or were preparing for a career in that field. Two students identified as native Hawaiian, one as a Pacific Islander, though all shared stories about their family's embrace of Hawaiian life and indicated having lived on the islands for many years, in some cases, generations. In their initial meetings and online postings, most were surprised by the choice to join ECE and sustainability, as it was out of the ordinary for majors in this field. Jennifer and Sharon indicated that they were taking the lead from a UNESCO report about promoting sustainability in ECE (Samuelsson & Kaga, 2008). But instead of preparing a syllabus for the students, they invited participants to draw from the report those questions that were most pertinent for study by the group. Jennifer described this process:

We did not create a syllabus. The only thing we gave them was the UNESCO report and we asked them to read it. They wrote about all the things that they noticed and what questions they had. Then we took all those questions and we coded, like qualitative research, to figure out what the big themes were. We got out all the questions that came out of the initial take and we sent them to everybody and asked them again for feedback. Then, we separated the students into four groups based on the emergent questions [see four framing questions above]. And they are now doing background research, developing reading lists and doing projects related to their questions.

One of the challenges noted by participants promoting sustainability in Hawaiian education generally is the symbolism of traditional culture and the coarse-grained reality of politics and funding. The faculty expressed genuine commitment to sustainability but perceived cultural values as mere window dressing to cover for grant proposals that would attract funding. The university's appointment of a native Hawaiian as president, for example, was symbolically significant though the reality of the need for increasing external grant funding weighed heavily on campus given the upstart status of New Kulanui. Sustainability, for example, was deployed by the university as an expression of Hawaiian values but more trenchantly, as a means of engaging in relevant research to attract attention and fiscal support. New Kulanui leadership believed an investment in sustainability would cement their image as an indigenous-serving institution that was in touch with Hawaiian values but which would, in turn, garner funding and prestige. The faculty accepted this as a reality of higher education in the US, though they said it generated skepticism about the actual depth and sincerity of support for sustainability; a suspicion that would come to fruition over the course of this study as New Kulanui eventually withdrew its overt commitment to sustainability within two years of my initial visit for research. Students typically do not develop awareness about the prestige-power-funding dynamic in higher education, mainly since it is often discussed out of public view and requires a longer time period than the four-year careers of most undergraduate students to witness. The same could be said of New Kulanui because the students focused mainly on the aspirational dimensions of sustainability and ECE and were very positive about the experience of the course.

Early Childhood Education and Sustainability Outcomes

I identify two insights from student experiences in the ECE course that will help to further illuminate the contours of the case. The first insight relates to how students developed a more complex grasp of sustainable development in relation to ECE. Students' initial online postings and face-to-face meetings indicated scant understanding about sustainable development. Students used phrases such as "make changes presently to influence a better future," "being self-supporting" and "journey to a better change." Many of the students tried to apply sustainability directly to ECE, or thought about it in terms of the field of ECE being sustained rather than as a way of thinking about the larger society and ECE's role within it. This illustrates that university students often assume hyper-specialization in courses in that what they study will not be related to the wider social context but only to the specific field (ECE). Also, this suggests that environmental discourse is typically not engaged in the preparation of educators, making this course a particular, if welcomed, oddity.

Jennifer and Sharon's choice to incorporate the UNESCO document and begin with a class inquiry was fortunate. The report speaks to the students' sense of disconnect between ECE and sustainability, suggesting that the fear of "doom and gloom" in environmental studies was a reason some ECE teachers did not embrace this area of curriculum (Samuelsson & Kaga, 2008, p. 11). Students generated questions based on the UNESCO document and in keeping with the local orientation of the course. One group, however, was tasked with learning more about sustainability in other parts of the world, so students reached out to Australia, New Zealand and Sweden, among other places, to enhance their understanding of how sustainability manifests differently in various contexts.

The culminating activity for students was to propose a course of study in ECE and sustainability. The student-designed courses were thoughtfully prepared, organized and impressive in their depth. The general pattern adopted by students was concentric circles, moving from self to world and in keeping with ECE principles, to interpret sustainability through the experience and examples of others. Most included Hawaiian cultural practices that symbolize a commitment to sustainability, from *malama aina* [caring for land] to *la'au lapa'au* [traditional healing practices] to *mahi'ai* [Hawaiian farmers and agriculture] and all included a dimension of community engagement and civic outreach. This was an important aspect of the work as it indicates that since the students themselves were engaged in fieldwork in the course, they learned and incorporated the value of field experiences into their planning as educators. The curriculum documents, taken together, demonstrate a substantial deepening and broadening of students' conceptions of sustainability and ECE over the four-month course of study.

The second insight relates to how students wove robust fi eld experiences into their emergent understanding of sustainable development. Students interviewed community advocates for sustainability and had co-participants in the course to serve as community liaisons with various learning centers, organic farms and new initiatives in sustainable living. Students gained important insights about the grounded nature of this type of work while being exposed to organizations nearby. Though there were real benefits to this approach, the uncertainty of bringing community members into an academic course appeared at various points in the course. One of the interviewees—a native Hawaiian woman who runs an indigenous aquaponics and food-sustenance education program—remarked on the questions raised by students in an interview that was later reposted by the student on the course blog:

> The worst thing in education is NO—"no can do this, no doing that"....
> Let *keiki* [children] get dirty and let them do what they are going to do,
> just give them a safe, enabling, positive environment to DO IT! And don't
> overthink it, you educators THINK TOO MUCH!

There was tension within the partnership between university culture and traditional Hawaiian culture in that the former prides itself on the development of a disposition of introspection (e.g. "thinking too much") while the latter is predisposed towards education through everyday experience, such as food production, that will germinate in proper habits and dispositions among children. There was a note of discord in the course as students struggled to reconcile their emerging identities as university students with their roles as practitioners. Similarly, students received a strong message from community members that a traditional way of life was simpler because it was less oriented towards *having* and more towards *being*, unburdened by the costs of environmental deterioration that consumerist avarice creates.

Students embraced the symbolism of Hawaiian culture as embodied in the readings/course materials. Jennifer and Sharon were very supportive of the community advocates' perspectives, however, because they were oriented towards both practice and application in their work as faculty members. That is not to say the course was enacted without deep reflection and lacking scholarly foundations, as both of the faculty members took their scholarly work seriously. But they did not position themselves or the students as university "know-it-alls" to critically observe practices from afar. Rather, they embraced the notion that they were partners with the community through the course and that their participation did not entail agreement with what community members said but acknowledgement of varied perspectives while truly being open to listen. Given that all of the students were practitioners while being university students, this stance resonated with them well.

While most universities espouse an interest in community partnerships, New Kulanui viewed a robust, community-based component as foundational to all programs and courses. A few of the participants in the ECE and sustainability were from Liliha Farms, an organic, cooperative farm located about an hour's drive from Honolulu on the leeward side of Oahu. The dry climate of this area makes agriculture an unlikely enterprise for the region. Keli'i, who started the farm and grew up in the community, dropped out of the local high school after a challenging adolescence. As he explained, "When you live in poverty, many things that seem crazy on the outside appear to be perfectly normal for you." He later joined with a group of others to found a cooperative, organic farm in 2000 in the hilly, dry terrain just above town. The farm was created to provide an opportunity for young people from this economically disadvantaged area to work, learn and thrive.

Keli'i explained that Laliha Farm is based on three pillars: heritage, entrepreneurship and social development. Heritage resonates with the organic farming that they engage in; entrepreneurship in the fact that the farm generates revenue from sales; and social development in the sense that students who work on the farm are also enrolled in the local community college with the possibility of matriculating at nearby four-year universities such as New Kulanui. The employees of the farm are mainly 17–25-year-old students who have or might otherwise have dropped out of high school and are native Hawaiians from the same Keli'i grew up. Students work on the farm three days per week reserving two days per week to attend classes, with majors ranging from organic agriculture, Hawaiian studies, native nutrition and lifestyle, and entrepreneurship. They are given a monthly stipend to cover expenses and free techniques tuition for their studies as compensation for work. The students were also given opportunities to visit the mainland and give presentations about their farm techniques, meeting other young people around the world engaged in organic, sustainable agriculture.

As we walked the farm and toured the production facility, the buzz of activity was noteworthy. Students seemed to work with a sense of purpose and spirit, calling out orders to one another, asking for help, and organizing the next activity. As Keli'i explained, "The students do everything, from planting and irrigation, to harvesting and packaging, to taking orders and distributing the food… everything!" The farm generated US $750,000 in revenue during the last fiscal year, selling crops to local markets, families and restaurants, particularly in the tourist areas.

Students who work on Laliha Farm have typical adolescent problems, of course, as young people will make decisions that negatively impact their ability to thrive and be productive. Keli'i explained, "They have a council, like a court, to decide whether or not the student can stay with the program." The self-regulating nature of the program speaks to the powerful civic dimensions of this type of arrangement such that students are themselves responsible for building and maintaining the culture of the organization. The council is also modeled on a Hawaiian elders forum wherein the conversation helps to articulate and solidify shared values of conduct. This aspect of Laliha is like the crops: organic, arising from the needs of the community and for the better of the social entity, the farm and its community members.

Global Youth Leaders and Sustainability Talk

In contrast to the case of sustainability education in Hawaii, Global Youth Leaders' digital film making program based in New York City presents another illustration of sustainability education in a sharply opposite context—one that took place in a metropolitan area and used digital media, virtual-world simulations, and field trips in the urban environment to foster students' understanding about sustainability.

GlobalYouth Leaders (GYL) is a nonprofit organization that aims to "ensure that urban youth have the knowledge, skills, experiences and values they need to succeed in school, participate effectively in the democratic process, and achieve leadership in their communities and on the global stage" by providing a variety of learning experiences, including global issue discussions, service learning/social action projects, and digital media literacy programs. Most GYL program participants come from low-performing schools and/or from communities whose members are historically marginalized. *Sustainability Talk* (ST), one of the Digital Leadership Programs, was a virtual talk show production program that aimed to introduce GYL to a broad range of concepts related to the topic of sustainability and to equip them with online broadcasting and virtual-world construction skills.

The program defined sustainability as "the ability to maintain a certain process or state. In reference to environmentalism, sustainability is a way of behaving that does not deplete natural resources faster than they can be renewed"—a similar conception to that employed by New Kulanui. The program framework was adapted from The Cloud Institute for Sustainability Education and included focuses on cultural preservation and transformation, responsible local/global citizenship, the dynamics of systems and change, sustainable economics, healthy commons, natural laws and ecological principles, inventing and affecting the future, employing multiple perspectives and a sense of place. At the end of ST, students co-produced a virtual talk show about three topics of sustainability chosen by them: food justice, global warming and e-waste. These talk shows were filmed in front of a live audience within the virtual-world *Second Life*, a once-popular online virtual world for youth.

The first phase of ST was designed as a five-week paid summer internship program. Students learned about various sustainability topics and online broadcasting skills in the *Second Life* virtual world, and prepared all preproduction materials such as scripts and settings for the virtual talk shows. There were two leading facilitators and several supporting and interning facilitators who took turns helping this program at different time periods. Each week students met for four days and worked 25 hours in this internship program. At the end of the program's summer phase, students completed draft scripts of their topic area and developed some preproduction visual materials for the *Second Life* sustainability talk show. The second phase of ST was an after-school program that met once a week in the following fall semester. At the conclusion of the program, two students attended and performed in the *Second Life* virtual talk show productions.

Students who joined ST had no prior interest or knowledge of environmental issues or sustainability but they gained new understanding through the ST program. These understandings made them care more about these public issues, as Shanice explained:

> I was aware of what's going on with ice caps melting and sea level rising, but I'm going to be honest and say that I didn't really care as much. But

because we spoke about it so much and we've gotten so much in depth with it, I care a lot more now.

Similar changes were found in other students who indicated that they were more aware of sustainable issues such as e-waste, factory farming and climate change, and were inspired to take action to address these issues. While they did act within the context of the ST program, there is no additional evidence around the claim that students' dispositions towards "caring a lot more" transferred beyond the program, yet they did report this change as a result of the program.

There are three forms of knowledge sources in ST's design—online videos, virtual-world simulations, and field trips—that merit further discussion as they are the means for students to grasp new sustainability concepts that are somewhat remote from their daily urban experiences. Online videos and documentaries were one of the major knowledge sources for students to learn about global sustainability issues in ST. From the beginning of this program, online videos about sustainability topics such as global warming, climate change, biodiversity, green movement and consumerism were viewed in class. GYL facilitators wanted to give students background knowledge and presented them with various perspectives about sustainability via this medium. After each screening, the facilitators discussed with students major ideas and messages from the videos and gave them opportunities to share any thoughts about the topics presented in the videos. The videos used included: *An Inconvenient Truth*, *The Story of Stuff*, *The Meatrix*, *e-Waste* and a TED Talk, *Greening the Ghetto*.

The videos helped to make the seemingly abstract concerns about e-waste more immediate through the examples provided, as student Javel noted:

> The videos are good because hearing about something and seeing it is very different 'cause when seeing it, you see the impact. [The] US exports waste to other countries, but like seeing it on the video is just different, seeing what's happening, is really bad, like smoke, what they burned and stuff.

The following texts from the global warming group's virtual talk show script illustrate a similar point around the grounding of the abstract:

> This video shows you how global warming is not only affecting us but also the animals, which leaves mankind with less species. It also shows habitats being lost and the world being overheated and melting. These are not fake events, these are real.

Marc's strong response to a video about the production of chicken nugget food from grinding eyeballs was another example of the power of video to draw youths' attention to issues that were less tangible in their daily experiences.

While online videos were effective in helping youth understand sustainability, they also presented a challenge of veracity. In a reflection after an online search activity, Ms. Chen asked students to think more about media format and information quality:

Ms. Chen: Ok, why YouTube?

Marc: As you know YouTube is a big website.

Ms. Chen: We all know.

Marc: It has videos, everything you could probably think about so a variety of things that you can look on, a lot of stuff that I don't know about.

Ms. Chen: But is every video on YouTube good quality?

Marc: No, some of them are real, some of them are not, you got to know what you're looking at; look at the sources on YouTube.

Despite this broad understanding of media skepticism, Marc did not investigate further to discover the fraudulence of the chicken nugget video. Students generally had vague ideas about the veracity of claims made in online video content. Javel shared a similar idea of how he would interpret the credibility of a video clip and said "When watching a video, I can tell what's true from fake stuff, but I don't have examples here; but I can tell when I see it." Laura thought YouTube provides some useful and helpful videos, "but some videos you cannot really trust because it could be someone who posts a random video because this is YouTube, everybody could post a video." When asked about her criteria for credibility evaluation, Laura replied that she paid attention to the name of the person who uploads the videos. "Say crazychick and he post up 'dance and some songs,' I'd go for it 'cause you name that and you post that video, but if you're posting something educational I don't think that I'll go for this." Overall, students understood the importance of determining the veracity of online videos but their demonstrated ability to interpret media at this level was limited.

Virtual-world simulation is another unique medium employed by ST to help students grasp issues of sustainability. The main reason for hosting activities in *Second Life* was to use the game-like virtual environment as "bait" (a problematic metaphor as it suggests gaming of students) to engage youth in learning about sustainability issues (Steinkuehler & Squire, 2014). As Ms. Chen put it "It's taking something that they are interested in and see how that can be used for educational purposes." The "bait" seemed to work well with these students. Most students enjoyed learning activities such as scavenger hunts and virtual field trips in *Second Life*, except during the moments when they encountered technical difficulties that interrupted the server connection. Mr. Gometz shared one student's response to a virtual field trip as an example of experiential learning in a virtual world:

Troy was talking about the rich experience of learning in *Second Life* about alternative energy sources. "You know, it would be different if I was in a classroom and somebody was talking to me about alternative energy sources," to which the student replied, "I saw them. They were represented. They were graphical." He indicated seeing a windmill, solar panels on top of a house and a hydroelectric plant. He was able to visualize those things, to actually see them. That for me was some of the power of the media in *Second Life*, these simulations that can happen.

The presumption about seeing/knowing in virtual space is laid bare in this comment. Mr. Gometz and his student Troy suggest that seeing a representation of a thing is equivalent to seeing the thing, which again illustrates the virtual/real tension present throughout the case.

Mr. Gometz was a strong advocate for simulated reality as equivalent to embodied experience, though his rationale was more tautological than reasoned through.

> With time, you could have really taken these to great levels. If the students are working on e-waste, you could have built a small city and begin to dump e-waste there little by little. You could simulate the impact of what that has been there, small builders. Can you see this potential? That could be really amazing and powerful. You build a little town, peaceful, with trees [laughing]. You go and let them stay for a little there. Suddenly, a cell-phone drops, then two and three and they begin to pile up and burn. Once they burn, a tree dies. That sort of simulation can be something that I think would be amazing, really powerful as a learning tool and as [an] experiential learning experience.

Mr. Gometz articulates what has been conceptualized by Jenkins et al. (2006) in digital simulations as "the ability to interpret and construct dynamic models of real-world processes" (p. 4). Advocates like him suggest that simulations can help students to "form hypotheses quickly and test them against different variables in real time" and can be effective in "representing known knowledge or in testing emerging theories" (p. 25). Complex sustainability such as global warming can become more comprehensible with such simulations. Yet, while the instructional goals of the activity might be achievable, the strategy is much less convincing for developing genuine environmental appreciation and embodied, aesthetic sensitivity.

While *Second Life* educators were generally advocates of simulated realities, even when exploring environmental issues which present a bit of an irony, there seemed to be a lurking sensitivity that being in a community means more than being online. Thus, various field trips and community service activities were planned to augment digital experiences. One of the field trips was to visit a local farmers' market. Students learned about farming, local food production and its effects on the environment along with the green market movement. They tasted a green salad made onsite with fresh produce from vendors while speaking with farmers about their production practices.

The theory behind farmers' markets, in comparison with supermarkets stocked with factory-farm products, establishes a more direct linkage between people and nature. Students were given opportunities at the farmer's market to see the rough results—rather than packaged products—of food production in their urban context. Students also expressed their preference to buy freshly picked fruits and vegetables at farmer's markets instead of traditional supermarkets after this field trip. Ironically, as they explored the locations of farmer's markets in the city, they learned that green markets were not a sustainable option for their daily grocery shopping because none of these markets were located near the under-resourced community neighborhoods in which they lived. This fact generated insights about the economic marginalization of students in various neighborhoods in NYC, a local finding with strong global resonance.

Moving Forward

Sustainability issues, including matters of development, equity and environment, are elemental to GCE. Given the significant challenges on the near horizon regarding global warming and its many incipient consequences, it is difficult to imagine education that is globally oriented not having a robust sustainability component. The cases presented herein represent starkly different illustrations of practice around sustainability, one in Hawaii that employs an online space for organized community-based learning and the other in NYC that is taught in a face-to-face environment but directed at developing media representations of issues. In Hawaii, indigenous culture, community and the natural environment provide support for understanding sustainability that was facilitated through an online component; the case of sustainability education in NYC by GYL relied heavily on virtual-world and online resources to foster understanding about sustainability. Technologies in this case helped students grasp remote, abstract and less tangible sustainability topics such as global warming, e-waste pollution and factory farming through graphics and simulations.

Both cases divergently illustrate the complexity of teaching and learning in mediated spaces about sustainability. The tangible–intangible element, or that which students can directly experience such as working on an organic farm or creating an online talk show, contrasts somewhat with the online activity of reading and participating in a-synchronous discussions. In New Kulanui's case, the online component was a mediated means to an end, which was to prepare educators to teach in early childhood settings about sustainability with community resources. Whereas in GYL, a face-to-face setting deployed online resources, such as environmental videos and simulations, to generate student representations of sustainability concerns, with the intention of having them read and interpreted by web-users. These divergent aims—one towards community engagement and the other towards mediaspace participation—raise important questions about where and how sustainability education can occur.

While there is no data to make definitive conclusions about "which works best," the notion of "what each means" can be ascertained from the views of educators and students engaged. All in unique ways are projects designed to refashion through synthesis learning objects. In New Kulanui, the objects are ECE, sustainability, online space and community resources, whereas in GYL, the objects are mediated instruction, sustainability and creating media representations. So while each program falls under the broad aegis of sustainability education in a GCE frame of learning and participation, the inflection was clearly on community in Hawaii and mediaspace in NYC. Ironically, while both were ostensibly about sustainability education, their key targets were within and beyond this content, viewing the learning as a means to community integration or media-savvy content consumers/producers.

A related insight from this comparison emerges from the intended participants as both programs were designed for historically marginalized people: Latino and African American youth in NYC and indigenous Hawaiian young adults. These were unlikely populations for GCE work given the long-standing trajectory of global learning being an elite education, albeit a lineage that is progressive in changing. But the subtext of each is quite different. In GYL, the added benefit of the ST program, and the key intention, was not on learning about sustainability in a global frame but on procuring ostensibly marketable skills with media tools in online, digital spaces. While at New Kulanui, the deeper aim was community participation, supporting educators and students while encouraging entrepreneurship among historically disadvantaged youths.

This raises an important conundrum that is frequently evident in GCE programming, or the deep structure that promotes economic development as part and parcel of any education effort. Learning about the environment, development and equity is necessary but insufficient in these cases as the deeper rationale is for continued economic productivity. Given the historical situation of poverty with these populations, this makes a great deal of sense. Yet, it does not interrupt, or even name, an economic development mantra that is generated by programming like this while it exists as part of the deep grammar of such programming. A notable exception to this theory is the fact that the teacher educators at New Kulanui had a different aim in mind than economic development, as they were more concerned with environmental sustainability and indigenous cultural flourishing. But they operated within a larger, university structure that rooted its work in economic development of indigenous peoples under a symbolic heading of sustainability and cultural preservation.

This analysis leads curiously back to the tensions raised at the outset of this chapter, between the fields of ESD and environmental education. The big question, one raised by Jickling and Wals (2008), is the possibility of teaching about the environment and sustainability in a way that does not get subsumed by an unexamined economic development imperative. Jickling and Wals (2008) do not believe this is possible and given the studies undertaken in this book, I am less sanguine than I once was about a workable synthesis. I am drawn to examples similar to those I found in Hawaii as being central aspects of GCE since it has the potential to regrow society in more just and humane ways and I am less persuaded by promise of hyper-mediated learning as developed in GYL. Yet, neither is able to resolve, or even fully recognize and name, the deeper dynamic, or is it a fissure, evident in efforts to teach for global citizenship in ways that are rooted in a reoriented sustainability ethic?

Note

1   Ching-Fu Lan co-authored the New York City case based on his dissertation study.

6

TEACHER EDUCATION

Teacher education is necessarily based in the local and national realities of a particular school system. Yet, calls for GCE typically invoke the need for teachers who are themselves globally competent, presenting a foundational disconnect (Merryfield, 2000; Zong, 2009). If teachers do not see themselves as global learners, their students may be unlikely to adopt a similar perspective. There has been attention to this conundrum recently in teacher education, shining the spotlight on a few programs. These efforts include cooperative exchanges among students and faculty in teacher education programs, attention to multilingual capacities of teacher candidates and the students they serve along with efforts to promote global learning in university-based programs (Buczynski et al., 2010). Professional organizations, such as the American Association of Colleges of Teacher Education (AACTE), have developed awards for exemplary programs, though by their own admission indicate that not nearly enough is happening to prepare teachers for building global learning capacity in the US (Robinson, 2012).

Why is preparing teachers for engaging learners as global citizens at the margins of teacher education? GCE is typically viewed as a pleasant addition that is not integral to a teaching life (Mundy & Manion, 2008), unless one happens to teach immigrant students or if the teacher is a "racialized immigrant" (Subedi, 2008). Multilingual and/or immigrant students within teacher education programs might be the focus of internationalizing efforts, for example (Colón-Muñiz et al., 2010), though attention to global learning is unlikely to be a broad focus for general teacher education programs (Mundy & Manion, 2008). Walter Parker (2011) found a tendency among schools that identify themselves as *international* for those schools to cater to diverse, multilingual students as a way of symbolizing what being international means in a school context. This orientation creates an ironic otherness among global programs within schools, as well as in teacher education, mirroring how international programs are often an adjunct, rather than integral, in universities and other educational institutions. The idea that US schools are set apart from global endeavors is a script not easily undone despite frequent and increasing exhortations otherwise.

A second plausible reason why teacher education institutions have not generally engaged with GCE is the recent raft of changes made related to teacher certification. Reforms like edTPA (Teacher Performance Assessment), the CCCS (Common Core Curriculum Standards) and assessments of teachers (e.g. Teachscape/Danielson Framework for Teacher Evaluation) and students (e.g. Performance Assessment of Readiness for College and Careers) have taken up much of the space for reform in education generally, focusing teacher education institutions and faculty on immediate concerns related to state licensure, early career success and newfound marketplace competition, all while helping to prepare novice teachers to navigate this new landscape. Teacher education is positioned reactively in this policy context, making changes that mirror what is happening in schools. There is some irony in the fact that the raft of policy changes have been largely precipitated by globally referenced standards regarding effective teaching, exemplary curriculum and notable instructional practices, even if these projections are suspect (see Steiner-Khamsi, 2004). These practices are circumscribed by the need to increase scores on internationally benchmarked exams such as the Programme for International Student Assessment (PISA) (Gaudelli, 2013). While US schools are becoming more directly integrated into a global system of teaching, assessment and evaluation by means of these evolving global norms, teachers are ironically not afforded learning opportunities to help them become knowledgeable actors or to grasp how their careers and lives are indeed globally connected. In this sense, *global* acts as a sort of null curriculum in teacher education, always present but rarely explicitly examined as a learning area.

A third explanation as to why teacher education has generally taken a reduced role in preparing teachers to engage students in GCE is the rise of nonprofits/NGOs to address issues related to this field. The increased presence of nonprofits/NGOs in teacher development illustrates what happens when a need is not addressed. Nonprofit/NGO efforts are often viewed as augmenting existing programs, such as when organizations such as the World Wildlife Fund, Teachers without Borders and Pennies for the Planet and hundreds of other nonprofits/NGOs organize programming for schools, from in-school fundraising for ecosystem protection to providing resources for teachers in economically impoverished areas to creating professional development forums for teachers about global issues. In addition, groups such as Teach for America/All, KIPP (Knowledge is Power Program) and Citizen Schools have become institutions in their own right as they establish schools, teacher certification programs and professional development courses for teachers in their networks.

A significant uptick in activity related to global learning and nonprofits/NGOs has occurred over the past decade as organizations outside universities that are focused on school-based professional development address a gap in teacher preparation for global teaching. The nonprofit/NGO sector has a freer hand with which to address teacher development in that they do not have to mediate university culture (e.g. faculty tenure, publishing demands, research expectations) and regulatory requirements for teacher education (supervised field experiences, instructional preparation). This fact alone may explain why there is a growing number of nonprofit organizations in the US and beyond that are active in teacher education activities or even wholesale licensure. As Mundy and Manion (2008) note, there has been growth in NGO involvement with Canadian schools, yet their participation is highly uneven, perhaps best described as episodic, and often oriented towards fundraising, which may uncritically support a global charity narrative all too common in the North (pp. 963–4). While their efforts are not as systematic as licensure programs within states, they warrant attention because of the sheer volume of the work being done along with how their increased presence demonstrates a dynamic of how schools react to external demands, such as globalization in education. Increasingly, scholars who study social change are examining the effects that tens of thousands of nonprofits/NGOs are having in shaping civil society (Iriye, 2002).

The cases in this chapter include two university-based teacher education programs with a global focus, one in the US and the other in Canada. These programs are treated comparatively as they are similar in important ways while offering points of contrast that arise from their diverse settings. I then turn to consider Poland's recent efforts to energize teacher education for global citizenship through the collaborative working of governmental and non-governmental sectors. There are three dilemmas that emerge from the conversations with participants in these three settings, ones that will support insights at the chapter's end. The first relates to the exclusivity and isolation that educators express about GCE discourse and indeed their own programming. This dilemma enfolds the tension of keeping the global distinct while recognizing that the values inherent in GCE point towards inclusivity and broad engagement of diverse people. The second dilemma relates to the broader development of critical, global sensibility among teacher candidates, students, teachers and schools. These conversations are rooted in concerns about equity at all levels of scale, the gross inequities that exist globally and the ability of educators to nurture this awareness through programming efforts. The third dilemma relates to the broad absence of systematic GCE efforts in schools. Since teacher education is necessarily focused on schools and teacher development, educators shared concerns that the exclusivity of GCE, noted above, typically manifest in schools themselves.

University-based Global Teacher Education in the US and Canada

I studied two programs, one at Midland University in the US and the other at Torg University in Ontario, Canada, as both were noted by colleagues in the field for having a strong commitment to developing globally minded teachers. Both programs operate in a cohort model as students seek admission, are offered coursework that is globally oriented and are given opportunities to work in schools and visit other places to augment their academic and field-based learning.

Midland University and the Global Learners Cohort

Midland University has a long tradition of engagement in international education. This commitment was strengthened in the past decade in the College of Education into a Global Learners Cohort (GLC). GLC has expanded to include a group of approximately 75 teacher candidates annually, mainly elementary teacher candidates with some secondary students, who apply to the program based on their academic achievement, motivation to learn about the wider world and interest in what it means to educate globally. Students begin with introductory courses in each of the four semesters during the first two years of their Baccalaureate degree followed by a study abroad/global experience in their junior year and a school-based field placement for student teaching that is designed to embody the aims of GLC. While these *global* courses are intended for students in GLC, they are not exclusive to the cohort so there are typically a few students from the general teacher education program in these classes. The field experiences—which include a visit to a nearby Arab American community and the possibility of an international placement—are reserved, however, for those in the GLC cohort.

The effort to be inclusive of the wider community in the GLC is purposeful, as faculty aim to avoid isolating the program from the rest of the College. Lydia explained the background of the College's global footprint, which was developed in tandem with the international impetus of the university over the past three decades. Lydia, a long-standing member of the faculty who co-directs and teaches in the GLC program, explained that the first wave of internationalization at the College was characterized by an *add-and-stir* approach of infusing topics here and there in an idiosyncratic fashion: "In the past, we would be studying special education led by a faculty member who had been to Belgium, so then students would read one article about special education in Belgium." In contrast to the current program, she was excited to see the amalgamation of these ideas in a coherent and cohesive way in GLC, while recognizing that their efforts were not without difficulty.

> My initial enthusiasm [for GLC] has not waned but my recognition of the complexity of what it means to take a social foundations [education] course

that has certain obligatory commitments, like certain things we have to do [for state requirements] and turn it into a global course…can lead to superficial attention of anything outside the US.

The initial choice to make the GLC a separate experience for students proved to be highly consequential in how the GLC has taken shape, one that mirrors a larger challenge in GCE. A recurring theme is the tendency to isolate global learning from other types of learning. This move creates an otherness to the learning, as if learning about becoming a teacher normally is best understood at a provincial or national level, rather than in broader terms. There are obvious benefits and insights yielded by studying education globally, such as helping prospective teachers see what is perceived as normal in one context as highly unusual in another. This ability to see and imagine otherwise is likely to be enhanced through global learning and such insights are of value to all who are becoming educators. But the choice to make this learning special, segmenting it out of a teacher education program, not only shapes the global learning experienced in programs such as GLC but also affirms the types of normative ways of thinking about teacher education, and education, in the *regular* program and ignores what other national systems do to prepare globally competent teachers (Darling-Hammond, 2010, see particularly Chapter 7; Dolby & Rahman, 2008).

Rory, an instructor of mathematics in GLC, shared his concerns regarding the cordoning off of regular teacher education from developing a global orientation.

> My fear is that GLC can quickly turn into a fancy club…giving students bragging rights and it ceases to be about understanding the world and your own place in the world and becomes "Oh, isn't that cool we have this Chinese food party!" I've noticed in some of the interactions in the classes where I have both GLC students and other students, that the global cohort students tend to set themselves apart as a special group because they get to do fancier things than what other people do. My feeling is that global awareness should be for all teachers considering the changing demographics in the US and it bothers me that we are talking a lot about this in the global sections, and not too much about it in the other sections, and yet the goal was to be inclusive.

This tension is not unique to Midland but characteristic of the way in which global learning is typically engaged, as a special topic or area that stands isolated from the core of learning, illustrative of an academic culture of fragmentation that houses teacher education (Goodwin, 2010). The in-group/out-group tension is not completely unexpected since the creation of a cohort invites a sense of being part of a club, even if it is not at all the intention of the faculty to create a sense of exclusivity. Students, too, are of course multiple in their identities, so belonging to the GLC at Midland enfolds within their ethnicity/race, gender and class sense of themselves.

One way devised by instructors to address isolation of GLC is through making direct connections between activities of the cohort and the wider community. There is particular interest in drawing upon the large number of international students as cultural informants. Daniel, a psychologist at Midland who is the key instructor for the GLC introduction to psychology course and also oversees psychology instruction for all teacher education students, devised a cross-cultural interview experience to help Midland students consider life from another's point of view. The students begin by identifying a person that they consider other, either owing to their being culturally different, an immigrant, practising a different religion, having a different sexual orientation or some other salient identity difference. Students then work in pairs around three planned interactions. The first has one person in the dyad positioned as the host in an activity that speaks to their identity, the second interaction flips these roles, and the third interaction asks each student to develop a metacognitive reflection on what they learned from the encounters captured with a videolog. Daniel noted that students are very uncomfortable with the idea of choosing an other as it tends to exoticize the familiar, yet he believes that the outcomes are worth the initially awkward exchanges. He also noted that the activity was so popular within the GLC cohort that it has now migrated to being used in all introductory psychology courses, a sign of the diffusion of global learning at Midland.

There is a sense among those involved in GLC at Midland that the work of educating globally should push students out of their comfort zones, to see their everyday lives as implicated in wider contexts. Faculty believe that students should be encouraged to see themselves in a global context and to consider their extensive privilege as university students, both in comparison to society generally and also in relation to each other (e.g. international students, members of historically marginalized populations in the US). Buon and Duwo, two doctoral students from Indonesia teaching in the GLC, talked about activities they organize to help students think about choosing as implicated globally.

> The novelty of global learning for these students provides opportunities while offering constraints. One activity I do is to pose the question, *Is there really such a thing as an American economy?* I have an activity to have them look at where their clothes are made, see where they are from and list countries and draw strings on a map, so in that way it's less of a distant thing, it's the stuff they wear every day, their bags, their smartphones. In doing that we're hoping to make the connection to understand and really have to think about where they are and connecting it to their lives.

This activity is typical of those used in the field to engage issues of global capital and considered in Chapter 2 (see Bigelow & Peterson, 2002). These types of activities attempt to breach the isolated way that global is treated by showing immediate, personal connections for students. It can also help model for future teachers how to create similar experiences for their students.

The principle that learning globally should purposefully move students out of their comfort zones is well established in the literature. Global educators have long-held the belief that placing students into situations of otherness will create dissonance and lead them to an awareness of their perspective and an appreciation of myriad other viewpoints (Coryell et al., 2010; Dwyer, 2004; Kissock & Richardson, 2010; Merryfield, 2001). As Dwyer (2004) noted in her study of 3,723 respondents drawn from a pool of 17,000 who studied abroad between 1950 and 2000, 98 percent self-reported that "study abroad helped them understand cultural values and biases," a finding which confirms how the dissonance of experiencing an other's life can shape one's views of oneself (p. 158). The challenge that GLC confronts is the degree to which experiences of otherness can be created/identified in a university program while students are living close to home. Or, are Daniel's dyadic videologs and Buon and Duwo's demonstrations of commercial linkages enough to connect—person to person as well as person to material goods—the GLC student to the world, to educate them both about their perspective and how they are implicated in the wider world?

GLC students engage with some of these issues in a course designed to address the citizenship dimensions of being global. *Global Service Learning* explicitly addresses issues of citizenship, interdependence and global engagement. Students consider service learning as a pedagogical practice and then design local projects that reflect their academic preparation. The syllabus and reading materials suggest a US focus to the work, however, and there is little attention to the problematic dimensions of North/South work globally, the alternative frame of working in solidarity as compared to service and the historical patterns that sit at the foundation of these efforts. Faculty view the service learning as critical to developing a global outlook, though, as it implicates the students by illustrating local–global connections while encouraging students to become active citizens.

Midland's service learning work was not overtly critical despite an expressed orientation in GLC to disrupt students' normative frames. Educating globally, GLC faculty believe, should push students out of their comfort zones while encouraging participants to see themselves in a global context, yet there was not a hard systems/capital critique as more critical versions of global learning suggest (Andreotti, 2010). There was a fear, however, that focusing on privilege would lead to "We're great and therefore should help the poor, global people" or as Lydia recounted from a previous trip, the paternalism of visiting a rural Chinese school and "wanting to give them things." In a similar vein, Karl was talking about a film that he uses in his foundations course called *The Short Life of Jose Antonio Gutierrez* (Specogna, 2006). He reflected on how challenging it is for students not to default to *I'm American* discourse in which they are already immersed and socialized.

After watching the film and getting back into discussion people very easily start speaking like an American. They start referencing *our* economy, and *our* jobs, and everything becomes taken for granted. One of our students said something about *our* jobs and *our* economy, and I felt like I had enough rapport with the class at that point that I could point-blank ask her: We just got done reading this stuff about interrelated global economies, inequities across the world, and different models of immigration, and do you really think it makes sense to talk about immigrants taking *our* jobs? And she honestly stopped and thought about it and looked at me and said, "That's a really good point."

The inclusion/exclusion dynamic has morphed in a number of interesting ways over the past two years of the GLC program. First, there is an intensive focus on how to support school-based efforts for global learning. Second, faculty are generally more concerned about intragroup dynamics in classes than the relationship of the GLC cohort to the college and university. The focus on school-based efforts grew out of a recognition that without school-based models for implementation, the GLC would create "lone wolves" of global educators rather than systematic agents of change, a paradoxical outcome given the aims of GCE around cooperation and systems-thinking/change (Tye & Tye, 1992). The concern about intragroup dynamics arose from a particularly challenging group of students that caused significant faculty concern.

Lydia noted that in teaching the first course of the new cohort in 2013, she found that students were being isolated, even ridiculed, based on existing social hierarchies that were reactivated within the GLC cohort by students themselves; an incongruous *clique-within-a-clique* dynamic. Lydia realized that this needed to be addressed, made her observations public and focused the introductory course on addressing the tensions that surfaced within the cohort. She facilitated this intervention mainly through dialog, making explicit behaviors and attitudes expressed in class and how they were damaging to the group's morale as well as hurtful to individuals. She thought this tension was largely reconciled but in a subsequent semester learned from her new colleague, Allison, that indeed the same group was demonstrating some of the same behaviors in class that they had the previous year, such as eye-rolling at comments made and social isolation of "othered" peers. Allison reflected on her first experience teaching in the cohort and witnessing this dynamic:

So the class is very divided, physically and what seems like emotionally and mentally. I've been working really hard to overcome some of that. I don't think it should happen in any class obviously but especially in a class that's about these [diversity] issues to have students of color on one side of the room and the white students on the other just blows my mind. Students have trouble listening to each other, so a lot of my white students will roll their eyes when other students talk, they'll turn their back, they'll talk over me and other students. If I let them get into groups themselves it would be all the white girls who are in sororities together, all international students together, and my one black student trying to figure out where she fits in. It's interesting too to see how they are using my thematic focus on Adichie's TED Talk, *The Danger of a Single Story* [Adichie, 2009]. Some of them have been using the concepts they have been taught to combat the single story of sorority girls as caddy or mean, and using Adichie's concept to explain that "sorority women are diverse and misunderstood." I have tried to help them consider how power dynamics works and the nature of hegemony, that the use of Adichie's concept is not appropriate in the case of privileged people, but it's been a challenge.

Faculty attributed these behaviors to the chemistry of the current cohort in particular but also to the student population at Midland generally, one that has limited exposure to difference from their pre-collegiate education. The GLC, thus, addressed students' experiential absences explicitly in the *Language, Immigration and Learning* class. When I visited, students were preparing for a two-day fieldtrip to an Arab American community wherein they would visit schools, interview teachers and principals, attend a museum and visit the local community center. There were moments of banter led by the instructor, Margaret, about visiting the "exotic others in Eberly," which generated laughter; a sort of insider's joke about the irony of studying others so close to home. When asked by Margaret how many had been to Eberly, however, none of the 20 students present indicated that they had ever been there.

This seemingly innocuous piece of information though may reveal what programs such as GLC are up against in countering the tide of mainstream culture, and particularly, the culture of becoming a teacher. The faculty had a shared sense of being on a mission in doing this work, raising global awareness and providing meaningful experiences with/of diversity. Yet, this was not typical behavior—to visit a nearby ethnic community—in the way that doing so is set aside as a *learning activity*, outside of the normal activity of undergraduate students. That such a visit is an a-typical activity and requires focused attention may further concretize the idea that Eberly is something fundamentally different, of *an other world* in a sense. This tension mirrors the consternation felt by faculty about the otherness of the GLC, a program designed to identify and explore difference but in a way that made the experience itself other within its host context.

The notion that the global is other relates to the relative absence of global learning within schools that partner with Midland. As Margaret explained, schools that embrace GCE in a wide, deep and interdisciplinary fashion are extremely rare, even non-existent, in Midland's service region and those that do exist tend to be elementary or middle schools that have either a large immigrant population and/or catalyzing teacher(s) who encourage global learning. Margaret offered an explanation:

At the elementary level historically, education was and continues to be a domestic endeavor and so, unless a given school had a particularly globally diverse student body, there was really no reason to focus attention outward. The CCSS [Common Core State Standards], which has provided a strong focus for what is taught in schools, does not integrate global competencies into the standards. CCSS does not prescribe content, of course, but global competencies are not included to the degree they could be. High-stakes testing in the state does not attend to global competencies either. Therefore, any global content needs to be voluntarily worked into the curriculum by teachers who are (a) committed to and recognize the value of global education and, (b) are sufficiently comfortable with the standard curriculum to recognize points of entry and develop supplemental experiences.

Margaret's survey of the challenging landscape casts doubt on the ability of GCE educators to fruitfully impact the situation.

I conducted a focus group interview with three teachers from Elmwood, a nearby elementary, who participated in Midland's summer study program in Tanzania. Nancy, Ralinda and Lisa talked about how the experience of visiting Tanzania for five weeks complicated their views about Africa. These teachers are now trying to migrate these insights into their classrooms through the use of children's stories, counting using Kiswahili numbers and helping students to critically read images of Africa. They talked about the misconceptions they previously had about Africa and how they critically examined these with their students.

> **Ralinda**: Yeah, so we are a Title I [additional federal funding] school and saw a lot of kids in this area don't get past Marlston or Walmart. Seriously they don't have experiences, so these kinds of things that I think you can share [from visiting Tanzania] are amazing.
>
> **Nancy**: The story with losing the tooth and putting it in under a gourd and getting a chicken, which is the tradition in Mali, the kids kept asking me even days after, "Like that's fantasy, right?! That doesn't really happen?!" And I said no, that really happens, that's what they do, that's part of their culture, in this particular area. I'm very careful about saying any time I post pictures that this is a picture of one small part. Doing that is one of the biggest eye-openers as you can get, since it's very easy to overgeneralize when teaching about Africa. That's probably one of the things that I become most aware of is trying not to overgeneralize.

Lisa, a fifth year Midland's student who is completing her student teaching practicum at Elmwood and a soon-to-be graduate of the GLC program, is a leader of this effort as she shares materials, practices and insights about how to help students think more globally through children's literature and mathematics. The teachers shared with me, however, that they were the only three who were engaged in this work at Elmwood, pointing to the summer study experience as a pivotal one in encouraging this transition. Margaret indicated that Midland was trying to connect Elmwood teachers with those at other nearby schools engaged in similar efforts, leveraging the thinking of one group to encourage more conversations about how to implement GCE in an elementary context.

Torg University and the Global Citizenship Cohort

Torg is located in southern Ontario and focuses on teacher education in the province since teacher licensure is controlled at this level in Canada. The Global Citizenship Cohort (GCC) at Torg, like Midland, is based on a cohort model. Students were somewhat older than those at Midland, being post-Baccalaureates with a median age of approximately 26 years. GCC students take a three-course sequence that includes *Teaching Seminar, Society and Schools* and *Psychological Foundations*. These courses are infused with content and approaches that "allow teacher candidates to make informed decisions about student learning, global and environmental awareness, advocacy, and community building for change. Our approach to GCE promotes advocacy towards equity, sustainable development, social justice, and systemic change." The courses are taken in conjunction with field experiences, or practicum, which constitute two months of classroom work over the period September through April in what is approximately a one calendar year program. Similar to the field experience at Midland, Torg's GCC seeks school placements where engaging in global learning is a high priority.

GCC is nested within a larger university that, like Midland, embraces global learning and supports relevant programming. The university has a broad commitment to serving the increasingly diverse province of Ontario and developing programs that respond to local needs while being globally connected. The approximate annual intake of 1,500 students in initial teacher education programs are exposed to a variety of globally infused courses; a range of electives, including aboriginal studies, comparative education and gender equity; internships in China, South Africa and Caribbean countries and in globally oriented community organizations; a bi-weekly seminar series on global issues for teachers and teacher candidates; access to international delegations and scholars representing some 25 countries; along with research opportunities in various global classroom initiatives. The context of GCE is significant at Torg and Midland as it provides built-in support for growing global cohorts while enabling existing programs, such as the seminar series at Torg, to be dually purposed.

Torg's GCC program began in the late 1990s and I had the opportunity to interview long-standing faculty as well as relatively new ones. The faculty spoke about their deep commitment to the work, how pressing it was that their focus be on teaching for equity and sustainability in an era of hyper-economic globalization and the challenges associated with doing this without it feeling as though it were an adjunct to the essentials of preparing to teach in Canada. All of the instructors spoke about the conceptual elusiveness of GCE and their efforts to keep open its meanings and emphases over time. Jackie, one of the co-coordinators currently, explained a previous effort by the faculty to "pin down" what was intended by GCE. Despite the uncertainty, there was a measure of comfort in the ambiguity, an outlook one might attribute to global learning generally since it encourages learners to move beyond their comfort zone to develop an understanding of how they are socially positioned.

Jodi, a long-standing faculty member in the program, described how four GCC faculty met to solidify a statement about what constitutes GCE and found it difficult to do, as their concerns involved social justice, sustainability, historically marginalized populations and pedagogical practices that address these concerns, such that no singular framework encapsulated what they valued educationally. What is very evident in Torg's approach, however, is a commitment to raising equity concerns in relation to the content of GCE and in the context of schools. Torg boasts developing pedagogues who attend to power relations into which schools and systems of education are spun. Darren, an instructor in the program for a good portion of its duration and a former classroom teacher, personalized this effort, seeing it as the work of teachers who undertake the challenge of unpacking their situated identity that implicates them in the wider society's choosing.

> Teachers can use the [prescribed] curriculum as a means to address these more critical issues and not feel constrained by it but see it as an opening and an opportunity. Unless you yourself have gone through that inside-out understanding and unpacking of your own social locations, identity, power and privilege, or your lack of privilege because you have been marginalized or oppressed because of your identity and truly have a more *critical* perspective then you're not going to go down that critical route in teaching. And what might happen is you reproduce the status quo. And so a lot of the work I have been trying to do with teacher candidates here in the politics and curriculum class is that process. What are our own political thoughts and ideas? How do we read what happens in the world? What's our own complicity in that? What's our own resistance to that? How are we political beings in a sense?

GCC faculty draw deeply on the theory that developing a global perspective among teachers must connect to their subjectivity, to highlight their positionality and to implicate their daily practice as teachers. Jodi, the current co-coordinator of GCC and instructor, explained a recent lesson focused on this dimension:

> Last week we talked about culturally relevant pedagogy and we looked at homework as a socio-cultural practice and as we did that we then looked at

How does this connect to our cohort theme of global citizenship education? And of course we can talk about how the diversity within Ontario, where people are coming from, how culturally relevant teaching would look if you were teaching internationally. And in some ways taking the homework piece by dissecting something as mundane as homework gets teacher candidates to recognize the assumptions and implications of every teaching strategy. So teacher candidates leave our cohort having seen the complexity and I think one of the key learnings with GCE is seeing the complexity and multiple perspectives in everything we're doing.

The focus on criticality and equity changes the way that GCE is talked about and enacted at Torg, focusing more intently on local dimensions, the profound changes economic globalization has brought upon communities and how people have been marginalized as a result of the changes. Magical, Pollyanna stories of how globalization *changed everything* (Friedman, 2005) are interrupted with critiques of globalization; its dislocations, distortions and discontent. A critical orientation towards globalization emphasizes the way that the spread of global capital and Western-style development has led to increasingly disparate incomes, the concentration of wealth in the hands of a few and increasing extreme poverty for hundreds of millions of others. As nations follow the lead of the US in defining the common good solely in light of individual, economic achievement while abandoning a safety net, labor is destabilized, especially among resident poor and dislocated economic migrants (Soysal, 2012). Typically teacher education is not engaged in a curriculum that explores these types of issues, abiding an implicit belief that such economic and political dimensions are auxiliary to teaching in a global era. But in Torg's GCC, these concerns are front-and-center as the faculty believe teachers need to develop critical sensitivities so they grow more aware of their own circumstances and better able to articulate and teach about systemic injustices.

The fact that Torg's GCC emerged in the late 1990s is notable. At about this time growing skepticism emerged particularly in North America about what had up until that point been an apparent consensus about the good of economic globalization, particularly market liberalization, the fall of the Soviet Empire and the expansion of free trade zones like the North American Free Trade Agreement (NAFTA). The Battle in Seattle of 1999, for example, which included some 40,000 protesters surrounding a meeting of the World Trade Organization (WTO), was the first widespread media recognition of a growing discourse in opposition to global economic liberalization—the mainstreaming of anti-globalization discourse (see Owens & Palmer, 2003). These foundational elements in GCC are present in current iterations of practice.

Darren, among the original coordinators and founders of GCC, reflected on how the cohort changed over time. He noted how Torg's program morphed as various discourses surrounding the work have taken shape.

Over the years, students read different things into that global piece and what ended up happening is you had groups that really represented different strands of whatever global education is coming together. So there were people who had come from an environmental background, people from overseas and NGO work, people interested in human rights, students interested in education equity, and people in terms of the peace education strand. But what I liked about all the global pieces was they always implied an action that you took when you learned something and that was part of what we did with students.

Torg students find a home in GCC because of its variegated call, with different streams coming together in a confluence of interest. Torg practised a sort of strategic ambiguity, lacking the fidelity of a proscribed conceptualization, which offered a wider expanse of opportunities to engage and inviting more educators into the work. Darren suggested that sustainability has become the center point of late due to funding and obvious warning signs regarding environmental degradation. He also observed that the rise of sustainability education as the dominant form of GCE "is partly a reaction to the global piece always interpreted as only global and not local. So the person starving somewhere far away was more important than the homeless person right inside your door." He noted too that more students have come to the cohort with the environment as a passion, one that is encompassing and immediate in terms of place.

Attention to local dimensions of GCE manifest most directly in GCC's field placements. I explored two of these, Vilmore Academy and Fairlawn School. Catherine, an instructor in the program, noted that GCC had challenges finding school placements due mainly to logistics, such as matching globally minded teachers and GCC students' needs. She noted that GCC has "an A list of schools, good placements where they do have global initiatives happening and strong faculty enacting those programs." Both Vilmore and Fairlawn shared an explicit commitment to GCE in their curricular offerings. Rosalind, the principal of Vilmore Academy, explained the rhetorical commitment to GCE that was not consistently enacted in the school, a problem she sought to address as head. She spoke about recent work ongoing in partnership with the faculty of Torg University to develop sustainable waste removal in communities with limited water access.

The first question students addressed was, *How do you get people to use the toilet?* The engineers [of Torg] said we can come up with a toilet that will meet all the sustainability criteria but it will sit unused. And so people working on this problem always go to education. You've got to educate the local population about sanitation. Every year there's a global challenge. We're a partner school with Torg's Global Center and we brought on board 14 other schools this year into the project. And the chemistry teacher got excited about it, and thought about it from the point of view of what is needed in terms of the developing world and sanitation and she got every kid as a project-based learning assignment to develop a toilet that would meet a set of criteria. So it became a curricular change to promote thinking more globally over a six to eight week unit. Last year we did sprinkles, which supports childhood infant malnutrition. We had ten schools participate and everybody looked at ways you could get mothers and fathers to think about using this micronutrient powder to enhance the vitamins and minerals that infants get in impoverished areas.

Rosalind's long-standing commitment to GCE practice in schools was tempered by her recognition that school leaders needed to motivate colleagues, such as those not in the humanities and social studies, to experience the value of global teaching.

My feeling is that there is significant interest and a willingness to get involved with global education/learning but opportunities are not always readily available. It has impressed me how so many schools when approached were willing to get involved with the most recent project (e.g. sprinkles/infant malnutrition). When support is lacking it may be related to a lack of time for teachers to collaborate, lack of local opportunities that are truly beneficial for students and periodic teacher job actions. People are looking for meaningful opportunities that engage students in authentic learning where students can develop understanding of global issues. Working with experts in the field, such as NGO's and professors, has proven to be an incentive. Teachers are looking to learn themselves from experts on global issues so this can inform their teaching.

Vilmore, however, is an independent school and thus fits a long-standing pattern of GCE in such schools. Rosalind noted this ongoing challenge, being a leader in practice but facing the challenge of encouraging other schools, particularly public schools that serve marginalized students, to participate in what is often situated as auxiliary education there.

Sharon, a teacher and alum of Torg's GCC program now nearly a decade removed from her teacher education program, invited me to visit Fairlawn, which is a public school, though one with a long-standing relationship with the university and drawing a student population of middle- to upper-middle-income families. I observed Sharon teaching a senior global issues course. Sharon recalled her participation in the GCC cohort as an opportunity to work with peers that had extensive international experience, mainly in the nonprofit sector who were shifting careers to work as teachers. She shared a great sense of connection to her student-teacher colleagues, pointing to this as the greatest strength of the program, a sentiment echoed by Jodi the current coordinator of the cohort. As Sharon explained, "GCC had lots of individuals like me, a real wide range of global experiences and all of us had this desire to learn more about the world. There was just a sense that people were all coming from the same place, that we had many common experiences." Not unlike the in-group/out-group dynamic of Midland, GCC students at Torg shared a common set of experiences that helped to coalesce an identity as global educators. Torg students, however, generally had much more global experience to draw upon from their work in the NGO sector than did students of Midland who were significantly younger as a group.

I observed as Sharon's students discussed a primer on globalization in small groups based on teacher-prepared questions. Sharon responded to some questions about specialized vocabulary, such as the International Monetary Fund (IMF) and World Bank. Students challenged the author's premise that globalization began in the 16th century, drawing evidence from their previous study of Rome to counter this assertion. There was clearly a sense that this type of critique was valued and invited in the class as student commentary was extensive. Sharon than pivoted to show students a brief excerpt of Michael Moore's (2009) provocative documentary *Capitalism: A love story*, which they then moved to discuss in groups. Torg's commitment to engaging in a critique of global capital around matters of social justice and equity was clear in this lesson, one that Sharon indicated was an ongoing theme for her class throughout the year.

Sharon raised the issue of isolation in GCE as she reflected on her experiences at Torg. She indicated that it was a benefit to be around like-minded university students as it helped her to sort through experiences beyond Canada while pushing her to learn more about issues previously unexamined. Those associated with the cohort program at Torg viewed themselves as having a special purpose in the university, arguably one that translated into their practice as teachers: to promote global learning that raised difficult questions about historical inequities, how this legacy was reinscribed in a global era, and echoing Darren's comments, so that young people will have a better sense of their subjectivity and positionality to act mindfully and differently in the world. GCC's orientation was summarized in the syllabus for *Teacher Education Seminar: Sustainability and Global Citizenship...*

> [It] Encourages teacher candidates to consider the interplay of school, community, and global forces and influences. Teacher candidates will examine approaches to teaching and learning that will allow them to make informed decisions about student learning, global and environmental awareness, advocacy, and community building for positive change. Our approach to GCE promotes advocacy towards sustainable development, social justice and systemic change.
>
> (Personal communication)

Torg's GCC faculty understood their efforts as developing teachers with global sensibility who grasp the connectivity of life on the planet, the long shadow of historical inequities and how those forces shape everyday life today, all focused on acting meaningfully in the world.

This agented orientation necessarily includes the local, particularly historically marginalized populations within a given community that are typically left out of conversations about GCE. Michael, one of the founders of GCC at Torg and current director of the program, shared this perspective and the challenges that it presents.

> One of the tensions we have is always trying to reinsert the issues of his-
> torically marginalized communities that are a mile from us and are directly
> involved in this thing we're calling the *global* that always seems like it is 9000
> miles away.

Their approach is realized to a degree in practicum placements located with stu-dents from historically marginalized groups as well as through the readings and discussions in the three core courses.

The program at Torg enacts a strong emphasis on critical and political dimen-sions of citizenship. The faculty at Torg, in fact, often qualified their use of GCE with the prefix *critical* to emphasize the distinction, apart from approaches that are more celebratory or surface. Faculty in the program spoke at length about this facet of the work, an orientation that is highly congruent with how faculty and students at Torg perceive the university in comparison to others. Anne, an instructor in GCC who recently completed her doctorate, contrasted Torg's GCC with a nearby teacher education program that she had experience in as a student.

> In the teacher education program that I'm currently studying in, the crux
> of everything we do is equity and anti-racism. But the only time *global*
> comes up it is separated from the discourse of urbanization and urban needs.
> I would call these things global citizenship education, talking about poverty,
> structural economic disadvantage and the like, but a lot of the teachers will
> not connect to it the way that it is interpreted.

Anne noted that this approach of segmenting racism and equity concerns from global ones, while typical in education generally, was not at all the case in her teacher preparation at Torg where these concerns were actively and purposefully comingled.

Catherine, also a recent doctoral graduate who taught briefly in the GCC, spoke of a related tension with her students. She explained that many of her students gravitated towards the global cohort because of previous experiences globally, either teaching or living abroad, a sense of the GCC affirmed by Sharon, an alum, and Jodi, the current co-coordinator. Catherine noted, however, that students' experiences resulted from their relative affluence and often abided by an implicit North/South, donor/recipient narrative. Catherine expanded on Anne's take:

> Who is the assumed citizen subject in global citizenship education? Underlying this conception of *global* is the privileged subject, the cosmopolite who is *supposed* to be learning about the world, but it [this approach] actually re-others people who are marginalized within national discourse while granting status to the international elite, say those pushing the International Baccalaureate program into schools. The class dimension is often ignored, yet these [economically poor] are the kids that need the global.

Noticeably absent at Torg, however, was discussion about how the space of GCC discourse was itself created by the privileged backgrounds of participants, postsecondary students who had opportunities to do year-long internships and work in global NGOs, due in part to their interest coupled with the means to pursue those interests. Given the amount of critical introspection in the GCC generally, this condition was taken for granted, as being how the reality of the world manifested at Torg.

Torg's emphasis on issues of equity—class, access and privilege—in the context of urban education was an ongoing concern in the course of study. Participants at Torg pointed to how this was enacted through critical engagement with the *Water for All* initiative under way throughout Canada. Anne summarized her take on the program:

> *Water for All* was started by a high school student and there are these basically rock concerts called *Water for All* days. *Water for All* day is the culmination of it…reminds me of Tony Robbins, like a spirit day, it has celebrities and there's a concert, it's like *you can change the world* and *you can change the world* and *you can change the world* [mimicking Oprah Winfrey]. It's great because the students get really excited. They show these videos with stars from *Degrassi* [Canadian teen television series] who spend a day in Kenya learning to fetch water with the mommas, as they call them, from the local village. They can't believe how hard it is, how they are exhausted at the end of the day and one of the Degrassi stars looks into the eyes of one of the mommas and says "now I really know" because like it is this personal enlightenment story for the Canadians. So we have teacher candidates do a comparison of soft/critical global citizenship education and there's *a big aha* moment that usually happens. And the message is not that you should not participate in the *Water for All* club but that we as educators need to think about what kind of conversation we are going to have on the subway or on the bus to and from these events.

The program positions high school students of the global North as the presumed subject of global learning and the Kenyan women as an object of pity requiring charity. Yet faculty tempered their critique of *Water for All* since the program was started by a high school student and embraced by current ones as well as educators. The aim to help their future teachers see the ways in which popular renderings of *global engagement* often reinscribe imperialist and Western views of the world, lacking GCE of a critical variety, was apparent (Andreotti, 2010; Subedi & Daza, 2008).

Michael, a lead faculty member in the program, had a deliberative stance about criticality.

> I think in our conversations here amongst the faculty it's about using a framework that helps us understand social phenomenon better. The other piece has more to do with educational change and implementation. When you are introducing young people to things global, where do you start? Are there values being enacted in the *Water for All* project that are actually helpful? They are certainly not the end goal, so it is trying to use a broad framework [soft/critical GCE] to locate that project while analyzing how it fits into the broader educational change paradigm as we move forward. So it's tricky. It's easy to come in and be very critical but at the same time you see people engaged in general understandings about the world that they wouldn't have otherwise.

Torg's priority for teaching GCE through a critical, equity lens is pronounced in all aspects of the program. Yet, they do so with awareness about the limits of such an approach. The thorniness of North/South charity, or gift-giving, is often bound up with GCE because of the field's focus on social engagement. Torg's faculty had similar and warranted concerns that programs like *Water for All* are heralded by schools engaging with GCE as a way of being active in the world, yet without the necessary awareness as to how student participation was wound within existing structures of dominance and well-worn grooves of who gives and receives and the implications of each.

Government Sector, NGO and Teacher Education Partnerships in Poland

Poland has long been viewed as a leading economic and strategic nation within the region and is seen as pivotal to the European Union's successful integration-by-addition strategy since it bridges East–West differences on the continent. Poland has also been recognized by the Global Education Network Europe (GENE) as an emerging leader in this curriculum area:

> Global Education (GE) in Poland, has developed significantly since 2004, and has been closely connected to the emergence of Poland's development cooperation programme and growing engagement by many actors, including key Ministries and Non-governmental Organisations (NGOs) as key actors, as well as other institutions.
>
> (GENE, 2009, p. 21)

Education in Poland has undergone dramatic changes following the 1947–89 Soviet period. The previous system was characterized by highly uniform methods, curricula and assessments along with bureaucratic regulations to insure compliance (Kozakiewicz, 1992). The formal learning of schools was supposed to be augmented by parallel education, or through the contents of film, theatre and television. Yet, despite the perception of outsiders, particularly in the West, of severe uniformity throughout formal and informal education in Poland, as Kozakiewicz (1992, p. 92) notes, "In practice such a system never really existed." As Wojcik (2010) offers through her qualitative study of teachers' recollections, they employed various strategies from different proportions of coverage to what they considered Marxist–Leninist scripts along with body language cues (e.g. eye winks) to communicate alternative versions of dogma.

Independence created a great deal of energy around remaking the educational system, a new one purposefully conceived in stark contrast to the previous regime. A key element of reconstruction was a policy move towards decentralization. As Edward Bodine (2005, p. 87) explains, "Postcommunist decentralization…needs to be understood within this socio-historical context: it was as much a project of deconstructing the workings of the socialist order as much as a project to forge new egalitarian and efficient institutions." Decentralization in Polish education has led to the growth of community schools which are highly varied in their orientations and largely unsupervised by the Ministry of Human Development despite receiving public funds and operating in a quasi-public role (Bodine, 2005).

Teacher development has received significant attention in Poland given a perceived need to "catch up" globally following the isolation that marked the Soviet era. Global learning has generated attention too, due in part to Poland's independence coming in an era of burgeoning globalization along with its recent inclusion in the European Union. There seem to be at least two strands, however, to these commitments. The first and primary one is based on the desire to promote economic development in Poland, again in keeping with the idea that education reforms are reacting to the Soviet era. Secondarily, there is a strand of commitment to being a regional leader within Europe and a vital member of the European community.

Teacher education for GCE is largely organized by governmental organizations working in cooperation with Ministry of Human Development training centers and partnerships with NGOs. The Ministry of Global Activities has been a policy leader in GCE throughout Poland. Jacek, a chief officer in this area, provided an overview of the state of global education, suggesting that most attention is geared towards teacher professional development.

> We work on two levels: formal education and informal education. Formal education means we go through a framework contract with the Ministry of Human Development. The Ministry offers us the services of its agency working on improving the capacity of teachers through a network of regional centers in every region of Poland. They are responsible for offering training to teachers. So we give them a grant yearly and they are providing teachers with specific training on what global education is, what are the tools to use, and what are the needs of kids. Recently there was an agreement signed between the Ministry of Human Development, Global Activities, and the organizations working on development cooperation basically saying we want to boost the presence of global education in formal education in Poland. So international development, cooperation and global education were introduced into the curricula. Then, NGOs work on specific guidelines for teachers and publishers to include global education in specific areas and topics of [existing] formal education, or how to use it [global education] across the board in geography, economy, even Polish history lessons, on every level.

Jacek noted that some teachers are more inclined towards global thinking, particularly around the major cities of Cracow and Warsaw as compared to rural areas.

Jacek explained that there was significant pushback to engaging in GCE among teachers in certain rural provinces, their opposition arising from a variety of perspectives. Jacek reflected on a recent trip that he took to work with school directors and the reactions that some of them shared about global education:

> Rural people claim that they are raising kids anyway and are doing a good job and what do I want from them in this respect? They basically said I invented a new term with other leftist psychos in Warsaw and now I am imposing it on them and they don't want it. "Global?!…everything is global. [*Speaking as if he's someone else.*] Do you think I'm not educating kids? Not raising them properly? Why do they need to be globalized? Everything is global anyway."

Jacek's recounting of the disagreement raised by school heads and teachers about the implication that they read into global efforts, namely that rural schools are not doing a satisfactory job of preparing students for the world beyond their community, is a critique that opens to a much wider conversation. There is a recurring national conversation about what is to be the role of Poland in the world. That efforts to teach for GCE trigger reactions like these is understandable given the recent past, a history that warrants suspicion from any authority heralding a *new idea*. Also, as Jacek later noted, the agenda for GCE is largely determined by the national government in Warsaw, and like other reforms in a centralized system, can be framed as being imposed from above. This reaction might also be read as another turn on the same conversation around isolation and exclusivity raised in Midland and Torg. The counter that GCE has a club-like quality, the brainchild of *leftist psychos*, could be interpreted as a populist response of resistance.

The metropolitan–global connection is common in many countries. The energy to establish programs in global education often draws from large population centers where an implied rationale for learning globally is clear in the diversity of people as well as the flow of consumer goods and media through urban areas. There is, too, a dimension of this interest that flows from the rise of neoliberal discourse and practices, or the sense that in order for a country/region/city to be a global player they need to participate, indeed compete, within the global marketplace that education is becoming (Spring, 2009). Yoon Ee-Seul, for example, found that Vancouver's efforts to gain recognition as a world-class global city led to the creation of mini/quasi-public schools that compete with community schools for the highest achieving students, purposefully creating a level-up tier of students. These schools offer special programming such as university transition, gifted education, technology and science, at times framed by a global theme, all of which contributes to the making of an ostensibly "world-class education" (Yoon Ee-Seul, 2011, p. 255). These types of educational strategies abound in cities around the world as the rising tide of global economic competition has created a sense of anxiety/opportunity to refashion schools in light of these changes. Yet, the hostility that may result, while often strategically read as being anti-global parochialism, may also be an expression of concern about the redefinition and deterioration of embodied community in the current global era.

What is meant by GCE and the ways that this field intersects with learning for global economic competitiveness is an area of uncertainty that arises from the multiplicity of meanings that *global learning* evokes. Teacher concerns about ambiguity resonated throughout Poland. Olaeda, who works for the Teacher Development Center that organizes GCE efforts throughout the country on behalf of the Ministry of Education, expressed the dual-edge that teachers experience when engaging in GCE:

> I think that the challenge, at least in the previous years, is explaining to the teachers *what is global citizenship education*? Because everyone has their own vision of what it means, what it is about, they did not understand what it is and what it is not. They had their different points, so that was the challenge for at least the last two years…the schools understand global education in their own way. Sometimes it is ecological education, sometimes it's about children in Africa, but they don't see the whole picture.

That GCE is supported at the urging of the Ministry of Global Activities complicates how it will likely be received by teachers and schools. The subject and aims of GCE are decoupled from each other in this scheme, since focusing on education for development (e.g. global poverty), sustainable development and human diversity (intracultural and intercultural education) does not necessarily equate with being economically competitive globally, though this is clearly the larger aim of the Polish government in pursuing this agenda.

While sustainability, development studies/human rights and human diversity may appear quite different on the surface, there is a clear, economic rationale undergirding each of these orientations and the combination of their integration generally in Poland. The focus on global poverty points to the overarching aims of GCE in Poland. Education about global poverty and its systemic dimensions, referred to as education for development, is very much in keeping with how GCE is understood in much of western Europe (Osler & Vincent, 2002). The NGO community associated with global relief organizations often advocate for a form of global learning that brings attention to economic interdependence, the wide and growing North/South affluence gap and efforts to address economic development. The shift in mindset from being a recipient nation in the 15 years immediately following independence towards being a growing economy repositioned as a donor nation in the past decade is a substantial societal change. In short, Poland's changed status on the world stage coupled with its aspirations to be a global player deeply informs the conception of GCE being promulgated.

However, others I interviewed disagreed about the extent to which Poland's status has changed internationally; or what also might be read as hesitation or even refusal to embrace an identity of Poland as global player. As I conversed with teacher educators in a focus group in Cracow, for example, they recounted their students' disbelief about Poland's purportedly new global position. They were incredulous that the economic situation of Poland was dramatically improved and viewed this as trumped up information touted by the government in pursuit of a global agenda. As Eryka noted:

> Yesterday I had a class of students and I asked them, "Do you believe that in the last year we made a change in the human development index (HDI), that we are at the 39th position right now and that Portugal is behind us?" and they told me "No, it's not possible, that's impossible…the factors are wrong. This change isn't reflected in our life, in our personal lives." I can't believe it too, myself, because we [teacher educators] have just been to Portugal as we were having classes and they have a really good quality of life there. This change may be true for a very few number of Poles but not for the society as a whole.

Interestingly, Eryka and her students' suspicions that the economic gap is widening between wealthy and poor Poles and thus distorting aggregate wealth gains in

Poland are supported by a recent OECD study (OECD, 2008). This situation has been reproduced throughout the world in a period of rapid economic globalization as national economies grow rapidly and with them, the gap between rich and poor too grows disproportionately within those same societies. The have/have not contrast within Poland is notable as it shapes the sense of civic duty that Poles have to the wider region and the European Union while creating points of tension with locals who feel that the governing elite are out of touch with the daily reality of a challenging economic situation.

The orientation towards understanding the world in terms of economic development also suggests a way of mediating the wider discourse of economic growth. Typically the *only* rationale for GCE is to prepare students for an interdependent, economically competitive world that they will inherit. Global learning befitting the mantra "learn-to-earn" is most common in educational policy circles. Those in the NGO sector, often beholden to financial support from governmental grants, private foundations and donors, recognize that the only way to approach a funder is on their terms, thus addressing economic development typically puts them in a positive light with those with financial resources. This is not the total picture, of course, as there are other notable dynamics, such as humanitarian motives, the desire to raise funds for international relief and a view that being involved globally equates with donating money for economic relief—all problematic stances as well since they abide a donor/recipient notion of global charity as opposed to one of solidarity and shared responsibility. But since support for work in Poland largely emanates from the Ministry of Global Activities, it is not surprising to see that it aligns with the larger geopolitical agenda of the state, and indeed as Jacek noted about reactions among rural people, the elite of the country.

In line with learning for economic development is the recent prominence of Poland's educational system in international benchmark examinations. Poland has witnessed an increase in international educational rankings as a result of PISA evaluations of leading economic countries. In 2009, for example, Poland ranked 12th, 19th and 13th, respectively, in reading, mathematics and science, ahead of countries like Germany, France, the UK and the US. In 2012, Poland improved in comparison to other nations, ranking 14th (reading), 12th (math) and 9th (science) (OECD, 2013). I attended two national educators' conferences in Cracow over the course of researching this book and this achievement is frequently noted as a mark of pride among educational leaders from throughout the country in attendance. Relatedly, Poland is increasingly acting as a gateway to nations to the east and south, both in terms of its economic and social relations but also as an interlocutor between western Europe and countries such as Ukraine and Turkmenistan. Jacek explained that since Poles do not have much of a colonizing past, they are viewed with less hostility and skepticism by their neighbors to the east compared to their EU allies from the west (e.g. Germany). Thus, Poland is increasingly viewed as a conduit of grant activity for those nations to the east, particularly since the Polish economy is performing better than many others in the region.

The way in which GCE flows out of the national agenda of international relations presents a series of questions and potential problems. Teachers and school leaders are likely to see GCE efforts as part of a national agenda or plan that implicates the way teachers have been engaging students in the past. Furthermore, concerns exist around tying global education efforts too tightly to a national agenda. Global education, in its origins, viewed the international system as problematic for a number of reasons; including that *international* education presumes the predominance of nation-states while nations have perpetrated mass violence, zero-sum competition and global dislocation since their creation in the 17th century and especially during the 20th century (Anderson, 1968). This tension is compounded in the context of teacher education and development since teaching is typically bound up with national educational priorities, which too are increasingly interwoven with international educational competition (Gaudelli, 2013).

Yet, the national organization of teacher development fits logically within the existing structure organized by the Ministry of Human Development. Kornelia, who coordinates the Ministry's teacher education outreach, explained that the Teacher Development Center is organized in 32 administrative units throughout Poland, with 16 lead schools along with 16 centers for teacher development organized throughout the country. She said they adopted a systemic pilot approach, wherein lead schools would be heavily engaged in promoting GCE and that their directors and teachers are directly involved in the process. Kornelia explained that much of what teachers do is to prepare after-school or auxiliary programs to support global learning as there is little opportunity for altering the course of study that is centrally governed by what is in published textbooks. This strategy provides teachers with expanded flexibility to choose contents that are timely and salient, allows teachers to introduce widely available materials (a significant problem for countries like Poland where materials published in Polish are limited) and permits choosing media for teaching that might not be typically employed, such as documentary film production. Yet, the auxiliary space of global learning also suggests a non-essential quality of GCE as practiced there.

The Teacher Development Center noted that there was a lot of energy and interest in GCE and that they were able to leverage grants from various government agencies and larger NGOs to support teacher development initiatives.

> The most effective way to change schools is to make projects like after-school projects and new schemes. Training funding through the Ministry of Human Development for the work of consultants to promote global learning, citizenship and social competency works best. We designed a turnkey model of professional development to invite school heads to take the lead and return to their schools to train their teachers.

Poland employs an attraction model of encouraging global learning by providing funding in small grants and attracting teachers and schools rather than coercing a much larger change in a system with over 30,000 schools. Jacek noted,

> Why we're doing support that way is because the teachers have incentive to go for training because it is not their free time they are investing, it is in the official path of their career. They get points for it and they are rewarded for it. So for us this is a teaser for them to come.

Educators at the Teacher Development Center indicated that there was a choir-preaching problem among teachers interested in global education that speaks to the relative isolation of GCE within the teaching profession generally. As Kornelia of the training centers noted, teachers were involved in training for GCE but many of them would have come to do this work even without an incentive.

The challenge therefore for those committed to engaging schools in GCE is to find points of connection and synergy between content that is a higher priority, like math and science, and GCE topics. The Civic Education Curriculum Center (CECC) is an NGO that promotes education for sustainable development, media education, human rights education and global education, all included as foci within civic education. Jakub, a curriculum director with CECC, noted the tension between math/science and what might be viewed as more humanistic offerings such as GCE. Jakub noted that there is currently a strong focus on educational value-added models as assessed by tests along with a rigorous external evaluation program organized by the Ministry of Human Development. Jakub also noted that this policy orientation, one increasingly common around the world, overrides attention to GCE of a humanistic sort. He commented that CECC shifted their attention from GCE exclusively, which he described as a "niche" activity, towards a broad-based approach to school reform.

> We are currently looking for ways to integrate GCE topics [development, sustainability, diversity] strategically in textbooks and in teacher development since they are not part of the curriculum that generally gets taught in schools. We're trying to help teachers to build it in. There is not much space in the curriculum for this with the accountability imperatives like math and science and not a great deal of capacity to do this work among teachers and schools.

Flowing from his own interest in ecology and development, Jakub noted that he attended a conference of the group Developing Europeans' Engagement with the Eradication of Global Poverty (DEEEP). He compared his experiences working in an educational NGO in Poland with those of his colleagues in Denmark, Finland and Sweden working on a vision statement. He said,

> If I came home and shared this vision for global learning in Poland, I would be called a radical, leftist activist…truly! So we need to take this into account in Poland, the conservative context in which we are coming from. Take for example climate change, there is still a discussion of what is causing this problem, which would not be the case in Sweden.

Jakub expressed that while there are groups of politically left-oriented people advocating for GCE, Poland is a politically and socially conservative country, making the implementation of GCE very challenging. Rather, it makes the argument for global learning in terms of economic competition, and thus supporting math/science learning, more appealing within this political and social context.

Moving Ahead

The three cases examined in this chapter, including two teacher education programs in the US and Canada as well as the ministry/NGO sector initiative in Poland, suggest a number of insights about GCE and developing teachers. As noted in the introduction, these interrelated problems center upon issues of exclusivity/isolation, criticality/equity, and primacy/absence of practice. The first insight is related to the tension between exclusivity and isolation. This multifaceted problem derives from a desire to keep global learning distinct from everyday learning, though in so doing, creates an inner/outer dynamic. This tension was most pronounced in the two teacher education institutions in Canada and the US although there were elements of exclusivity in Poland's teacher education work as well. Global educators were aware of the irony of this situation given the close alignment of inclusiveness and diversity in GCE efforts, yet these cohort programs were exclusive and this is typical of similar efforts (UNESCO, 2014). Separating global learning from all other learning is problematic in light of expressed values since exclusivity creates a clique-like environment. This tension was noted among students and alum of Torg, the faculty at Midland as well as the advocates in the governmental and NGO sectors in Poland.

This tension mirrors the complex identity that is increasingly evident in a global age. People affiliate with many changing and diverse identities, a sense of who one is mirrored in larger social bodies. Part of what makes people feel connected are these similar and shared experiences, of which traveling globally to learn about and engage with others still remains a-typical for the majority of people. So it is not surprising that young people at a university who share having studied abroad would wish to affiliate with similar students. At least part of the rationale for segmenting GCE from other efforts, however, is based on the fact that the world is truly complex and multifaceted in ways that belie full understanding. The programmatic efforts at Midland and Torg were both geared towards orienting teacher candidates to live with complexity and recognize the impossibility of knowing fully.

GCE's exclusivity problem points to at least two interventions that educators should consider as new initiatives are developed: (1) the dissociative tendency of GCE and (2) the need to widen the circle broadly and continuously in GCE efforts. As to the first, the conceptual slippage between what is local and global is a core problem of GCE work. Setting up special programs, institutes and activities that are globally focused creates an otherness quality to the work. This categorical distinction is problematic because of the very fact that it denotes separation, and is typically focused on areas apart from the immediate concerns of local places. Thus, a dilemma for those preparing teachers for GCE is to maintain healthy attention to those immediate concerns while connecting these issues or concerns meaningfully to global dimensions so as not to disassociate but synthesize.

Comingling as opposed to disassociating as a strategy for GCE suggests an even more delicate issue: widening the circle of GCE. There is a certain understanding among global educators that presumes that *"eventually, they will all come around."* While I agree to a large extent that education is moving towards being more globally informed and connected, I disagree that we should wait for it to occur. So it's less a matter of if education will become more global, as that transition is already well under way, but rather which version of globally oriented schools will emerge. The risk of promoting GCE to be practised, theorized and reworked in an expanding variety of contexts is that it may lose its fidelity, which is no small matter among those who feel wedded to very particular, and often over-prescribed, interpretations of what GCE ought to be.

The trouble here lies in a core, implicit notion in GCE claiming that it is a specialization rather than imagining it as a generalization. Much of the conversation about what it means to be a global citizen, for example, presumes a degree of specialized knowledge—from global political structures to economic institutions to social and cultural relations. But as a generalization, GCE implies a way of being in the world that, simply put, "opens people's eyes and minds to the realities of the world" (O'Loughlin & Wegimont, 2002, p. 13). The specialist may scoff at these generalizations as being too simplistic though I would suggest that this way of opening up the field of GCE is a productive direction for future efforts. A good case can be made, for example, that all teacher education students at Midland and Torg should be enrolled in their respective global cohorts as these are simply effective, thoughtful and meaningful ways of being a teacher today, regardless of the way it is labeled. To segment off GCE in teacher education belies the very conceptual foundation of GCE—of the interdependence of our being, the systems into which we are engaged and the need for a shared commitment to improving our collective situation in a compromised biosphere. In those senses, GCE is remarkably simple.

The second insight is drawn from the domain of being critical about GCE and its relative attention to issues of global equity. Teacher educators, particularly among those in Canada and to a lesser degree in the US, interpreted GCE as necessarily including knowledge of global inequities, how those manifest locally while connecting beyond, and what can be done to address those issues. Interestingly, this was less of a concern in Poland though still present in the focus on development education, which may speak to the relatively new global position of Poland as a donor nation or perhaps a hesitancy among Poles to view themselves as part of the North. Educators shared a concern that economically poor, urban and rural people in the global North are frequently omitted from conversations about GCE. Educators were very sensitive to this omission and interpreted their work as reaching out beyond a presumed typical audience for GCE—white, middle- to upper-middle-income students whose families work internationally and value such pursuits—towards students who are typically left out of GCE learning. Developing critical sensitivity to inequities, at home and globally, has emerged as an increasingly salient dimension of GCE.

Two decades ago there was an ongoing squabble in the US between the value of learning globally and multiculturally, as if the fields ought to be mutually exclusive. Global education has a legacy of being associated with diplomatic education, intended solely for those who were likely to live in countries outside of their origin and typically of people with financial means to do so (Gaudelli & Wylie, 2012). This lineage contributed to some degree to the initial separation of global and multicultural discourses, though there is increasing evidence in scholarship and practice that the fields are being comingled (Banks, 2008). The interactivity of these discourses has much to do with the recognition by global educators that inherent to their field are concerns about global inequities, growing wealth disparities and the deep impact of frivolous consumption on the biosphere. Furthermore, for multicultural and social justice educators, a growing awareness that injustices are not nationally bound nor historically disconnected but far-reaching and themselves interdependent has led to an outward turn (Andreotti, 2010; Subedi, 2010).

The internal dynamic at Torg around the critique of *Water for All* is a prime illustration of how problematic addressing equity can be. The faculty wished to dually engage the project, both as an illustration of youth engagement and also as a point of critical inflection about how the positionality of being from the North perpetuates privilege in donor–recipient relationships. They were, in effect, raising the question of who benefits from aid. And, Torg faculty wrestled with the question of how one critiques such programs without sapping the goodwill and enthusiasm of young people in the global North who may lack the patience for solutions that require a much wider, systemic grasp of issues than donations alone can ever accomplish. These problems are not easily resolved and may push against my argument for widening the circle of GCE. Does widening the circle necessarily invite superficial engagement in the world?

The confounding dimensions here are what I would characterize as a culture of instantaneousness and the phenomena of the spectacle. As the world has grown increasingly interconnected, time is collapsing and increasingly commodified. This is not new to the most recent global age but endemic throughout human development, particularly in the industrial era that began marking time with greater precision for economic purposes, like trade. The results are all too familiar as the incessant rush of a now-culture has created a hyper-environment that can lead to exhaustion. One should note that most youth under the age of 25 have not experienced a slower world such that the *need for speed*—in interactions, activity, engagement, learning—can be all consuming. If there are no quick fixes to long-standing problems of social exclusion, growing inequality and a beleaguered environment, then it requires citizens prepared and patient for long-term changes not realized through inspiring, one-day conferences or quick visits to a country. This point of tension is one that remains a strong undercurrent, perhaps even an undertow, in the socially engaged GCE that one might envision for teachers and students to create.

A second social dynamic at work in preparing teachers to develop youth for civic engagement is living in an age of spectacle. Guy Debord offered social analysis of spectacle and how it prefers appearance over reality and emerged as a function of late capitalism's fixation on image, commodification and consumption. As Debord notes:

> The spectacle manifests itself as an enormous positivity, out of reach and beyond dispute. All it says is: "Everything that appears is good; whatever is good will appear." The attitude that it demands in principle is the same passive acceptance that it has already secured by means of its seeming incontrovertibility, and indeed by its monopolization of the realm of appearances.
> (Debord, 1966/2000, stanza 12)

The desire for events, happenings, moments of fullness or what Debord has called "fully equipped blocks of times" (stanza 152) contributes to this sense of the spectacle. This social attribute is related to a perpetually fast society, as people move incessantly from one moment of ostensibly full living to another and another, a chaining of experience that devalues ordinary time, everyday existence as being simply time to be gotten through, ever in pursuit of the next event.

An orientation towards learning that draws on high-profile events or spectacle is an exasperating dimension of the contemporary scene in education, one that is counter-productive to learning, actually, as the seemingly fallow periods of less activity can give the mind a chance to work out what has been experienced (Gaudelli, 2016; Gaudelli & Laverty, 2015). Also, the slow pace of change can be symbolized in bold events that showcase change-becoming but what happens behind the scenes, away from the spotlights and in the routines of activities in institutions. The *hard-to-witness* changes are the foundation for much of what we might momentarily see as change, or that which garners the spotlight of a big event. Critique, critical examination, asking questions and thinking twice, or revisiting an issue at a later point, all suggest an inefficiency that is not befitting a social moment of spectacle.

So given this social context, reorienting teacher education for GCE around issues of critique towards social justice is a desirable path. Yet, the mediating social context of speed and spectacle needs to be made explicit by educators working in this space, a counter-practice of sorts given the sweeping tide of a wider culture. Furthermore, the efforts of Torg faculty are admirable in a sense though they are countering a much more powerful social flow that begs the seemingly simple question: "How can *Water for All* be bad if so many people think that it's good, wrapped in the spectacle that it is?" This tautological way of thinking about the world, or that it must be right if so many believe it to be right, is a significant challenge for GCE programs wishing to swim upstream against the well-worn grooves of North/South donor/charity.

The last insight that I draw from these teacher education cases for GCE is the need for primacy amid a relative absence of practice. GCE is still relatively rare in schools with episodic programs offered piecemeal as compared to sweeping, comprehensive and systemic implementation. The same cannot be said, however, about how globalization has shaped the global playing field upon which education is increasingly understood (Darling-Hammond, 2010). The main point of difference between these two types of global education is the latter's focus on education as a preparation for global economic competition and the former's orientation towards promoting peace, diversity, justice and sustainability, or a humanistic foundation. Neither the economic rationale nor what I offer as a humanistic rationale for global learning is mutually exclusive. But the primacy of the economic rationale for global learning often leads to a diminution of humanistic orientations as economic dimensions of these foci are less obvious, such as human rights and addressing global injustices, or in fact contrary to the continued expansion of development in a Western frame.

Global learning, particularly in the second decade of the 21st century, has come to be paired with an economic imperative to change schools and teachers to confront the flat-world of a single market, governed by rapacious competition. The US Council for Economic Development, for example, articulates this stance plainly:

> To compete successfully in the global marketplace, US-based multinationals as well as small businesses must market products to customers around the globe and work effectively with foreign employees and business partners. Our firms increasingly need employees with knowledge of foreign languages and cultures.
>
> (Development, 2006, pp. 1–2)

This way of thinking about the world, and therefore thinking about preparing teachers, is difficult to reconcile with the pressing needs for a new global ethics that is not rooted solely in economic development (see Singer, 2002). Also, the environmental costs of more of a *business-as-usual approach* seem not to take into account the stark realities that confront humanity in the 21st century, not the least of which is a warming atmosphere and all the social dislocation likely to accompany this shift.

The whole of this discussion about teacher education for GCE in the US, Canada and Poland ought to be understood within the wider view of the policy context for educational reform and teacher education reform generally. The extraordinary attention given to how teacher education is being reformed to address globalization far outweighs teacher education efforts around social justice, peace, human rights and environmental sustainability (Darling-Hammond, 2010). The loose use of *global* and *international* in education discourse is abundant such that one is compelled to ask, "How do you mean that?" when it is raised. As Zygmunt Bauman explains, "All vogue words tend to share a similar fate: the more experiences they tend to make transparent, the more they themselves become opaque. The more numerous are the orthodox truths they elbow out and supplant, the faster they turn into no-questions-asked canons" (Bauman, 1998, p. 1). I once gave a talk in North Carolina about global education and its looseness was most evident. The first two speakers, educational officials from the state and the host university, spoke about global learning in decidedly economic terms. At my opportunity to talk about global education, I started by saying, "and now for something completely different!"

In retrospect I think my comment was in error, since the economic and humanistic orientations towards global learning are not opposed necessarily. As there are material conditions to being human so is there a need to earn to live adequately. And too, as there are economic costs to avoiding injustice, engaging in mass violence, denying or failing to uphold the rights of others and in ignoring environmental concerns, a humanistic orientation to global learning is not cleaved off from an economic one. The challenge is to encourage discourse that is more inclusive, diverse and expansive about GCE such that these tradeoffs cannot be ignored in siloed conversations.

7

INSIGHTS FOR PRACTICE AND A HABIT OF EVERYDAY TRANSCENDENCE

Looking back over the GCE cases, certain patterns emerge that deserve the attention of educators in many venues: those teaching in P-12 classrooms, teacher educators and educators in postsecondary contexts, professional development leaders, curriculum developers, those working in nonprofit/after-school programming sectors as well as policymakers interested in GCE. I offer these insights not as rules-to-follow but as tools-to-think with, in the development of learning opportunities for those inheriting a troubled yet awesome world. I have organized the patterns from those of immediate concern to GCE educators to those that have broader applicability to all interested in the nature of education. These heuristics will be more or less relatable to new situations depending on the contours and contexts where they might be relocated which is ultimately in the interpretive domain of educators. I briefly discuss each heuristic with regard to the cases from which they are drawn and the ways in which they can give volition and orientation to GCE practices. The last of these recommendations is one that subsumes all of the other patterns and provides an ending point for the book around developing a habit of thought around *everyday transcendence*.

1. Inclusion of Historically Marginalized Populations in GCE and the North/South World Situation

GCE programs examined herein highlight the learning of historically marginalized populations, including African American and Latino secondary students in two New York City learning venues, slum dwellers in Mumbai, students at Marjoon in Bangkok, native Hawaiian postsecondary students along with the preparation of teachers in Ontario to educate urban students informed by GCE.

This is a welcome change in the field, one that has a long history of being the sole domain of globally mobile families of economic means. I am not suggesting that GCE programs are typically enacted with students who are relatively disempowered within their social contexts since that would misrepresent the field of GCE practice. Rather, my purposeful selection of cases like these is meant to highlight the possibilities of working in and about such contexts as well as the way that GCE has shifted from an elite-oriented education to a broad-scale program. GCE is even more vital to students at the economic margins of society since those students are less likely to have the ability to insulate themselves from adverse conditions of living in a hyper-networked era of fast capitalism that disproportionally harms people at the economic margins. If any child can be said to be in need of knowledge, skills and dispositions about how the world is being reconfigured in a global era, then it would be slum dwellers in Mumbai, youth in Bangkok, indigenous populations such as native Hawaiians and urban students in Ontario along with their hundreds of millions of peers the world over.

Privileging the education of those at the economic margins with opportunities for thinking and doing related to issues of our global inheritance of class-divided societies is paramount to meaningful GCE. Attention to deep patterns of an imperial past that continues to cast a long shadow on how education categorizes, subjugates and divides the world among curriculum developers and educational material producers is vitally important (Willinsky, 1998). Yet, undoing a deep-seated mindset particularly in the North that even talking about GCE summons a typical audience—Northern/Western, European/North American/Asian, wealthy/privileged—is a significant challenge, one that can only be resolved by pushing the deep and growing inequalities to the fore of the discussion (MacDonald, 2013). I do not recommend this as a tool for its symbolic value, as that reeks of the sort of window dressing of including historically marginalized people at conferences simply to say they are in attendance to validate the representative aura of the conference (Visvanathan, 1997). Rather, like Darpali's efforts to have students study the excesses of globalization in the issue of sex trafficking/trade, the intention should be to educate reflexively and discursively towards undoing these modes of oppression; developing a critical read of the world they inhabit that leads people to act.

This type of pedagogical practice—one that implicates students into the social dimensions of being at many turns—creates a certain tension. Inviting people who might otherwise not recognize a problem out of their insulated realities into the full throes of trying to grasp the excesses and deformities of contemporary globalization, while helping those who already know of a problem, such as slum dwellers, with a way of naming and knowing in a broader, socially intelligible way can create anxiety. Pedagogically this works against the tendency to categorize or curate the world in ways that reinforce a belief in the lifestyles of the North as the pinnacle of human achievement *qua* modernity while compelling people to leave their isolation and experience a wider, if discomforting, world.

GCE ought to highlight the vast global inequalities that rapid economic globalization has exacerbated, working against an otherwise detached way of treating poverty and dislocation particular to the contemporary global era. The stunning images of the collapsed clothing factory in Dhaka, Bangladesh in April 2013, where 1,129 were killed and 2,500 sustained injuries, garnered worldwide attention in the immediacy of the events and are an illustration of how this highlighting might occur ("Savar Building Collapse"). Subsequent news reports, though, failed to demonstrate a strong link between demand for low-priced clothing at shopping outlets (e.g. H&M and Walmart) and race-to-the-bottom conditions in factories (e.g. those in Bangladesh.) Horrible events like this are generally not what people have in mind when they invoke being global, evidence of how *global deflection* is built into normal conversation about what the term connotes. GCE educators must be mindful of this tendency to avoid or deflect and the absences that such deflections create.

GCE in this formulation requires highlighting positionality and how one's location in the world determines how one sees and participates. I often wonder how some journalists and academics adopt such a rosy-colored way of seeing how the world is being reconstituted by globalization. This type of cheerleading is difficult to reconcile when the signs of dislocation and turmoil are starkly evident. My assumption is that those who abide the triumphal globalization script, though substantially quieted by the financial meltdown of 2008 and subsequent years, choose to ignore how they are positioned in the world. Sampling culinary delights from far afield in a luxury seven-star hotel having just arrived refreshed from premier-class travel on a brand new aircraft is literally a different world than claiming to have access to fresh water in a slum since it is available for two hours per day. And while this positioning is not solely prefigured by class, as ethnicity, race, gender, gender orientation and sexual orientation factor in intersectionally, the failure of GCE to explore class stratification and economic dislocation in the world we inherit is a critical, indeed intolerable, oversight. Yet, there seems to be an emerging consensus around poverty as the recently released Sustainable Development Goal 2015–30 makes "eradicating poverty everywhere" Goal 1. This is an essential priority for the world and therefore a critical element of GCE.

2. Safeguarding Against Othering Practices

To venture into studying and acting in a deeply inequitable world can potentially lead to othering the same people and situations that one is aiming to understand. But to meaningfully engage in GCE, which presumes knowing and doing in a way that is globally resonant, requires that this venture be undertaken. The *pitiful other* problem encountered in Canada is instructive about this dilemma. As ICHRP staff indicated, this was the default setting for students and teachers in studying issues such as poverty, waste disposal, access to clean water and infectious diseases.

Faculty at Torg in Canada also managed this charitable impulse as they engaged their students in a critical examination of the widely popular global youth social action project, *Water for All*. Repositioning students to think about how they can work in solidarity and through commonality, rather than for charity and out of pity, is especially challenging.

One technique that helps to address an othering stance is to examine issues of equivalency, or to seek out comparable situations that students already encounter. The Elmwood Elementary teachers affiliated with Midland University's GCC, for example, teaching their students about a practice in Mali of placing a lost tooth under a gourd to receive a chicken, while a banal illustration, makes a poignant example of cultural context that seeks strong parallels in the other and self. Similarly, in Midland's teacher education course wherein students were reanimating in miniature the othering dynamic of the university as a whole, Lydia and Allison troubled the students in the global cohort with their observation and implicated teaching and learning through this episode. The ways of challenging otherness may not always be so seemingly readymade for comparison as these two episodes suggest, and yet the heuristic indicates how to develop educational programming that does not distance the acts of others as radically different but rather as forms of cultural adaptation that beckon further investigation.

As a secondary teacher, I recall bringing my students at the invitation of an Imam to a mosque for a Friday call to prayer. We were participant-observers in the prayer, seated in the rear of the mosque. While we were only 30 kilometers from our high school, the palpable sense that we were elsewhere resounded throughout this experience. This visit represented a point of discomfort for students since they had to dress differently than they would for school for the visit. I was always concerned about the way that the mosque visit positioned us as observers if not handled properly. Upon debriefing the fieldtrip with students, however, many would remark on the basic similarity they experienced in this setting, one that was compatible with their own religious participation rather than what it appeared on its exterior, as fundamentally different. This same experience could have been highly inappropriate if my co-teacher and I framed it as a voyeuristic visit with an exotic group of others. Rather, we safeguarded against this in a way that allowed our students to see the basic similarity of faith while developing an inkling of understanding of the differences also present.

But this illustration draws from the knowing end of the GCE spectrum rather than the action end, the latter being degrees more difficult with respect to sensitivity issues. As to this, the need to bring young people into communication and relationship with those whom they aim to assist is of utmost importance. The youth of the Darpali program, for example, learned about issues from the intersection of their personal experience and the explanation of fellow residents, giving them insights about how the sex trade shapes Mumbai and their community. Or similarly, the faculty of New Kualani building into their global sustainability courses a community-informed viewpoint addresses the same need. A way to simplify this heuristic is to always assume that if there is a social problem in a community or region, there are already existing efforts to address those problems. Then the task of GCE educators and students/agents is to identify these groups, communicate about the nature of the problem and act in solidarity with them to address it rather than to presume to act on their behalf.

3. Development of Space for Intersectionality and Hybridity of Identity to Flourish

GCE invites a discussion of identity, or what it means to belong to and/or affiliate with a social group. GCE may also advocate the emergence of a new identity, of being a *global citizen*. There is evidence to suggest that students, when confronted with the idea of what it means to be a global citizen, reconfigure without jettisoning other identities seeking a way to think of themselves as multiple rather than singular (Myers et al., 2015). This finding suggests that there is a degree of plasticity to civic identity, one that can be nurtured actively through experiences that expand people's thinking about themselves. An illustration of this from the cases appears in the comparison of the global magnet school in New York City and the elementary through postsecondary school in Bangkok. These cases contrasted rather sharply in that students in the GEA of New York were largely interacting superficially around well-established identity categories, such as being from a particular borough, practicing a religion or speaking a language other than English. Educators at GEA frequently missed opportunities to help students think more deeply, connectedly and discursively about these social categories as they were treated as solids rather than fluids. In comparison, the focus in Marjoon in Bangkok was away from the social categories of the West and towards a deeper understanding of oneself that can be located in one's thoughts, actions and inner-self, excavated through the practice of ongoing meditation. Yet, an internalized way of seeking identity can undermine the social necessity of group identification that can spur needed social action to redress discrimination.

This contrast, one that speaks to an East–West difference in how identity is theorized, suggests a possible hybrid approach around identity development. Rather than positing identity as ascribed through social category, or as solely a journey within, GCE that invites students to examine intersectionality in their own lives may move in a discursive direction. The advantage of intersectionality is that it does not presuppose social groups as categorically determinant but suggests that how one belongs to a group is always contingent on the many other categories that a person simultaneously is. Germinating awareness of this can also move students to a greater awareness of how their perceptions of what is socially diffused about their identities, or in light of Steele's (2010) stereotype threat research, can work to inoculate them against facilely "taking in" social scripts about who they are because of a given identity.

Recognizing the temporal dimension, or how a sense of self is determined in various identity iterations but also by the temporal and spatial context that surrounds what it means to be of particular social groups, is an important dimension of this work. Identity understood this way is not completely untethered from some characteristics of a person, while also not being over-determined by the same. Multiplicity, then, creates space for new identities to emerge, such as thinking of oneself as a global citizen and learning, being and acting in the world with that piece of understanding about oneself. Making space for identity work, a crucial element of GCE, may allow for fledgling notions of being a global citizen to take shape in a manner not adjunct but integral to the unfolding of who one is in space and time.

4. Deploying Mediation Pragmatically While Recognizing the Limits of All Forms of Mediation

The contemporary global era emerged with the expansion of mediation. The media age is an apt description of the past three decades such that GCE and digital technology are often comingled in educational programming. The sustainability chapter, for example, illustrates two uses of educational technology/media: namely the use of *Second Life* in NYC and an online teacher education course about sustainability and early childhood education. In both cases, the digital tools of mediation helped to facilitate interactions over distance, in keeping with the global value of building interconnections. The contrast of these cases points to a rub in digital technology, however, or that the technology itself is a means of distribution while also being a content. Mediation in this sense is interchangeably content and form, one that does not replace embodied interactions with digital ones but can lead to mutually enhancing interactions between these two spheres.

There is reason to proceed with caution when using tools of mediation in education so that programs are not mindlessly developed around and for gadgets. And educators would also be wise to trouble the mediation that occurs within seemingly unmediated spaces, such as face-to-face conversations in a meeting, or classroom conversations that occur in real time, or any of our daily interactions that appear as unmediated but are indeed mediated by so many factors. Social interactions are mediated by the context in which they occur, the participants that engage them, the language that is used to communicate and through any number of other forms of "media" in the broadest sense of this term. So while there is a sound, pragmatic reason for employing mediation in digital and online fashion to bridge the gap of time/space differences, these interactions are not a magical cure-all to address extant problems of any interaction. One tremendous value afforded through the rise of digital mediation is the way in which it casts doubt on what it means to participate, to engage, indeed to learn, at a distance, making more evident the "space," "people" or "contents" of interaction that otherwise recede into a normative context. This same doubt, however, should be cast on face-to-face classrooms or community-based interactions as well, since these are mediated differently, but mediated nonetheless, which allows for divergent interpretations of the various texts in flow.

The flow of texts around the world has indeed created many diverse opportunities to learn and to act as a global citizen, ones that educators ought to fully embrace in their wide and discordant reach. Appadurai (2013) describes the current media/text situation as one that is "the relationship between the forms of circulation and the circulation of forms" (p. 64). The forms of circulation are best thought of as the circuitry that operates global text flows, such as the internet and how media has filled this space. But in this process of circulation, the forms or contents are essential components, as they are the stuff that is being downloaded, read, processed, refashioned and reimagined in the context of divergent locales that themselves become nodes of redistribution. Examples of global text flow are seemingly endless, from the rise of legal documents (a circulation of form) in the discourse of human rights (a form of circulation) to the rise of feature-length films (a circulation of form) as a vehicle for pervasive narratives (a form of circulation). But as Appadurai notes, these flows do not happen in unimpeded ways, but ironically create eddies and obstacles that redirect and block their continuation, such as when ISIS employs social media to grow a revanchist regime. The surprise regarding ISIS's deployment of media is evidence of the continued belief that the tools are good when in fact they represent a comingled presence of contents and forms, a persistent condition that deserves the full recognition of GCE educators.

5.   Balancing Exclusivity and Inclusivity in Participation of GCE

GCE suffers from a series of exclusivity problems. First, as examined in the first heuristic, is the tendency to reserve global learning for elites on the misguided assumption that "global leaders" can be identified by dint of their birth. There is growing awareness within GCE to address this shortcoming as the interplay of this type of educational practice and matters of educational equity intersect. The second exclusivity problem is the tendency to isolate and make global learning a pleasant addition (Mundy & Manion, 2008). This issue arose in the GCE cases examined herein, specifically in the GCC of Midland and Torg. This area of exclusion is due in part to those outside GCE who do not see the point of learning about the world they inhabit or have not experienced being an other or being taken out of their comfort zone.

Flipping the equation are those inside the discourse in some manner, though my conception of who would be sympathetic if not fully engaged is outlined in the range of meanings of what constitutes *global education* (see Chapter 2). These insiders have often fashioned an identity around their *global* orientation, see themselves as part of something larger and often derive benefits from being the global person within their institutions or in their communities. Their voice is one recognized for expertise in global affairs, perhaps since they are multilingual, lived and worked outside their home country, or engaged in partnerships with institutions in other parts of the world. There is a certain cache that comes with this institutional positioning and therefore it is in the interest of these insiders to maintain this status.

This dynamic, both inside and outside global discourse and practices, is highly problematic. For the insider, the fidelity test is one that undoes otherwise good beginnings that can eventually lead to meaningful efforts. The field has long lamented, for example—and with good reason for doing so—the superficial "foods, festivals and fairs" approaches to global learning. Yet, in dismissing these first steps, insiders have unintentionally thwarted people's impulse to learn beyond themselves for fear of being criticized for not doing it properly. This has created an ironic us/them dynamic that only serves to isolate GCE and related efforts from educational primacy. I am not suggesting that global learning or GCE should be an "anything goes" affair since some surface efforts can be harmful to the larger aims of the work (Pike, 2013). But I do believe that a rigid fidelity test as to what does and does not constitute global learning is an error that only serves to isolate GCE from necessary first steps on the part of those who might otherwise become engaged.

The recent attention surrounding the Global Poverty Project and the Global Citizen Project is a good illustration of the popularization of the movement. The projects are organized around the UN Sustainability Goals, 2015–30 and leverage media personalities, famous musicians, political celebrities and spectacle events like the recent concert in NYC's Central Park to raise awareness about the goals and subsequent campaign. While these sorts of events may not create depth of thinking and inquiry around perplexing global problems, there is something to be said for the energy and attention that they help to focus.

GCE is a remarkably broad field of discourse and practice such that no single program will ever rise to the level of comprehensively addressing all reasonable contents. Not unlike the conundrum experienced by Torg faculty over the *Water for All* campaign, the feel-good effort that some wished to upend while others saw a potentially useful beginning point, one that could reorient away from charity and towards acting in solidarity over time, GCE needs similar bearings. In this sense I am an avowed pragmatist, and therefore an incrementalist, who would prefer some change rather than none remaining mindful that the desire for the ideal situation ought not foil efforts towards the good.

6. Planning for Sustainability of Programmatic Efforts

GCE, as for most suffixed educations, can ebb and flow in a faddish manner. Indeed, the fad-orientation of education is among its most consistent historical characteristics (Tyack & Cuban, 1997). Those involved in developing an educational initiative like the many presented herein would be wise to develop plans to make the effort sustainable when the inevitable shifts occur while thinking about how the work can morph into a second or third act beyond the original one. In the relatively short four-year period of this book's development, two of the examples are completely sunsetted (e.g. early childhood education course in Hawaii) or significantly altered (e.g. CRP in Canada). In all of the others, the programs remain in place but there have been alterations, including new staff, foci and venues for the work.

GCE will likely grow in importance in the years ahead despite the rise and fall of efforts within particular institutions and among certain regions of the world. The significant challenges the world confronts in the next 50 to 100 years, especially global warming and its many ancillary harms, will require a sustained effort in education that addresses shared problems. The unending chase for the *next-best-thing* in education, a pattern that mirrors consumption habits in market economies, can lead to reform exhaustion and a feeling of being overwhelmed among educators. The ensuing dynamic to close one's classroom door, or from a larger perspective a school leader's choice to close the schoolhouse gate despite all that's happening around, is readily witnessed in contemporary schools. Yet, the era of connectedness and networked interactivity makes this response increasingly impracticable and beckons a new openness on the part of teachers and students, educators and learners.

One way to build sustainability in a GCE program is to encourage educators to witness their lives and those of their schools as interdependent with the wider world. Schools, despite a parochial tendency to focus on the immediate situation and environment, are increasingly tied into networks. As pointed out in Chapter 2, policymakers are now tightly coupling school performance and economic growth, however misguided that way of thinking may be, such that the performance of schools is directly linked to global comparisons of effectiveness and competitiveness (Gaudelli, 2013; Spring, 2009). When schools are understood in this manner and educators, students and parents are engaged in conversations of how these macro forces are shaping their immediate surroundings, the tendency to think the global as a passing fancy is likely to dissipate. Globalization is a condition of how the world operates and education is deeply implicated in those operations, such that the stance of being non-involved is not a realistic option.

The close-the-classroom-door/schoolhouse-gate mentality is not unlike *global deflection* that focuses on situations far away rather than problems nearby. The tragedy of certain global conditions, from the rise of fundamentalisms, degrading labor conditions to the specter of a warming planet due to overconsumption of fossil fuels, may be a source for the unsustainability of GCE programs. The learning may be too confounding, overwhelming or generative of hopelessness that it turns people off just at the moment when they need to be more tuned in. Global problems like those represented herein are not likely to resolve themselves, regardless of humanity's willful denial of them. GCE educators, then, would be wise to build into their programmatic efforts more plasticity and modularity. Like an aircraft whose wings are designed to bend many degrees off center in order that they not snap in extreme weather conditions, GCE programming needs more flexibility so that changes in the wider field of education do not upend otherwise promising efforts. This type of forward thinking is far from easy to achieve since predicting what might come next is impossible, particularly as the time horizon expands. But what-if contingency planning would go a long way to insure that otherwise strong educational programming not be moth-balled due to a sudden change in the educational landscape.

7. Incorporating a Habit of Everyday Transcendence in GCE

I grew up in a time in the US when it was very common for people to use highways as garbage pails. I can vividly recall my dad driving, rolling down the window and tossing out some piece of trash. I probably did the same but I cannot recall doing so, perhaps an illustration of our tendency to selectively remember those elements of our biographies that neatly fit with our current selves. Even recounting this, now nearly five decades later, is a source of embarrassment. But it happened and I can feel the slippage of time in the fact that such behavior, while unfortunately not unheard of today, is remarkably less common. What changed? There was an iconic TV commercial that began broadcast in 1971 known as the "Crying Indian" commercial. It depicted an apparently Native American man (Iron Eyes Cody, an actor who portrayed Native Americans but was himself of Italian/Sicilian lineage) paddling a canoe in a picturesque stream that spills into a dirty harbor with cargo ships, factories and soot. He pulls the canoe ashore, walks next to a crowded highway when a passer-by rolls down his window and throws trash at his feet, while then looking into the camera as a tear rolls down his face. The ad would be considered hokey in the contemporary context but it was very effective, along with a number of other public service announcements that echoed and created greater environmental consciousness generally, specifically changing attitudes about littering and recycling.

The gradual change in littering behavior speaks to the shift that I believe is needed with respect to global awareness, what I am calling a *habit of everyday transcendence*. First with regard to habit, I employ the term in the spirit of Dewey, who attempted to redefine this common term, as was his approach generally, towards a heightened level of refinement and understanding. Habit for Dewey was not mere repetition absent thought, but rather a way of being in the world that is aim oriented. A teacher who routinely gives a test on Friday or requires a monthly essay or regularly groups students to read a document may not be in possession of habit in Dewey's sense. Their behaviors may originate from an idea they picked up from a colleague or through a professional network, the rationale and mindfulness of the act long disassociated from the act itself. In this sense, it is a habit for Dewey (1902/1990) in the typical and thoughtless sense of its meaning, a behavior that rather than being possessed by a teacher indeed possesses her. "Habit in any act is a sort of routine or groove in which the mind works. It marks a channel in which the activity goes on almost unconsciously or automatically" (p. 299).

The aim of a habit, or that attempt to resolve a problem such as opening a door in a particular way or solving a quadratic equation, is initiated by the aim whose success is achieved at first by reasoned chance and increasingly by plan and coordination. Habits are not mere repetition but are success-oriented behaviors that seek an aim. In this sense habit accompanies a conscious and active awareness of what one is trying to do. Dewey distinguishes between the degree of attentiveness or focus brought to that aim as a qualifying characteristic of what makes an aim solidify into an expressed habit. He describes getting "white heat" attention on the aim such that the habituation of a thoughtful act will result more quickly (Dewey, 1902/1990, p. 302). The repetition of habit, in Dewey's sense of the term, ought not be a mindless one since every new context and situation demands an attention to small adjustments and subtle recalibrations required to fit a way of doing and thinking out of the abstraction of one's past experiences into the immediacy of a present circumstance.

The habit that GCE aims to encourage is simply mindfulness about how the world is present in all material and relational interactions, a habitual way of thinking that actively works away from the way we tend to see ourselves in the world and towards the way that we need to perceive ourselves: from isolated to integrated, disconnected to interconnected and separate to inseparable. A simple illustration from physics can help to illustrate this in a somewhat profound manner. Since matter cannot be created or destroyed, each of us is constituted by matter that has always been on the Earth, simply recycled and reorganized over eons to make one the person that they are. And the same is true that upon the death of a person, they eventually disintegrate to return matter to the cycle. The organization of distinct organisms such as people offers an illusory sense of being distinct, perhaps alien, from the biosphere, each other and all that came before. But taking from this simple fact, we can and ought to make a habit of thinking of ourselves as metabolized from the flora, fauna, minerals and water of the planet to which we ultimately return.

This way of thinking, mind-bogglingly complex and banal in other ways, is the habit that I have in mind. How does one develop such a transcendent habit of thought in the presence of an everyday existence characterized by routines? This is perhaps more of a puzzle than most are willing to admit. I used to think that exposing students to an episode of interconnectivity—such as having them trace the origins of a simple school item such as a backpack or lunch-bag—would then diffuse and germinate in their thinking generally. Generally it did not. In some ways I still believe in this way of thinking as I teach courses in GCE both in face-to-face and online environments, with current and soon-to-be educators from a variety of places, while using this very technique to explore the fundamental interdependence of being. Yet, I know that this perpetual sense of interconnectivity is an insight I cannot keep ever-present in my mind despite a long-standing commitment to being a global educator.

I locate the crux of habitualizing such thinking as a challenge that traipses along the boundary of *everyday transcendence*. What I mean by the phrase *everyday transcendence* is a dual and discursive sense of how the transcendent arrives in the same container as the everyday, or that there is a co-presence of mundane and sublime in all things. A method for developing insights of co-presence is through estrangement, a process that sits at the core of everyday theory (Highmore, 2002). As Henri Lefebvre notes:

> Of course details retain their brutal reality; this wheelbarrow is still creaky and cumbersome, this peasant's life is still harsh and that worker's life is still dull and joyless. Things have not been transfigured and we do not get carried away by mystical joy. And yet our consciousness of these things becomes transformed and loses its triviality, its banality, since in each thing we see more than itself—something else *which is there* in everyday objects, not an abstract lining but something enfolded within which hitherto we have been unable to see.
>
> (Lefebvre, 2014/1958, p. 154)

Taking a commonplace item and considering its profundity is a process of estrangement, of noticing what is physically present but often overlooked or taken for granted, a way of thinking that is subtext to the classroom activity of exploring how materials are aggregated and distributed in the world. The commonality of the object coupled with the heightened awareness of its rare qualities is a way of juxtaposing *taken-for-grantedness* and exceptionality, which are present in literally every thing.

Everyday, mundane objects can give young people an enriched sense of what the global means in their lives and how they are interconnected to all that surrounds them, immediately, more distantly and even remotely. The area where one lives, the yard of a home, lobby of a building, center of a village or places that surround a school all have possibilities that point to locales and times beyond the immediate objects. Our yard, for example, has a square stone deeply buried in the front corner that borders intersecting roads. We learned from the local mail carrier that these were mileage stones that denoted the point at which parcels cost an additional half-cent to reach. And we grow tomatoes in the summer, connecting our very small and limited experience of crop raising with vast systems of hydrology, photosynthesis and food production on the planet. The examples that can be drawn are numerous but reframing everyday objects as those which point in myriad directions outwards and to multiple points of contact beyond themselves suggests limitless opportunities to see the connectedness of all that we encounter in the everyday.

As I am writing this paragraph, I glance at a pencil. The pencil represents a technology of communication although we rarely think of it in this manner. As such it is quite an amazing tool as it once provided easy codification of thought that extended well beyond the momentary. The pencil surely wowed initial users with its ease of use, portability and utility compared to a printing press, not unlike how people perceive digital devices today. When one is able to focus attention, white hot in Dewey's words, on a pencil, one can derive many questions that speak to its transcendent qualities along with its mundane nature. Where was this pencil made? How did I get it? How is it like or unlike other writing instruments? Why did forms of writing instruments change over time? What texts do we read today that were formed by these instruments? How does the absence of tools that create such texts illustrate the erasure of process from a product-oriented culture? How did pencils emerge from England and Germany around the 16th century and why then? Where was this particular pencil made and what are its components? And on and on. The point (if you'll forgive the pun) is that the most mundane of elements in the world have rippling significance that stretches across time and space and speaks to the transcendent possibilities present all around us and in the simplest of things.

Social science of the 20th century has had a particularly strong orientation towards the everyday as it was there that studies would be conducted—in regular classrooms, ordinary clinics, run-of-the-mill offices and the like—to analyze and theorize the goings-on of modern life. Anthropology as a field, for example, emerges concomitantly with industrial capitalism as a means of relocating the mystery of daily living in the lives of "exotic others." Anthropology's focus on daily life, particularly as behaviors and rituals point to something more mysterious beyond such routines, illustrates a germ of thought that took root in this era. Social sciences generally are focused on what is commonplace among people and in society, though the distillations and abstractions inherent in the methods of social science (e.g. anthropology, sociology, political science) all suffer the loss of so much data that it renders them somewhat stick-like, fragmentary and shadowy beyond the tightly defined boundaries of their own landscapes. G. W. Hegel's oft-cited phrase illustrates this limitation well, that "the familiar is not necessarily the known" (Lefebvre, 2014/1958, p. 152).

Social science falls short of capturing the totality of everyday existence due to its textual and visual orientation, one that obscures aurality and vocality, haptic and kinaesthetic sensations and olfactory matters (Highmore, 2002). The aim to capture everydayness is perhaps also attributable to modernity such that "everyday life might be the name for the desire of totality in postmodern times" (p. 25). But a difference here is that those who have theorized everydayness recognize the fundamental haziness of the inquiry along with the unrepresentability that it invites. All of the in-betweens of life, which are not textualized, visualized or even verbalized, are the beginnings of where everydayness occurs and yet its ephemerality makes it difficult to grasp and make socially intelligible through tools, such as language, image and speech, that we have at our disposal. Everydayness is an abstruse uncertainty that is difficult to adequately represent. As Henri Lefebvre (2014/1958) suggests, the everyday is what is left over after analysis, or after the activities of the social scientists have exhausted the subject.

It seems fitting to think with everyday theory when considering GCE since both are very much results of the 20th century. GCE emerges from an increasingly interdependent world that surfaced the complex problem of how to educate people to live with the capacity to destroy our species and others. And everyday theory too grew up alongside the industrial modernity of the last century. Ben Highmore (2002) points to the ubiquity of institutions, atomized work and the routines of bureaucracy that create charged tensions in the humdrum, daily existence therein. The sense that industrial culture had peaked in modernity which resulted in a longing for something more fulfilling led to an anomic search around the existential question, "what else?" or "is that all?" My sense is that GCE's aura is too glowing amid this despair, that there is not enough attention to the more fundamental questions that confound and challenge modernity, such that the field is often cast as cheerleading for global capitalism. I do not see GCE in that way but it is my view that the absence of consideration of the transcendent in the day-to-day, and indeed the tragic in both, results in a certain hollowness of GCE.

GCE can move from a desolate condition of knowing without fully being towards one of *everyday transcendence* that occupies the space of being and knowing with an awareness of what is unknowable. Being global in this sense is not simply a rational matter of knowing about the world but a stance of knowing in and with the world with a great deal more humility than certainty. In this formulation of GCE, the fullness of life and its material and metaphysical elements are not to be factored out as noisy interferences that need to be excised from the data but as the occurrence of not-yet-known, perhaps unknowable presence of the stuff of life. The stuff of life is understood as an alternative aesthetic experience for attending to the everyday, one that does not abide the instrumental attempts to catalog it, nor the expressive artistic version of everyday that appears in art forms nor the claims of positivism on totality. Rather, it is an aesthetic that inhabits an awareness that "actuality always outstrips the procedures for registering it" (Highmore, 2002, p. 23). But even the metaphor invoked by "outstripping" is problematic as it gestures towards a race of exhaustion. That is not the point. Rather, the point is to live fully in the present in the same sense of Dewey's call to honor the child's life lived, not some abstract future life.

David Hansen (2009), who draws upon Diogenes to examine cosmopolitanism as a way of being in the world, suggests that ancient versions of cynicism unlike contemporary ones offer hope and value, rather than nihilism and abyssal thought. And a location of that hope and its attendant possibility draws decidedly from the everyday or mundane aspects of daily life.

> Human culture also features unfathomable creativity…no more visible than when individuals and communities intersect. These intersections generate not just sparks of strife and violence, although that obviously happens. They

also trigger new, unanticipated modes of mutual learning, appreciation, and fulfillment, as people strive to inhabit an ever-changing, ever-unpredictable world. Cosmopolitanism can denote cultural beginnings at the crossroads of human interaction…as a dynamic openness to the new fused with loyalty to the known.

(Hansen, 2009, pp. 7–8)

The new and the known in all their various forms are indeed the stuff of life that call upon us to enter conversations that move towards shared understandings of our common existence.

My call in this book, one made in light of nine emergent practices drawn from various corners of the world, is rather simple: the future of GCE lies in a robust and centered view of the present, everyday circumstances that we all inhabit divergently, the stuff of our lives. GCE in this sense is a form of education that embraces recognition of the local as profoundly interdependent upon myriad other locales; the presence of vast, inherited and perpetuated historical injustices and building the capacity to act in solidarity to address these injustices; the reliance of our species on the biosphere for its sustenance and continuance in a rapidly deteriorating environment; and the possibility of achieving these understandings through habitualized attention to everyday transcendent materials, events and conditions. The extent to which these aims are realized will foretell how a peaceful, sustainable and just global society may emerge.

I believe this is some of what Diogenes had in mind when he declared himself a citizen of the world. While the times of ancient Greece are seemingly far removed from the current global moment, the congruities are notable. The ancients witnessed, just as we do, intolerance, war, injustice and environmental harm. Our technological capacity far exceeds theirs and yet these tools of modernity in and of themselves do not constitute a better world. This fact is perhaps most evident in the devastation of Hiroshima and Nagasaki at the conclusion of World War II by atomic weapons. This recently commemorated event fundamentally altered the course of humanity while ushering in the nuclear age. R. Buckminster Fuller, a visionary and early intellectual leader of what we now call globalization, heard the news of the bombing of Hiroshima in August, 1945. "Bucky" Fuller reflected on that event by saying, "Humanity is in 'final exam' as to whether or not it qualifies for continuance." These prophetic words are both a searing commentary and a strident call to action, how to think and act in ways that human life, in balance with the biosphere, is indeed granted continuance. And if those lessons are to be learned and abided by, then educators will play a pivotal role in that teaching. I hope to see a time where we no longer use prefixes in education, such that *global citizenship* and all of the other valuable and numerous qualifiers are no longer needed. I hope for and work towards the day when what it means to be *educated* will necessarily include all of these qualifiers such that education alone will be enough.

APPENDIX

METHODOLOGY

Three studies constitute the basis of the data-oriented chapters (3 through 6) in this book. While the studies are distinct, the perspectives and methods that undergird each are similar enough to be treated in a composite fashion here. The theoretical framework that informed the design and implementation of the research is rooted in pragmatism, hermeneutics and a critical orientation. The pragmatist bearings flow from the interactive and theorizing aspects of the research, wherein participants engaged in reflexive interviews designed to encourage theorizing experience through subsequent articulation. Participants were purposefully asked to look at their work problematically and inspect the points of incongruence that exist within their intentions, the activities of the programs and feedback from students. A core principle in pragmatist thought is that educational research, like life, is transactional and iterative and therefore that knowledge is not a description of reality but an examination of what one does and the happenings related to that doing (Biesta & Burbules, 2003). Furthermore, the intention of the studies and this book is not to prescribe actions related to GCE but rather to provide illustrations that can be used to think within the development of new and refashioned programming.

The study was also informed by hermeneutic theory as participants were invited to interpret their work through the materials, documents and experiences they created around the question of *What do these mean*? Theoretically this approach issues from the belief that educators and participants are mindfully engaged in reflexively altering their work over time, in new situations and as a result of observing and analyzing student/participant feedback. Therefore, to best understand programs is to enter into the space of interpretation that participants themselves engage while developing and implementing educational programs. The hermeneutic orientation also emerges from the fact that the book and research are interpretations of interpretations, or what Hans-Georg Gadamer (1960/2011) has referred to as the doubleness within hermeneutic theory, indeed within all language. The interpreters, in this case the researchers, are presented with an interpretation of experience that they must then interpret, to move the texts offered by participants from their alien otherness to our own (Hermans, 2009).

Last, the third element of the theoretical framework is criticality. The research is critical in the sense that the cases were purposefully drawn from programming designed with and for historically marginalized populations to examine practices in this domain. The intention of including examples from the South and among historically marginalized populations in the North seeks to remedy a persistent gap in GCE scholarship and discourse. Interview questions, activity observations and data analysis were conducted with mindful attention to issues of equity, positionality and injustice as these issues are necessarily co-animated by examining a problematic concept such as GCE. The research is entirely drawn from the qualitative tradition. Qualitative research is used to describe and understand a social phenomenon and make sense of the phenomenon according to the meanings participants have brought to it, a way of conducting research that is appropriate given the theoretical orientation of the work (Denzin & Lincoln, 2005; 2011). Qualitative research emphasizes "episodes of nuance, the sequentiality of happenings in context, and the wholeness of individuals" (Stake, 1995, p. xii).

I relied on existing contacts in many countries and friend-of-friend recommendations that snowballed the sample. I asked colleagues if they knew of people doing global citizenship education in NGO, IGO, IHE, community-based and primary/secondary education sectors (Bogdan & Biklen, 2007). The relatively large sample of cases drawn herein is somewhat a-typical for this type of research. Yet, the need to comprehensively address the wide range of foci within GCE made this a necessary design choice. The following data points including the number of each type served as the basis for analysis and development of the studies: Skype interviews (N=7), face-to-face interviews (N=68), focus group interviews (N=9), email correspondence (N~200), activity observation (N=13), website content maps (N=9) over a total of 83 research/person days. In each case, I made a minimum of two visits ranging between three and nine research days per site. All participants were contacted following initial interviews through email exchanges to extend and clarify remarks and observations made in situ. Program websites were reviewed for content and to develop specific questions and follow-up queries about activities of the organizations. The protocol included mapping of contents with particular attention to statements of principal goals and content that revealed prior or existing practices. All data was collected in English with the exception of four interviews and four classroom observations in Bangkok and an activity observation in Mumbai that was translated simultaneously from Hindi. Translations were not verbatim but in summary style and there was no independent check for veracity of translations.

Data transcription of interviews was done verbatim by a research assistant and periodically by the researcher with attention given to preserving remarks, significant gestures and verbalisms that supported analysis. Data analysis employed various strategies that aimed to fracture collected data and rearrange them in categories that help explicate dynamic relationships between different pieces of data while providing a theory for the workings of the case investigated. The coding strategies included direct coding, categorical aggregation, pattern analysis and case description (Creswell, 1998; Stake, 1995).

I analyzed the data following a complete transcription of all digitally recorded interviews. In the case of email correspondence, these texts were preserved and included in the database for this study. Analysis was conducted by identifying recurrent patterns in the data, both within a particular interview and among a set of materials from a particular site, such that there was confidence that the information gleaned was emblematic rather than idiosyncratic utterances of passing thoughts. Codes were modified following initial coding.

I relistened to audio files of participants in each case to holistically determine if the descriptions adequately and comprehensively matched the data. This was an effort to avoid stilted, text-only renderings while reanimating the feel of the interview, including laughter, background noise and voice inflections to assist with properly contextualizing the texts. This technique was particularly helpful in reminding me of individual events or contextual considerations that had fallen out of the initial analysis process. In each case, I returned for a second visit of an equal number of research days to re-interview key participants and note changes and development of the program since my first visit. All three studies drawn upon in writing this book were conducted under the auspices of the Institutional Review Board of Teachers College, Columbia University who reviewed and approved procedures for the protection of participants. All proper nouns are pseudonyms with the exception of those referring to actual places (e.g. Teachers College).

REFERENCES

2013 Demographic Report. (2013). New York City: NY Department of Education.

Adichie, C. N. (2009). The danger of a single story. *TED Talk.* Retrieved from http://www.ted.com/talks/chimamanda_adichie_the_danger_of_a_single_story?language=en (December 11, 2015).

Akomolafe, B. (2014). Pppppppppppppdtggvv pppppnjp+ sspelalaa: Keynote address of the 2nd edition of the DEEEP Global Summit. Retrieved from http://www.deeep.org (December 11, 2015).

Anderson, L. F. (1968). An examination of the structures and objectives of international education. *Social Education,* 32(7), 639–47.

Andreotti, V. (2010). Postcolonial and post-critical global citizenship education. In G. Elliot, C. Fourali, & S. Issler (eds.), *Education and Social Change.* London: Continuum, pp. 223–45.

Appadurai, A. (1996). *Modernity at Large: Cultural Dimensions of Globalization.* Minneapolis: University of Minnesota Press.

Appadurai, A. (2013). *The Future as Cultural Fact: Essays on the Global Condition.* London/New York: Verso.

Appiah, K. A. (2006). *Cosmopolitanism: Ethics in a World of Strangers.* New York: W.W. Norton & Company.

Apple, M. (2011). Global crises, social justice and teacher education. *Journal of Teacher Education,* 62(2), 222–34.

Asher, N. & Crocco, M. S. (2001). (En)gendering multicultural identities and representation in education. *Theory and Research in Social Education,* 29(1), 129–51.

Banks, J. A. (2008). Diversity, group identity, and citizenship education in a global age. *Educational Researcher,* 37(3), 129–39, doi:10.3102/0013189x08317501.

Banks, J. A. (2009). Human rights, diversity and citizenship education. *The Educational Forum,* 73, 100–10. Retrieved from http://www.tandfonline.com/doi/full/10.1080/00131720902739478 – abstract (December 12, 2015).

Barber, M., Donnelly, K. & Rizvi, S. (2012). *Oceans of Innovation: The Atlantic, the Pacific, Global Leadership and the Future of Education.* London: Institute for Public Policy Research.

Bauman, Z. (1998). *Globalization: The Human Consequences.* Cambridge: Polity.

Biesta, G. (2013). Knowledge, judgment and the curriculum: On the past, present and future of the idea of the practical. *Journal of Curriculum Studies*, 45(5), 684–96.

Biesta, G. & Burbules, N. (2003). *Pragmatism and Educational Research.* Lanham: Rowman & Littlefield.

Bigelow, B. & Peterson, B. (2002). *Kids for Sale: Child labor in the Global Economy Rethinking Globalization.* Milwaukee, WI: Rethinking Schools, pp. 190–221.

Bodine, E. (2005). Radical decentralization and the role of community in Polish educational Reform. *European Education*, 37(1), 83–102. Retrieved from http://eduproxy. tc-library.org/?url=http://search.ebscohost.com/login.aspx?direct=true&db=eft&AN =507984601&site=ehost-live (December 12, 2015).

Bogdan, R. & Biklen, S. (2007). *Qualitative Research For Education: An Introduction to Theories and Methods* (5th edn.). Boston, MA: Allyn & Bacon.

Boulding, E. (1990). *Building a Global Civic Culture: Education for an Interdependent World.* Syracuse, NY: Syracuse University Press.

Brewer, M. B. (2007). The importance of being we: Human nature and intergroup behavior. *American Psychologist*, 62(8), 728–38.

Bromley, P., Meyer, J. & Ramirez, F. (2011). The worldwide spread of environmental discourse in social studies, history, and civics textbooks, 1970–2008. *Comparative Education Review*, 55(4), 517–45. Retrieved from http://www.jstor.org/stable/10.1086/660797 (December 12, 2015).

Buczynski, S., Lattimer, H., Inoue, N. & Alexandrowicz, V. (2010). Developing a policy for an international experience requirement in a graduate teacher education program: A cautionary tale. *Teaching Education*, 21(1), 33–46, doi:10.1080/10476210903466935.

Burack, J. (2003). The student, the world and the global education ideology. In K. Porter-Magee, J. Leming & L. Ellington (eds.), *Where Did Social Studies Go Wrong*, Fordham Foundation. Retrieved from http://edexcellence.net/publications/where-didssgowrong.html (December 12, 2015), pp. 40–69.

Case, R. (1993). Key elements of a global perspective. *Social Education*, 57(6), 318–25.

Castells, M. (2010). *The Network Society.* Oxford: Blackwell.

Castles, S. & Davidson, A. (2000). *Citizenship and Migration. Globalization and the Politics of Belonging.* New York, NY: Routledge.

Christian, D. & McNeill, W. (2011). *Maps of Time: An Introduction to Big History.* Berkeley, CA: University of California Press.

Collins, A. & Halverson, R. (2009). *Rethinking Education in the Age of Technology: The Digital Revolution and Schooling in America.* New York: Teachers College Press.

Colón-Muñiz, A., SooHoo, S. & Brignoni, G. (2010). Language, culture and dissonance: A study course for globally minded teachers with possibilities for catalytic transformation. *Teaching Education*, 21(1), 61–74, doi:10.1080/10476210903466976.

Committee for Economic Development. (2006). *Education for global leadership: The importance of international studies and foreign language education for US economic and national security.* Washington, DC: Committee for Economic Development. Retrieved from https://www.actfl.org/sites/default/files/pdfs/public/Finalreport.pdf (December 12, 2015).

Coryell, J., Durodoye, B., Wright, R., Pate, E. & Nguyen, S. (2010). Case studies of internationalization in adult and higher education: Inside the processes of four universities in the United States and the United Kingdom. *Journal of Studies in International Education*, 16(1), 75–98, doi:10.1177/1028315310388945.

Cowperthwaite, G. (Writer). (2013). *Black Fish*. In C. Films (Producer): Magnolia Films.

Creswell, J. W. (1998). *Qualitative Inquiry and Research Design*. Thousand Oaks, CA: SAGE.

Crutzen, P. J. & Stoermer, E. F. (2000). The "Anthropocene". In T. I. G.-B. Programme (ed.), (Vol. 41) Stockholm: The Royal Swedish Academy of Sciences, pp. 17–18.

Dagger, R. (1997). *Civic Virtues: Rights, Citizenship, and Republican Liberalism*. Cary, NC: Oxford University Press.

Darling-Hammond, L. (2010). *The Flat World and Education: How America's Commitment to Equity will Determine Our Future*. New York: Teachers College Press.

Darwin, C. (1909/1859). *The Origin of Species*. New York: P.F. Collier & Son Company.

Davies, I., Evans, M. and Reid, A. (2005). Globalising citizenship education? A critique of "global education" and "citizenship education". *British Journal of Educational Studies*, 53(1), 66–89.

Davies, L. (2006). Global citizenship: Abstraction or framework for action? *Educational Review*, 58(1), 5–25, doi: http://dx.doi.org/10.1080/00131910500352523.

Denzin, N. K. & Lincoln, Y. S. (eds.) (2005). Introduction: The discipline and practice of qualitative research. *The SAGE Handbook of Qualitative Research* (3rd edn., pp. 1–32). Los Angeles, CA: SAGE.

Denzin, N. K. & Lincoln, Y. S. (2011). *The SAGE Handbook of Qualitative Research* (4th edn.). Thousand Oaks, CA: SAGE.

Deutsch, M., Marcus, E., & Brazaitis, S. (2012). A framework for thinking about developing a global community. In M. Deutsch & P. Coleman (eds.), *Psychological Components of Sustainable Peace*. New York: Springer Science+Business Media, pp. 299–324.

Dewey, J. (1902/1990). *Habits John Dewey: The Later Works* (Vol. 17, 1885–1953, *Miscellaneous Writings*). Carbondale, IL: Southern Illinois University Press.

Dewey, J. (1916/1944). *Democracy and Education*. New York: Free Press.

Dewey, J. (1969). *The Child and the Curriculum: The School and Society*. Chicago: University of Chicago Press.

Dolby, N. & Rahman, A. (2008). Research in international education. *Review of Educational Research*, 78(3), 676–726, doi:10.3102/0034654308320291.

Dwyer, M. M. (2004). More is better: The impact of study abroad program duration. *Frontiers: The Interdisciplinary Journal of Study Abroad*, 10, 151–63. Retrieved from http://eric.ed.gov/?id=EJ891454 (December 12, 2015).

Ee-Seul, Y. (2011). Mini schools: The new global city communities of Vancouver. *Discourse: Studies in the Cultural Politics of Education*, 32(2), 253–68, doi:10.1080/01596 306.2011.562670.

El-Haj, T. R. A. (2010). "The beauty of America": Nationalism, education and the war on terror. *Harvard Educational Review*, 80(2), 242–74.

Engelman, R. & Terefe, Y. (2014). Will population growth end in this century. *Vital Signs*. Retrieved from http://vitalsigns.worldwatch.org/vs-trend/will-population-growth-end-century (December 12, 2015).

Etzioni, A. (2004). *From Empire to Community*. New York: Palgrave-Macmillan.

Fahrmeier, A. (2007). *Citizenship: The Rise and Fall of a Modern Concept*. New Haven, CT: Yale University Press.

Foucault, M. (1986). Of other spaces. *Diacritics*, 16(1), 22–7.

Francis, P. (2015). Laudato Si' On Care for our Common Home. Retrieved from the US Conference of Catholic Bishops, http://www.usccb.org/about/leadership/holy-see/francis/pope-francis-encyclical-laudato-si-on-environment.cfm (December 12, 2015).

Fraser, S. (1964). *Juliene's Plan for Comparative Education 1816–17*. New York: Teachers College, Columbia University.

Freire, P. (1993/1970). *Pedagogy of the Oppressed*. New York: Continuum.

Friedman, T. (2000). *The Lexus and the Olive Tree* (rev. edn.). New York: Farrar, Straus & Giroux.

Friedman, T. (2005). *Ten Forces that Flattened the World. The World is Flat*. New York: Picador.

Gabay, C. (2008). Anarcho-cosmopolitanism: The universalisation of the equal exchange. *Global Society*, 22(2), 197–216. Retrieved from http://oro.open.ac.uk/10714/1/Microsoft_Word_-_Anarcho_Cosmopolitanism_31.10.07%5B1%5D.pdf (December 12, 2015).

Gadamer, H.-G. (1960/2011). *Truth and Method*. London: Continuum International.

Gaudelli, W. (2003). *World Class: Teaching and Learning in Global Times*. Mahwah, NJ: Erlbaum.

Gaudelli, W. (2007). Global courts, global judges, and a multicitizen curriculum. *Theory and Research in Social Education*, 35(3), 465–91.

Gaudelli, W. (2013). Critically theorizing the global. *Theory and Research in Social Education*, 41(4), 552–65.

Gaudelli, W. & Laverty, M. (2015). What is a global experience? *Education and Culture*, 31(2), 13–26.

Gaudelli, W. (2016). *People, Pope and Planet: A Pedagogical Reading of Pope Francis' Encyclical on Global Warming*, Laudato Si' [unpublished manuscript/in review].

Gaudelli, W. & Wylie, S. (2012). Global education and issues-centered education. In S. Totten & D. Pedersen (eds.), *Educating about Social Issues in the 20th and 21st Centuries: A Critical Annotated Bibliography*. Charlotte, NC: Information Age, pp. 293–320.

Gay, G. (2000). *Culturally Responsive Teaching: Theory, Research and Practice*. New York: Teachers College Press.

Gee, J. P. (2000). Identity as an analytic lens for research in education. *Review of Research in Education*, 25(2000–01), 99–125.

(GENE), G. E. N. E. (2009). *Global Education in Poland*. Retrieved from Amsterdam: https://www.polskapomoc.gov.pl/Global,Education,165.html (December 11, 2015).

Gettleman, J. (2013). Silence on awkward topics at inauguration of Kenya's president. *The New York Times*, April 9.

Goodwin, L. (2010). Globalization and the preparation of quality teachers: Rethinking knowledge domains for teaching. *Teaching Education*, 21(1), 19–32, doi:10.1080/10476210903466901.

Gopaldas, A. (2013). Intersectionality 101. *Journal of Public Policy and Marketing*, 32, 90–4.

Guilford, G. & King, R. (2013). Peak meat? The world eats 7-times more animals than we did in 1950. *The Atlantic*. Retrieved from http://www.theatlantic.com/business/archive/2013/06/peak-meat-the-world-eats-7-times-more-animals-than-we-did-in-1950/276846/ (December 12, 2015).

Gur-Ze'ev, I. (2010). Philosophy of peace education in a postmodern era. *Policy Futures in Education*, 8(3/4), 315–39.

Hansen, D. (2009). Walking with Diogenes: Cosmopolitan accents in philosophy and education. *Philosophy of Education Yearbook*, 14(1), 1–13.

Hanvey, R. G. (1975). *An Attainable Global Perspective*. (ED 116 193). Denver, CO: Colorado Center for Teaching of International Relations.

Hargreaves, A. & Shirley, D. (2012). *The Global Fourth Way: The Quest for Educational Excellence*. Thousand Oaks, CA: SAGE.

Hayden, M. (2011). Transnational spaces of education: The growth of the international school sector. *Globalisation, Societies and Education*, 9(2), 211–24, doi:10.1080/1476772 4.2011.577203.

Heinberg, R. (2011). *The End of Growth: Adapting to Our New Economic Reality*. Gabriola Island, Canada: New Society.

Hermans, T. (2009). History. In M. Baker & G. Saldanha (eds.), *Routledge Encyclopedia of Translation Studies* (2nd edn.). New York: Routledge, pp. 133–5.

Highmore, B. (2002). *Everyday Life and Cultural Theory: An Introduction*. London: Routledge.

Hung, R. (2012). Being human or being a citizen? Rethinking human rights and citizenship education in the light of Agamben and Merleau-Ponty. *Cambridge Journal of Education*, 42(1), 37–51, doi:10.1080/0305764x.2011.651202.

Iriye, A. (2002). *Global Community: The Role of International Organizations in the Making of the Contemporary World*. Berkeley, CA: University of California Press.

Iyengar, R. & Bajaj, M. (2011). After the smoke clears: Toward education for sustainable development in Bhopal, India. *Comparative Education Review*, 55(3), 424–56. Retrieved from http://www.jstor.org/stable/10.1086/660680 (December 12, 2015).

Jaffe-Walter, R. (2013). "Who would they talk about if we weren't here?": Muslim youth, liberal schooling and the politics of concern. *Harvard Educational Review*, 83(4), 613–62.

Jagodzinski, J. (1981). Aesthetic education reconsidered or please don't have an aesthetic experience! *Art Education*, 34(3), 26–9.

Jenkins, H. (2006). Convergence Culture: Where old and new media collide. NY: New York University Press.

Jickling, B. (2010). Reflecting on the 5th World Environmental Education Congress, Montreal, 2009. *Journal of Education for Sustainable Development*, 4(1), 25–36.

Jickling, B. & Wals, A. E. J. (2008). Globalization and environmental education: Looking beyond sustainable development. *Journal of Curriculum Studies*, 40(1), 1–21.

Jones, J. M. (2015). In US, Concern about Environmental Threat Eases. Retrieved from http://www.gallup.com/poll/182105/concern-environmental-threats-eases.aspx (December 12, 2015).

Kahneman, D. (2011). *Thinking, Fast and Slow*. New York: Farrar, Straus & Giroux.

Kimmelman, M. (2013). Going with the flow: Water governance in the Netherlands. *The New York Times*. February 19.

King, M. L. (1967). A Christmas Sermon. Retrieved from The King Center, http://www.thekingcenter.org/archive/list/4999 (May 25, 2015).

Kirkwood, T. F. (2001). Our global age requires global education: Clarifying definitional ambiguities. *The Social Studies*, 92(1), 10–15.

Kissock, C. & Richardson, P. (2010). Calling for action within the teaching profession: It is time to internationalize teacher education. *Teaching Education*, 21(1), 89–101, doi:10.1080/10476210903467008.

Kiwan, D. (2005). Human rights and citizenship: An unjustifiable conflation? *Journal of Philosophy of Education*, 39(1), 37–50, doi:10.1111/j.0309-8249.2005.00418.x.

Korf, B., Habullah, S., Hollenbach, P. & Klem, B. (2010). The gift of disaster: The commodification of good intentions in post-tsunami Sri Lanka. *Disasters*, 34, S60–S77, doi:10.1111/j.1467-7717.2009.01099.x.

Kozakiewicz, M. (1992). Educational transformation initiated by the Polish "Perestroika". *Comparative Education Review*, 36(1), 91–100, doi:10.2307/1188091.

Kymlicka, W. & Walker, K. (2012). *Rooted Cosmopolitanism: Canada and the World*. Vancouver, BC: UBC.

Lakoff, G. (1987/2008). *Women, Fire and Dangerous Things: What Categories Reveal about the Mind*. Chicago, IL: University of Chicago Press.

Lamy, S. L. (1987). Teacher training in global perspectives education: The center for teaching international relations. *Theory into Practice*, 21(3), 177–83.

Learning Metrics Task Force 2.0. (2015). *Center for Universal Education*. Retrieved from http://www.brookings.edu/about/centers/universal-education/learning-metrics-task-force-2 (December 11, 2015).

Lefebvre, H. (2014/1958). *Critique of Everyday Life*. Translation by John Moore. London: Verso.

Little, A. W. & Green, A. (2003). Successful globalisation, education and sustainable development. *International Journal of Educational Development*, 29(2009), 166–74.

Louv, R. (2008). *Last Child in the Woods: Saving our Children from Nature-Deficit Disorder*. Chapel Hill, NC: Algonquin.

Luke, T. (2005). Neither sustainable nor development: Reconsidering sustainability in development. *Sustainable Development*, 13(4), 228–38, doi:10.1002/sd.284.

MacDonald, A. (2013). *Considerations of Identity in Teachers' Attitudes toward Teaching Controversial Issues under Conditions of Globalization: A Critical Democratic Perspective from Canada*. (PhD), OISE/University of Toronto. Retrieved from https://tspace.library.utoronto.ca/bitstream/1807/35891/1/MacDonald_Angela_M_201306_PhD_Thesis.pdf (December 11, 2015).

McLuhan, M. (1964). *Understanding Media: The Extensions of Man*. New York: McGraw-Hill.

Marche, S. (2012). Is Facebook making us lonely? *The Atlantic*, August 15.

Meier, D. (1995). *The Power of their Ideas*. Boston, MA: Beacon.

Merryfield, M. M. (2000). Why aren't teachers being prepared to teach for diversity, equity and global interconnectedness? A study of lived experiences in the making of multicultural and global educators. *Teaching and Teacher Education*, 16(2000).

Merryfield, M. M. (2001). Moving the center of global education: From imperial world views to double consciousness, contrapuntal pedagogy, hybridity and cross-cultural competence. In W. B. Stanley (ed.), *Critical Issues in Social Studies Research for the 21st Century*. Greenwich, CT: Information Age, pp. 179–208.

Merryfield, M. M. & Subedi, B. (2001). Decolonizing the mind for world-centered global education. In E. W. Ross (ed.), *The Social Studies Curriculum: Purposes, Problems and Possibilities*. Albany, NY: State University of New York Press, pp. 277–90.

Miller, J. (2005). The American curriculum field and its worldly encounters. *The Journal of Curriculum Theorizing*, 21(2), 9–24.

Mohanty, C. T. (1988). Under Western eyes: Feminist scholarship and colonial discourses. *Feminist Review*, (30), 61–88.

Mohanty, C. T. (2003). "Under Western eyes" revisited: Feminist solidarity through anticapitalist struggles. *Signs: Journal of Women and Culture in Society*, 28(2), 499–535.

Moore, M. (2009). Capitalism: A Love Story. Documentary by Overture films.

Mosley, S. (2010). *The Environment in World History*. New York: Routledge.

Mundy, K. & Manion, C. (2008). Global education in Canadian elementary schools: An exploratory study. *Canadian Journal of Education*, 31(4), 941–74.

Myers, J. P., McBride, C. E. & Anderson, M. (2015). Beyond knowledge and skills: Discursive construction of civic identity in the world history classroom. *Curriculum Inquiry*, 45(2), 198–218.

Myers, J. P. & Zaman, H. A. (2009). Negotiating the global and national: Immigrant and dominant culture adolescents' vocabularies of citizenship in a transnational world. *Teachers College Record*, 111(11), 2589–625.

NASA, NOAA Find 2014 Warmest Year in Modern Record. (2015). Retrieved from http://www.nasa.gov/press/2015/january/nasa-determines-2014-warmest-year-in-modern-record (December 11, 2015).

NBC. (2012). Alabama Presidential Election Results. Retrieved from http://elections.nbcnews.com/ns/politics/2012/alabama/president/-.VWix-lxVikp (December 11, 2015).

New Country Classifications. (2013). New York, NY. Retrieved from http://data.worldbank.org/news/new-country-classifications (December 11, 2015).

O'Loughlin, E. & Wegimont, L. (2002). *Global Education in Europe to 2015: Strategy, Policies and Perspectives*. Paper presented at the Europe-wide Global Education Congress, Maastricht, Netherlands. Retrieved from Maastricht: http://www.coe.int/t/dg4/nscentre/Resources/Publications/GE_Maastricht_Nov2002.pdf (December 11, 2015).

OECD. (2008). Growing unequal: Income distribution and poverty in OECD countries. Retrieved from http://www.oecd.org/els/soc/41494435.pdf (December 11, 2015).

OECD. (2013). PISA 2012 Results. Retrieved from http://www.oecd.org/pisa/keyfindings/pisa-2012-results.htm (December 11, 2015).

Osler, A. (2011). Teacher interpretations of citizenship education: National identity, cosmopolitan ideals, and political realities. *Journal of Curriculum Studies*, 43(1), 1–24, doi:10.1080/00220272.2010.503245.

Osler, A. & Vincent, K. (2002). *Citizenship and the Challenge of Global Education*. Stoke: Trentham.

Our Common Future: Report of the World Commission on Environment and Development. (1987). Retrieved from Oslo: http://www.un-documents.net/our-common-future.pdf (December 11, 2015).

Owens, L. & Palmer, M. (2003). Making the news: Anarchist counter-public relations on the world wide web. *Critical Studies in Media Communication*, 20(4), 335–61.

Oxfam. (2015). Global Citizenship. Retrieved from http://www.oxfam.org.uk/education/global-citizenship (December 11, 2015).

Oxley, L. & Morris, P. (2013). Global citizenship: A typology for distinguishing its multiple conceptions. *British Journal of Educational Studies*, 61(3), doi:10.1080/00071005.2013.798393.

Parker, W. J. (2011). "International education" in US public schools. *Globalisation, Societies and Education*, 9(3–4), 487–501, doi:10.1080/14767724.2011.605330.

Pearce, F. (2013). Has the Kyoto Protocol done more harm than good? *New Scientist*. Retrieved from http://www.newscientist.com/article/dn23041-has-the-kyoto-protocol-done-more-harm-than-good.html-.Uu-6OrR4X1E (December 11, 2015).

Peters, M. A., Britton, A. & Blee, H. (eds.) (2008). Introduction: Many faces of global civil society; possible futures for global citizenship. *Global Citizenship Education: Philosophy, Theory and Pedagogy* (pp. 1–13). Rotterdam: Sense.

Pike, G. (2013). Global education in times of discomfort. *Journal of International Social Studies*, 3(2), 4–17.

Pike, G. & Selby, D. (1999). *In the Global Classroom* (Vol. 1). Toronto: Pippin, pp. 9–30.

Pinar, W. F. (2013). *Curriculum Studies in the United States: Present Circumstances, Intellectual Histories*. New York: Palgrave-Macmillan.

Pizmony-Levy, O. (2011). Bridging the global and local in understanding curricula scripts: The case of environmental education. *Comparative Education Review*, 55(4), 600–33. Retrieved from http://www.jstor.org/stable/10.1086/661632 (December 11, 2015).

Popkewitz, T. S. (1980). Global education as a slogan system. *Curriculum Inquiry*, 10(3), 303–16.

Pro-Con.org. (2013). *State by State Chart of Felon Voting Laws*. Retrieved from http://felon-voting.procon.org/view.resource.php?resourceID=286 (December 11, 2015).

Quoidbach, J., Gilbert, D. & Wilson, T. (2013). The end of history illusion. *Science*, 339(6115), 96–8, doi:10.1126/science.1229294.

Rios-Rojas, A. (2014). Managing and disciplining diversity: The politics of conditional belonging in a Catalonian institute. *Anthropology and Education Quarterly*, 45(1), 2–21.

Robinson, S. (2012). *Commit to International Study Cultures*. Retrieved from http://aacte.org/news-room/aacte-in-the-news/sharon-p-robinson-commit-to-international-study-cultures.html (December 12, 2015).

Rose, O. H. & Bridgewater, P. (2003). New approaches needed to environmental education and public awareness. *Prospects*, 33(3), 11.

Samuelsson, I. P. & Kaga, Y. (2008). *The Contribution of Early Childhood Education to a Sustainable Society*. Paris: UNESCO. Retrieved from http://unesdoc.unesco.org/images/0015/001593/159355E.pdf (December 12, 2015).

Savar Building Collapse. (2013). Retrieved from http://en.wikipedia.org/wiki/2013_Savar_building_collapse (December 12, 2015).

Shiva, V. (1997). The Greening of Global Reach. In G. Otuathail & S. Dalby (eds.), *Geopolitics Readers*. London: Routledge.

Silova, I. & Steiner-Khamsi, G. (2008). *How NGOs React: Globalization and Education Reform in the Caucasus, Central Asia and Mongolia*. Bloomfield, CT: Kumarian.

Singer, P. (2002). *One World: The Ethics of Globalization* (2nd edn.). New Haven, CT: Yale University Press.

Slaughter, A.-M. (2004). *A New World Order*. Princeton, NJ: Princeton University Press.

Sniegocki, J. (2008). Neoliberal globalization: Critiques and alternatives. *Theological Studies*, 69(2), 321–40.

Societies, (2015). Mission and Objectives. World Council of Comparative Education Societies. Retrieved from http://www.wcces.com/mission.html (December 12, 2015).

Sousa Santos, B. d. (2014). *Epistemologies of the South: Justice against Epistemicide*. Boulder, CO: Paragon.

Soysal, Y. (2012). Citizenship, immigration, and the European social project: Rights and obligations of individuality. *British Journal of Sociology*, 63(1), 1–21, doi:10.1111/j.1468-4446.2011.01404.x.

Sparshott, F. E. (1972). Figuring the ground: Notes on some theoretical problems of the aesthetic environment. *Journal of Aesthetic Education*, 6(3), 11–23.

Specogna, H. (Writer). (2006). The Short Life of Jose Antonio Gutierrez. Documentary film. Retrieved from https://en.wikipedia.org/wiki/The_Short_Life_of_Jos%C3%A9_Antonio_Gutierrez (December 12, 2015).

Spivak, G. C. (2004). Globalicities: Terror and its consequences. *The New Centennial Review*, 4(1), 73–94.

Spivak, G. C. (2012). *An Aesthetic Education in the Era of Globalization*. Cambridge, MA: Harvard University Press.

Spring, J. (2009). *Globalization of Education: An Introduction*. New York: Routledge.

Stake, R. (1995). *The Art of Case Study Research*. Thousand Oaks, CA: SAGE.

Steele, C. (2010). *Whistling Vivaldi: How Stereotypes Affect Us And What We Can Do*. New York: W. W. Norton.

Steiner-Khamsi, G. (2004). *The Global Politics of Educational Borrowing and Lending*. New York: Teachers College Press.

Steinkuehler, C. & Squire, K. (2014).Video games and learning. *Cambridge Handbook of the Learning Sciences*, 2nd edn. Cambridge: Cambridge Press.

Subramanian, A. & Kessler, M. (2013). The Hyperglobalization of Trade and Its Future. Working Paper 3, Global Citizen Foundation. Retrieved from http://www.colorado.edu/AmStudies/lewis/ecology/hyperglobalization.pdf (November 15, 2015).

Sustainable Development Goals. (2015). Retrieved from http://www.un.org/sustainabledevelopment/education/ (September 27, 2015).

Subedi, B. (2008). Contesting racialization: Asian immigrant teachers' critiques and claims of teacher authenticity. *Race Ethnicity and Education*, 11(1), 57–70.

Subedi, B. (2010). *Critical Global Perspectives: Rethinking Knowledge about Global Societies*. Charlotte, NC: Information Age.

Subedi, B. & Daza, S. (2008). The possibilities of postcolonial praxis in education. *Race Ethnicity and Education*, 11(1), 1–10.

Tabb, W. (2012). *The Restructuring of Capitalism in Our Time*. New York: Columbia University Press.

"Thousands of Newark students leave school in protest, block major intersection". Bill Wichert, May 22, 2015. NJ.com. Retrieved from http://www.nj.com/essex/index.ssf/2015/05/newark_students_leave_school_in_protest_block_majo.html (August 4, 2015).

Totnes, T. T. Transition Town Totnes. Retrieved from http://www.transitiontowntotnes.org/ (December 12, 2015).

Tyack, D. & Cuban, L. (1997). *Tinkering towards Utopia: A Century of Public School Reform*. Cambridge, MA: Harvard University Press.

Tye, B. & Tye, K. (1992). *Global Education: A Study of School Change*. Albany, NY: SUNY Albany.

Undocumented Immigrants in the US. (2013). Retrieved from http://www.pewresearch.org/daily-number/undocumented-immigrants-in-the-u-s/ (December 12, 2015).

UNESCO. (2014). *Global Citizenship Education: Preparing Learners for the Challenges of the 21st Century*. Retrieved from Paris: http://unesdoc.unesco.org/images/0022/002277/227729E.pdf (December 12, 2015).

UNICEF. (2012). Progress on Drinking Water and Sanitation. UNICEF and the World Health Organization, New York: UNICEF. Retrieved from http://www.unicef.org/media/files/JMPreport2012.pdf (December 11, 2015).

UN Millennium Development Goals. (2000). Retrieved from http://www.un.org/millenniumgoals/.

United States Court of Appeals, F. C. (1996). *Kaepa, Inc. v. Achilles Corporation*.

Visvanathan, S. (1997). Mrs. Brundtland's disenchanted cosmos. In G. Otuathail, S. Dalby & P. Routledge (eds.), *Geopolitics Reader*. London: Routledge, pp. 237–41.

Waldow, F. (2012). Standardisation and legitimacy: Two central concepts in research on educational borrowing and lending. In G. Steiner-Khamsi & F. Waldow (eds.), *World Yearbook of Education 2012: Policy Borrowing and Lending in Education*. Florence, KY: Routledge, pp. 411–27.

West, C. (1993/2001). *Race Matters*. Boston, MA: Beacon.

Wiggins, G. & McTighe, J. (2005). *Understanding by Design*. Alexandria, VA: Association for Supervision and Curriculum Development.

Willinsky, J. (1998). *Learning to Divide the World: Education at Empire's End*. Minneapolis: University of Minnesota Press.

Wilson, A. (1998). Oburoni outside the whale: Education: Reflections on an experience in Ghana. *Theory & Research in Social Education*, 26(3), 410–29.

Wojcik, T. (2010). When curricular objectives collide: The official, enacted, and experienced curricula in schools during the People's Republic of Poland (1952–89). *Curriculum Inquiry*, 40(5), 600–13, doi:10.1111/j.1467-873X.2010.00513.x.

Zembylas, M. & Vrasidas, C. (2006). Globalization, information and communication technologies, and the prospect of a "global village": Promises of inclusion or electronic colonization? *Journal of Curriculum Studies*, 37(1), 65–83, doi:10.1080/0022027032000190687.

Zong, G. (2009). Developing preservice teachers' global understanding via communication technology. *Teaching and Teacher Education*, 25(5), 617–25.

INDEX